The Lineup Card

The Lineup Card
An Illustrated History of the Baseball Collectible

Tom O'Reilly

McFarland & Company, Inc., Publishers
Jefferson, North Carolina

Unless otherwise credited, all images are from the author's collection, .

LIBRARY OF CONGRESS CATALOGUING-IN-PUBLICATION DATA

Names: O'Reilly, Tom, 1969– author.
Title: The lineup card : an illustrated history of the baseball collectible / Tom O'Reilly.
Description: Jefferson, North Carolina : McFarland & Company, Inc., Publishers, 2024 | Includes bibliographical references and index.
Identifiers: LCCN 2024004591 | ISBN 9781476691602 (paperback : acid free paper) ∞
ISBN 9781476650869 (ebook)
Subjects: LCSH: Baseball—Collectibles—United States. | Baseball—United States—History. | Lineup card. | BISAC: SPORTS & RECREATION / Baseball / General
Classification: LCC GV875.2 .O74 2024 | DDC 796.357075—dc23/eng/20240224
LC record available at https://lccn.loc.gov/2024004591

BRITISH LIBRARY CATALOGUING DATA ARE AVAILABLE

ISBN (print) 978-1-4766-9160-2
ISBN (ebook) 978-1-4766-5086-9

© 2024 Tom O'Reilly. All rights reserved

*No part of this book may be reproduced or transmitted in any form
or by any means, electronic or mechanical, including photocopying
or recording, or by any information storage and retrieval system,
without permission in writing from the publisher.*

Front cover images: (top) Lineup card collection (Jeffrey Lazarus and Rick Levy);
(bottom) Panoramic view of Fenway Park for Game 3
of the 1914 World Series (Library of Congress)

Printed in the United States of America

*McFarland & Company, Inc., Publishers
Box 611, Jefferson, North Carolina 28640
www.mcfarlandpub.com*

Table of Contents

Acknowledgments	vi
Preface	1
Lineup Cards Defined	5
How to Read a Lineup Card	25
The History of Lineup Cards	38
The Use of Lineup Cards in Other Sports	67
A Day in the Life of a 2022 Lineup Card	84
Famous Lineup Cards	88
Lineup Card Artistry	107
Minor League Lineup Cards	123
The Lineup Card Collectors	140
Signatures/Autographs on Lineup Cards	203
Authenticity: Caveat emptor ("Let the buyer beware")	213
Lineup Cards: What Are They Worth, and Where to Buy/Sell	223
The Future of Lineup Cards	238
Notes	241
Bibliography	247
Index	251

Acknowledgments

The most enjoyable part of writing this book was the people I got to meet along the way, including current and former Major League Baseball and minor league managers, coaches and umpires, league officials, sports memorabilia sellers, collectors and historians. I was fortunate that so many people were gracious with their time, knowledge and general support.

Two people went above and beyond in terms of their help with information, pictures and offering sanity checks along the way. Jeff Garfinkle has an amazing collection of sports ephemera, of which lineup cards are a significant piece. Jeff was generous with his time as well as his experience as both a collector and seller of lineup cards.

And then there is Jeffrey Lazarus. I loved hearing about all the lineup card collections I came across during this journey, but Jeffrey's collection is above and beyond any of them, not only in quantity—he has more than 3,000 cards at last check—but also quality; Jeffrey has managed to collect lineup cards from many of baseball's historic moments, and a who's who of baseball's most iconic names. Many of the lineup card pictures throughout this book, especially the older ones, are cards in Jeffrey's personal collection.

When I had questions, Jeffrey typically either already knew the answers, or if he did not, had cards that helped get me what I was looking for.

Finally, the ultimate acknowledgment is to my family—Julie, Kate and Sean—who have supported me going to games and chasing lineup cards since 2013, and sometimes even joined me.

One lineup card stands out from the others in my collection, an August 2021 lineup card from a Southern League game featuring the Birmingham Barons and Tennessee Smokies. It is the only lineup card in the collection from a game we were all at.

Acknowledgments

Birmingham's dugout lineup card from their loss to the host Smokies in the first game of a doubleheader on August 19, 2021.

Preface

Lineup cards have played a small but important role in baseball games played since the late 1800s. Not only are they necessary to play the game, but lineup cards also help tell the story of some of the sport's greatest moments. Yet when baseball's story is told through stories and memorabilia, lineup cards have flown under the radar.

On its web page about baseball book reviews, *Baseball Almanac* writes: "Over 70,000 books have been written covering every facet of our national pastime."[1] Hold on, *Baseball Almanac*. None of the 70,000-plus books have ever focused on lineup cards.

My interest in lineup cards started in 2013 when I found out that you could ask a manager, coach or umpire for his lineup card(s) after a game, and he might give it to you. My kids, Kate and Sean, and I have collected about 400 cards since then by asking managers, coaches and umpires for them after a game we were at.

If I am going to collect something, I want to know as much about the item as I can. How are lineup cards used and by whom? What is their history? How and where do you get them? What are they worth? How have they evolved over time? Who else collects them, and what lineup cards do they have?

These were just some of the questions I had about lineup cards. I was disappointed to find that there was little information available, just a few articles and some pictures. I was very surprised that no one had written anything in-depth about them, such as a book or journal article. I was certain lineup cards not only had a story to tell, but a good one.

So in 2020, I set out to write the first book about lineup cards. I had to do a lot of digging. Thankfully, there are various resources available on the Internet, such as

- Net54baseball.com, an online baseball forum with a few interesting threads about historical lineup cards
- KeyMan Collectibles (*http://keymancollectibles.com/*), a vintage baseball memorabilia portal that has posted some lineup card information and pictures over the years
- Free newspaper databases, including Chronicling America (https://chroniclingamerica.loc.gov/) and Fulton Search (https://fultonhistory.com/Fulton.html)
- Sports auction houses, which have information on current and sold auction items, including lineup cards
- The National Baseball Hall of Fame, which has a searchable online digital collection (https://collection.baseballhall.org/), although only a few lineup cards are included

Preface

SYRACUSE CHIEFS at LEHIGH VALLEY IRONPIGS
COCA-COLA PARK • ALLENTOWN, PA • JULY 26, 2016

Game #2

LEHIGH VALLEY IRONPIGS

#	ORIGINAL	POS.	CHANGE
1	SWEENEY	5	
2	CRAWFORD	6	●●
3	WILLIAMS	7	●
4	RUF	3	
5	ALTHERR	9	●
6	~~R___~~ KNAPP	2	
7	PERKINS	8	
8	VALENTIN	4	●⑥
9	MURRAY ~~MORGAN~~	1	
P			

AVAILABLE POSITION PLAYERS

LEFT-HANDED	SWITCH	RIGHT-HANDED
MOORE	BURRISS	
STASSI		
LOUGH		
~~HUNTER~~		

AVAILABLE PITCHERS

LEFT-HANDED	RIGHT-HANDED
ARAUJO	GARCIA
RUSSELL	MARIOT
	HERRMANN
	~~MURRAY~~
	~~H___~~

SYRACUSE CHIEFS

#	ORIGINAL	POS.	CHANGE
1	BOSTICK	5	
2	LOMBARDOZZI	4	
3	GOODWIN	8	
4	SKOLE	3	●●
5	MARTINSON	6	
6	SOLANO	2	●
7	COLLIER	9	⑥
8	RAMSEY ~~D___~~	7	●
9	~~CARPEY~~	1	●●
P			

AVAILABLE POSITION PLAYERS

LEFT-HANDED	SWITCH	RIGHT-HANDED
~~RAMSEY~~		SEVERINO
~~D___~~		SANCHEZ

AVAILABLE PITCHERS

LEFT-HANDED	RIGHT-HANDED
HARPER	~~GLOVER~~
GRACE	MARTIN
	RUNION
	DAVIS

MANAGER SIGNATURE _____

Kate and I snagged this dugout lineup card from an International League game at Lehigh Valley in 2016.

But the best information I got was from talking to people: collectors, sellers, auction house executives, coaches, managers, umpires, sports memorabilia experts, etc. Some had more to offer than others, largely because lineup cards are inconspicuous in the big picture of baseball memorabilia. But collectively, the story started to come together.

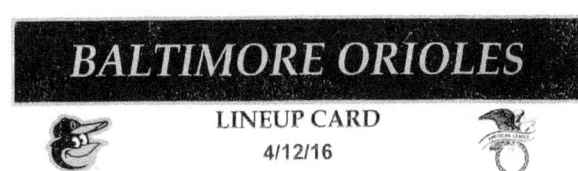

Sean and I got Baltimore's bullpen lineup card from David Ortiz's 506th career home run game.

While many lineup cards from before the 21st century are long gone, often thrown in the trash after a game, there are enough surviving to piece together an interesting account of baseball's history, such as the official batting order cards from Major League Baseball's (MLB) first All-Star Game in 1933, both dugout lineup cards from Sandy Koufax's 1965 perfect game, the blank Orioles dugout lineup card from September 11, 2001, and the 2004 World Series Game 4 card from the Red Sox dugout that a lifelong Boston fan paid $165,010 for to celebrate the first Red Sox world championship in 86 years.

If *Baseball Almanac* is correct about there being more than 70,000 baseball books written, then it is long overdue that lineup cards get their moment in the sun, and I am happy to be the one to tell their story.

Lineup Cards Defined

A baseball lineup card is a physical document, either handwritten or computer printed before a game, that includes at least one team's lineup. It contains information including the starting lineup, batting order and positions, and reserve players. Lineup cards are used by managers, coaches, players, and umpires for reference before and during a game.

There are different types of lineup cards, which are further defined and explained in the sections below.

Lineup cards have evolved over the years, so there are differences between, for example, a lineup card from the 1960s and a lineup card today. The definitions and explanations below are based on current lineup cards. The evolution of lineup cards over the years is covered in the chapter "The History of Lineup Cards."

Official batting order cards

The MLB "Official Baseball Rules" addresses lineup cards under the title "Exchange of Lineup Cards," which notes in part that each manager should give his batting order to the umpire-in-chief five minutes before a game starts.[1]

This card is known as the official batting order card. Batting order cards are also colloquially referred to as lineup cards.

Each team keeps one copy of its batting order card and gives the home plate umpire three or four copies: one for the home plate umpire, one for the opposing team and one or two for the base umpires.

As of 2021, MLB batting order cards include the following information (as indicated on the Mariners batting order card shown below):

1. Team name and logo
2. The date of the game
3. In the upper right-hand corner, an "H" if it is the home team's card, or an "A" if it is the visiting, or away, team's card
4. The starting lineup, including positions, in the order the players will bat; the starting pitcher's name is last
5. Righties indicated by "black" ink
6. Lefties indicated by "red" ink
7. Switch-hitters indicated by "blue" ink
8. The designated hitter spot highlighted
9. A list of eligible reserves, broken out as position players and pitchers

The Lineup Card

10. Each player name in the format of last name and the first initial of their first name
11. A version number, date and time stamp at the bottom of the card
12. The manager's signature at the bottom; the signature may be handwritten or digitally copied and pasted

The version and time stamp were first added in 2020. The idea is that they make it

OFFICIAL BATTING ORDER
Seattle Mariners
A

Sunday, April 25, 2021

	ORIGINAL	POS.	CHANGE		ALSO ELIGIBLE
					POSITION PLAYERS
1	Haniger, M	DH	B		
			C		Marmolejos, J
2	France, T	4	B		Trammell, T
			C		Torrens, L
3	Seager, K	5	B		PITCHERS
			C		1. Gonzales, M
4	Lewis, K	8	B		2. Kikuchi, Y
			C		3. Misiewicz, A
5	White, E	3	B		4. Sheffield, J
			C		5. Dunn, J
6	Moore, D	9	B		6. Flexen, C
			C		7. Graveman, K
7	Haggerty, S	7	B		8. Middleton, K
			C		9. Montero, R
8	Murphy, T	2	B		10. Newsome, L
			C		11. Sadler, C
9	Crawford, J	6	B		12. Steckenrider, D
			C		13. Vest, W
P	Margevicius, N	SP	B		14. Margevicius, N (SP)
			C		
			D		
			E		

Version 1 - 4/25/2021 at 11:46 AM

MANAGER'S SIGNATURE _____

Seattle Mariners batting order card from a 2021 game against the Red Sox.

Lineup Cards Defined 7

OFFICIAL BATTING ORDER
Seattle Mariners

A

Thursday, July 01, 2021

#	ORIGINAL	POS.	CHANGE	ALSO ELIGIBLE
				POSITION PLAYERS
1	Crawford, J	6	B	
			C	Trammell, T
2	Haniger, M	DH	B	Murphy, T
			C	**PITCHERS**
3	Seager, K	5	B	1. Gonzales, M
			C	2. Misiewicz, A
4	France, T	3	B	3. Santiago, H
			C	4. Sheffield, J
5	Bauers, J	9	B	5. Chargois, J
			C	6. Flexen, C
6	Moore, D	4	B	7. Gilbert, L
			C	8. Graveman, K
7	Long Jr., S	7	B	9. Middleton, K
			C	10. Montero, R
8	Torrens, L	2	B	11. Ramirez, Y
			C	12. Sewald, P
9	Fraley, J	8	B	13. Steckenrider, D
			C	14. Vest, W
P	Kikuchi, Y	SP	B	15. Kikuchi, Y (SP)
			C	
			D	
			E	

Version 1 - 7/01/2021 at 11:25 AM

MANAGER'S SIGNATURE _____

A Seattle Mariners batting order card from a July 1, 2021, game against the Toronto Blue Jays at Sahlen Field. The game was played in Buffalo due to Canada's COVID-19 travel restrictions.

easier for the managers and umpires to be certain that they all have the correct version of the cards before the game.

The size and formatting of the cards has varied over the years, but MLB created a uniform template for all teams to use starting in 2021. All cards are digitally printed, and the size of the cards is 5.5" × 8.5".

Aside from the "H" and "A" designations on the card, home team cards are white and visiting team cards are light blue.

The Lineup Card

OFFICIAL BATTING ORDER — Baltimore Orioles
Monday, May 30, 2022

	ORIGINAL	POS.	CHANGE	ALSO ELIGIBLE — POSITION PLAYERS
				Mullins II, C
1	Hays, A	9	B / C	Odor, R
2	Mancini, T	DH	B / C	Chirinos, R
3	Mountcastle, R	3	B / C	**PITCHERS**
4	Santander, A	7	B / C	1. Akin, K
5	Urias, R	5	B / C	2. Perez, C
6	Rutschman, A	2	B / C	3. Zimmermann, B
7	Mateo, J	6	B / C	4. Baker, B
8	McKenna, R	8	B / C	5. Bautista, F
9	Owings, C	4	B / C	6. Bradish, K
P	Wells, T	SP	B ABC / C / D / E	7. Diplan, M
				8. Gillaspie, L ②C
				9. Krehbiel, J ⑦B
				10. Lopez, J
				11. Lyles, J
				12. Sedlock, C
				13. Tate, D ④
				14. Wells, T (SP)

Version 1 - 5/30/2022 at 6:01 PM

MANAGER'S SIGNATURE

OFFICIAL BATTING ORDER — Boston Red Sox
Monday, May 30, 2022

	ORIGINAL	POS.	CHANGE	ALSO ELIGIBLE — POSITION PLAYERS
1	Hernandez, E	8	B / C	Arroyo, C
2	Devers, R	5	BC	Dalbec, B
3	Martinez, J	DH	B / C	Plawecki, K
4	Bogaerts, X	6	B E / C	**PITCHERS**
5	Verdugo, A	7	B / C	1. Davis, A
6	Story, T	4	B / C	2. Diekman, J
7	Cordero, F	3	B / C	3. Barnes, M ①
8	Vazquez, C	2	B / C	4. Brasier, R ① B
9	Bradley, J	9	B / C	5. Danish, T
P	Hill, R	SP	B ABD / C / D / E	6. Eovaldi, N
				7. Houck, T
				8. Pivetta, N
				9. Sawamura, H ④A
				10. Schreiber, J
				11. Valdez, P
				12. Wacha, M
				13. Whitlock, G
				14. Hill, R (SP)

Version 1 - 5/30/2022 at 5:56 PM

MANAGER'S SIGNATURE OMG

Lineup Cards Defined

OFFICIAL BATTING ORDER

NEW YORK — **NEW YORK** — DATE 8/14/16

#	ORIGINAL		CHANGE		ALSO ELIGIBLE
1	ELLSBURY (L)	8	B 3		3 ROMINE
					HEADLEY (S)
2	HICKS (S)	7	B		TEIXEIRA (S)
			C		GARDNER (L)
3	GREGORIUS (L)	6	B		
			C		
4	CASTRO	4	B		1 CESSA
			C		2 PARKER
5	McCANN (L)	DH	B		SWARZAK
			C		WARREN
6	SANCHEZ	2	B		CLIPPARD
			C		BETANCES
7	AUSTIN	3	B		LAYNE (L)
			C		4 SHREVE (L)
8	JUDGE	9	B		
			C		PINEDA
9	TORREYES	5	B		SABATHIA
			C		TANAKA
	SEVERINO	1	D A		
			E		

MANAGER'S SIGNATURE _____

Umpire batting order card from a game during Aaron Judge's rookie season. Note the lineup changes during the game written by the umpire (courtesy Jeffrey Lazarus).

The cards used by the home plate umpire are the game's official record, with one or two base umpires also keeping notes on a pair of cards to help the home plate umpire keep track of lineup changes and other rules such as mound visits taken and the three-batter minimum rule.

Opposite page: **Umpire Adrian Johnson's batting order cards from a 2022 Baltimore at Boston game. Johnson began the game as the second base umpire, but replaced home plate umpire John Tumpane after Tumpane took a foul ball to the mask in the seventh inning.**

Batting order cards are exchanged before the beginning of not only MLB games, but also nearly every baseball and softball game from Little League on up. However, there are differences between the batting order cards used by MLB teams and those used by minor league and amateur teams. Minor league and amateur teams typically produce three batting order cards: one for each manager and one for

```
Chi            Cin
3-PC           3-C
8-PC           9-C
               9-PC
```

Notes written by an umpire on the back of an "away" batting order card.

NY PENN LEAGUE — OFFICIAL BATTING ORDER — 8/20/2017

Home Team ☒   Visiting Team ☐

#	POS	Player
1	2 2B	Brujan, Vidal
2	13 CF	Chester, Carl
3	21 SS	Walls, Taylor
4	6 C	Law, Zacrey
5	4 RF	Rojas, Oscar
6	24 LF	Benard, Isaac
7	28 DH	Lorenzo, Rafelin
8	20 1B	Eureste, Matt
9	9 3B	Tansel, Deion
P	38	McKay, Brendan

BENCH
22	Perez, Angel
10	Pujols, Bill
27	Ramirez, Jean

BULLPEN
35	Gist, Andrew	31	Mozingo, Zack
29	Pflughaupt, Blake	26	Rosillo, Eduard
46	Schryver, Hunter	43	Salinas, Jhonleider
37	Fulenchek, Garrett	18	Vogel, Matt
25	Lopez, Hector		

MANAGER

New York Penn League — OFFICIAL BATTING ORDER — August 20, 2017

Home ☐   Visitors ☒

BATTING ORDER		POS	NO.	SUBSTITUTE
1	MOESQUIT	4	9	
2	NICHTING	8	40	
3	McCOY	6	6	
4	CRAPORT	5	54	
5	COPELAND	DH	12	
6	RINGHOFER	3	45	
7	FERGUSON	7	18	
8	CARRILLO	2	51	
9	JARRETT	9	48	
SP	HANIFEE	1	23	A B

REMAINDER OF ROSTER
11	BREAZEALE	UTL	39	
12	RIPKEN		58	
13	ORTEGA		13	
14	GRAHAM		17	
15				
16	MUCKENHIRN	P	37	
17	HANIFEE		23	
18	KEATON		41	
19	MING		49	
20	GARCIA		31	
21	HAYES		28	B
22	JOBST		62	
23	JOHNSON		19	
24	GRUENER		32	
25	TEAGUE		38	
26	BURKE		46	
27	KNUTSON		34	A
28	BISHOP			
29	VESPI		36	
30	MURPHY		29	
31	BONILLA		64	
32	LOWTHER		57	
33	BAUMANN		26	
34	HARVEY		24	
35				

Manager: Kevin Bradshaw #25
Designated Manager: RAMBO SAMBO #16
Pitching Coach: MARK HENDRICKSON #30

Game 1 ☐   Game 2 ☐

A pair of computer-printed batting order cards from a 2017 New York–Penn League game.

A pair of handwritten batting order cards from a 2021 Frontier League game. Note that Wite-Out was used to make a correction on the left-hand card.

the home plate umpire. Amateur teams sometimes make a fourth card for the scorekeeper.

While most affiliated minor league teams digitally print their batting order cards, the majority of independent minor league teams and amateur clubs still handwrite their cards.

12 The Lineup Card

Dugout lineup cards

As the name suggests, dugout lineup cards are posted in the dugout. They are larger than batting order cards—MLB dugout cards are typically 11" × 17"—and usually include the starting lineups and eligible players for both teams.

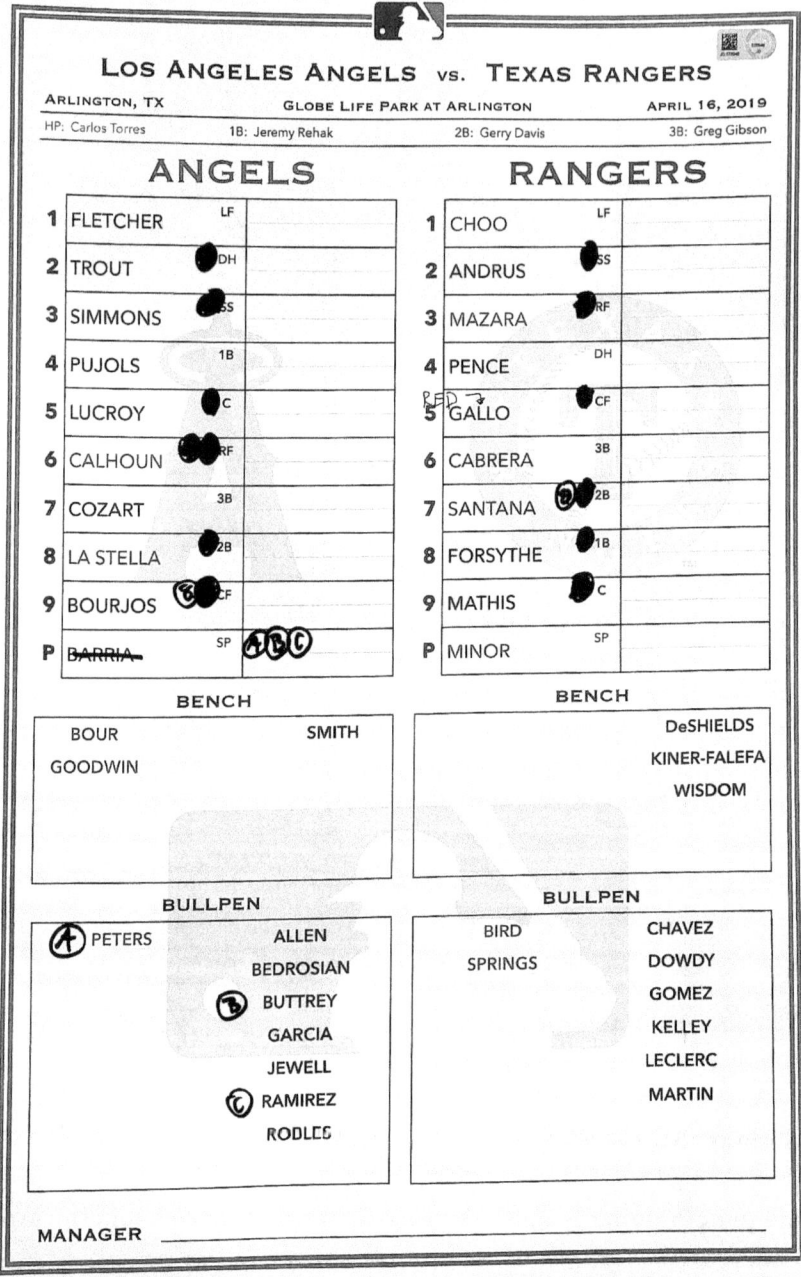

Albert Pujols and Mike Trout highlight this 2019 Los Angeles Angels dugout lineup card.

Lineup Cards Defined

MIAMI MARLINS AT NEW YORK METS
CITI FIELD • FLUSHING, NY • SEPTEMBER 28, 2022

HP -   1B -   2B -   3B -

MIAMI MARLINS

#	ORIGINAL	POS.	CHANGE
1	Berti, J ●●	6	
2	Leblanc, C	4	
3	Anderson, B ●●	9	
4	Fortes, N ●⑬	DH	
5	De La Cruz, B	8	
6	Bleday, J ●	7	
7	Stallings, J ●●	2	
8	Groshans, J ●	5	
9	Diaz, L	3	
P	Luzardo, J / Scott, T / Bleier, R / Nardi, A / Brazoban		Brigham / Floro

NEW YORK METS

#	ORIGINAL	POS.	CHANGE
1	Nimmo, B ●	8	
2	Alonso, P ●	3	
3	Lindor, F ●	6	
4	Canha, M ●●	7	
5	McNeil, J	9	
6	Escobar, E ●⑥	5	
7	Vientos, M ●	DH	
8	Guillorme, L ●	4	
9	Nido, T ● / Gore	2	McCann
P	Walker, T / Lugo		Ottavino / Diaz / Smith

AVAILABLE POSITION PLAYERS — MIAMI MARLINS

LEFT-HANDED	SWITCH	RIGHT-HANDED
		Burdick, P
		Cooper, G
		Encarnacion, J
		Rojas, M
		Williams, L

AVAILABLE POSITION PLAYERS — NEW YORK METS

LEFT-HANDED	SWITCH	RIGHT-HANDED
Naquin, T	Vogelbach, D	Gore, T
		McCann, J
		Ruf, D

AVAILABLE PITCHERS — MIAMI MARLINS

LEFT-HANDED	RIGHT-HANDED
Bleier, R	Alcantara, S / Brazoban, H
Fishman, J	Brigham, J / Cabrera, E
Garrett, B	Floro, D / Hoeing, B
Nardi, A	Lopez, P
Okert, S	
Scott, T	

AVAILABLE PITCHERS — NEW YORK METS

LEFT-HANDED	RIGHT-HANDED
Peterson, D	Bassitt, C / Carrasco, C
Rodriguez, J	Diaz, E / Lugo, S
	May, T / Megill, T
	Ottavino, A / Scherzer, M
	Smith, D / Williams, T
	deGrom, J

MANAGER SIGNATURE _____

This Miami Marlins dugout-style lineup card includes both teams' and MLB's logos as watermarks.

Dugout lineup cards may include notes or color-coding, either preprinted (e.g., whether batters are righty, lefty or switch-hitters; whether pitchers are right or lefty) or written during the game (e.g., cross-outs for the name of players who left the game; notes on which player made the last out in an inning) to help the team with lineup

Date: 6-10-16 **Opponent:** MISSIONS

FRISCO ROUGHRIDERS		OPPONENT	
1	CHOO — RF	1	STEVENS — 3B
2	CORDELL — CF	2	RONDON — SS
3	GUZMAN — 1B	3	TORRES — LF
4	VAN HOOSIER — 3B	4	SCHULTZ — RF
5	JACKSON — DH	5	OLT — 1B
6	IBANEZ — 2B	6	GORIS — C
7	MENDEZ L. — SS	7	LINDSEY — 2B
8	DEGLAN — C	8	SMITH — DH
9	GARIA — LF	9	WARD — CF
P	MENDEZ Y. — P	P	LAMET — P

RESERVES (Frisco): BECK, BURG, TRINAFEL
RESERVES (Opponent): QUINTANA, BONSFIELD, DEL CASTILLO

The Frisco Roughriders, the Double-A team of the Texas Rangers, used a black-and-white dugout lineup card that measured 8.5" × 14" during the 2016 season.

decisions during the game. Twenty-first-century MLB dugout cards are typically colorful and have logos, including watermarks.

Lower-level professional and most amateur teams also use dugout lineup cards. Their dugout cards are generally smaller—most are 8.5" × 14"—and not as decorative as MLB cards.

CORNELL BIG RED — THE IVY LEAGUE

OPPONENT: YALE DATE: GAME 1

#	Player	Pos
1	SAKS	8
2	FLEMATTI	DH
3	SIMONEIT	2
4	GARZA	9
5	ARNDT	3
6	TAYLOR	6
7	COLLINS	5
8	CARNEGIE	4
9	BINNIE	7
P	WYATT	1

B	#	NAME	POS
L	25	Apostle	OF
L	6	Arndt	1B
R	2	Binnie	OF
R	3	Carnegie	INF
R	41	Charles, A	OF
R	11	Charles, L	OF
R	15	Collins	INF
R	35	Flematti	C
R	21	Garza	INF/OF
L	17	Guiliano	OF
R	37	Hernandez	INF
L	19	Lepper	OF
R	4	Matton	INF/OF
R	23	Rodriguez	C
R	33	Simoneit	C
R	9	Taylor	INF
R	12	Yacinich	INF
R	1	Lillios	INF

PITCHING

#	NAME	THROWS
16	Arnold	L
29	Bailey	R
22	Bemiss	R
39	Brown	R
8	Cushing	R
26	Davis	R
40	Ellison	R
27	Gilbert	R
36	Jarrett	R
38	Kirton	R
1	Lillios	R
34	Natoli	R
13	Saks	R
20	Urbon	R
31	Wyatt	R
12	Yacinich	R
32	Zacharias	R

A Cornell University baseball team dugout lineup card.

Unlike batting order cards, which are rarely sold, MLB dugout lineup cards are almost always sold. Exceptions include giving a card to a player who made his debut or reached a milestone during a game.

Detroit's dugout lineup card from the game in which Miguel Cabrera recorded his 3,000th career hit, signed and inscribed by Cabrera. The Tigers gave Cabrera the milestone lineup card during a ceremony a few months after the achievement (courtesy Detroit Tigers).

Other types of lineup cards

Bullpen lineup cards function similarly as dugout lineup cards, just in the bullpen. They are almost exclusively used at the MLB level, as few non–MLB teams have a dedicated bullpen coach.

A Miami Marlins bullpen lineup card from a 2015 game against the Washington Nationals.

According to MLB coaches and managers interviewed, it is up to the bullpen coach to decide if he wants to use a bullpen card, and if he does, what it will look like. Some bullpen coaches design their own, while others use an extra copy of the dugout lineup card.

For example, Seattle Mariners bullpen coach Trent Blank did not keep a bullpen

A 2019 Minnesota Twins bullpen lineup card.

lineup card in 2022. Jeremy Hefner, bullpen coach for the Minnesota Twins in 2019, created his own lineup card for the bullpen.

Chris Young used a dugout-style lineup card when he was bullpen coach of the Chicago Cubs in 2022.

The emphasis on bullpen lineup cards is the opposing team. In fact, the card may not include any of a team's own lineup/reserves as their bullpen is most interested in who is coming up to bat for the other team; who the potential pinch-hitters are; and whether the other team's hitters are righty, lefty or switch-hitters for

Lineup Cards Defined

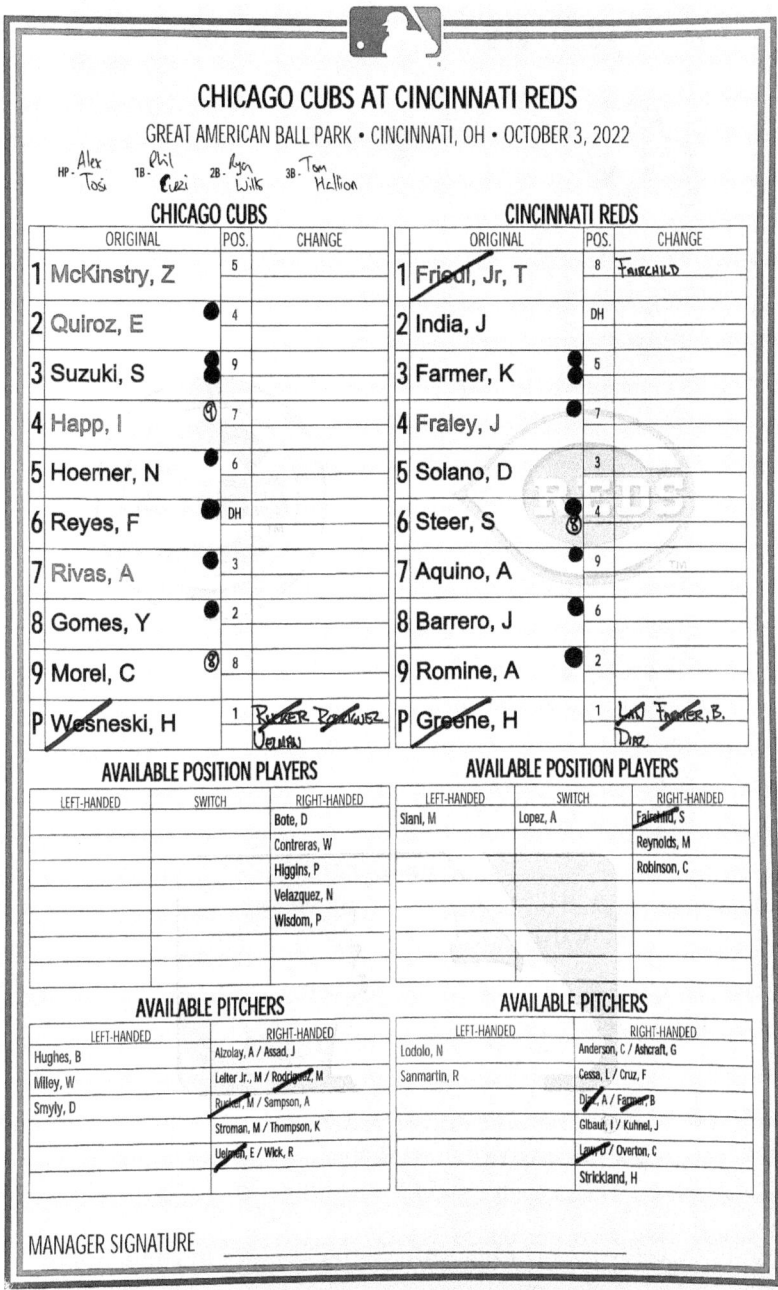

The Cubs used a dugout-style lineup card in their bullpen for this 2022 game against the Reds.

potential matchup purposes. MLB bullpen cards are typically either given away or thrown out after a game, although there are teams that sell them and others that keep them.

Some type of clubhouse or today's lineup card can be found in an MLB team's locker room or press room.

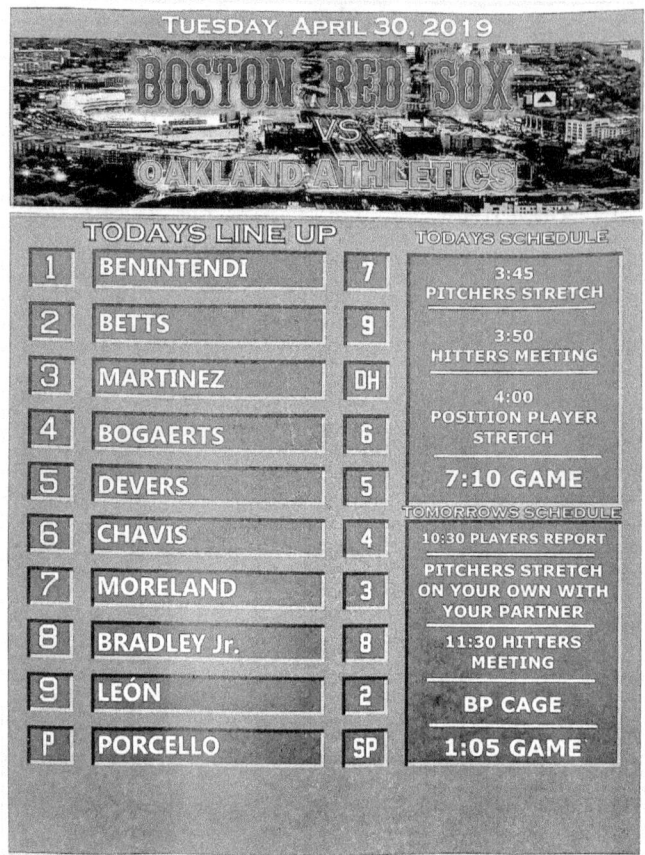

The daily lineup card posted in the Red Sox clubhouse on April 30, 2019. It includes the pre-game schedule for both that day and the next.

There is no set format for a clubhouse or today's lineup card. The card might look similar to a batting order or dugout lineup card, or it may look completely different and include information such as the schedule for warm-ups/batting practice, batting practice groups, the schedule for the next day's game, etc.

Replica lineup cards are typically offered for sale or as a giveaway for a notable game (e.g., the game Adrian Beltre collected his 3,000th career hit) or if there is great demand (e.g., Game 7 of the 2016 World Series when the Cubs won for the first time in 108 years).

The replica card is a facsimile of the actual dugout lineup card, including any markings made on the card during the game. Some replica cards are even authenticated by MLB, and some are signed by players to increase the value. But as replica lineup cards are created after a game, and often mass-produced, they do not fit under the definition of a lineup card as defined earlier in this chapter.

Finally, some teams will keep a pitchers' relief usage card in the dugout to keep track of recent use of their relief pitchers so they are easily able to determine who is available to pitch in that day's game. In most cases, this information will be kept on a separate card. However, in the example below, the information was taped onto the back of a batting order card.

Lineup Cards Defined 21

HP - KERWIN DANLEY
1B - WALLY BELL
2B - BRIAN RUNGE
3B - ROB DRAKE

NEW YORK METS at WASHINGTON NATIONALS
NATIONALS PARK · WASHINGTON, DC · SEPTEMBER 30, 2009

WASHINGTON NATIONALS

#	ORIGINAL	POS.	CHANGE
1	HARRIS	8	
2	DUKES	9	
3	ZIMMERMAN	5	
4	DUNN	3	
5	WILLINGHAM	7	
6	BARD	2	
7	DESMOND	6	
8	GONZALEZ	4	
9	LANNAN	1	

NEW YORK METS

#	ORIGINAL	POS.	CHANGE
1	PAGAN	7	
2	HERNANDEZ	4	
3	WRIGHT	5	
4	BELTRAN	8	
5	FRANCOEUR	9	
6	TATIS	3	
7	SANTOS	2	
8	VALDEZ	6	
9	REDDING	1	

AVAILABLE POSITION PLAYERS

LEFT-HANDED	SWITCH	RIGHT-HANDED
ORR	GUZMAN	BURKE
		NIEVES
		MAXWELL
		PADILLA
		MORSE

AVAILABLE POSITION PLAYERS

LEFT-HANDED	SWITCH	RIGHT-HANDED
MURPHY	CASTILLO	EVANS
REED		SHEFFIELD
SCHNEIDER		
SULLIVAN		
THOLE		

AVAILABLE PITCHERS

LEFT-HANDED	RIGHT-HANDED
VILLONE	ESTRADA
GARATE	CLIPPARD
	BERGMANN
	RIVERA/KENSING
	SEGOVIA
	MACDOUGAL

AVAILABLE PITCHERS

LEFT-HANDED	RIGHT-HANDED
FELICIANO	DESSENS
TAKAHASHI	STONER
	BROADWAY
	PARNELL
	GREEN/STOKES
	RODRIGUEZ

MANAGER SIGNATURE *Jim Riggleman*

Replica lineup card from Gary Sheffield's final MLB game.

CINCINNATI REDS
Great American Ball Park

DUGOUT AND PHOTOGRAPHERS' AREAS
- Ball striking padded railings or netting around dugout or photographers' area: **In Play**.
- Ball striking facing over dugout or recessed steel railing: **Out of Play (Award by Book Rule)**.
- Ball on top step (lip) of dugout: **In Play**

BACKSTOP AREA
- Pitched or thrown ball resting on top of padding or on ledge of signage: **In Play**.
- Pitched or thrown ball lodging in padding or signage: **Out of Play (Award by Book Rule)**.

TARP AREA
- Thrown or fair ball that lodges behind or under canvas on field tarp: **Out of Play (Award by Book Rule)**.
- A Catch may be made on canvas.

OUTFIELD AREA
- Batted ball in flight going over horizontal yellow line on top of outfield fence: **Home Run**.
- Batted ball striking horizontal yellow line: **In Play**.
- Batted ball in flight striking vertical yellow line in left-center field and caroming over outfield fence: **Home Run**.

Book Rul	8/15	8/14	8/13	8/12	8/11
Fassero	1-16p		up 2		
Walker	1/3-4p			1-13p	1-8p
Chrstnsn			2/3-16p		up 1
Eyre	11/3-19p		1-16p		
Hawkins	11/3-27	up 1			1-2p
Benitez					
Accardo		up1/1-8	1/3-7p	2/3-1p	

	8/15	8/14	8/13	8/12	8/11
Belisle	1-10p	0-10p	1-10p		
Merckter		1/3-16p		1/3-13p	
Weathers			1-9p	12/3-23p	
Keisler	1/3-14p				
Coffey	2/3-8p	1-5p			
Shcktford	2-17p				
Stndrldrge		2/3-7p	1-9p	1-12p	

The Giants charted the usage of both teams' relievers and taped the info to the back of their lineup card (courtesy Zack Hample).

A scorecard is not a lineup card

While there is some overlap, scorecards have a different purpose than lineup cards—they are used to record each play of a baseball game—and therefore scorecards are not included in this book.

New Britain Bees manager Stan Cliburn kept score for his batters in this 2016 Atlantic League game.

A summer college league manager or coach kept score for both teams on the lineup card.

That said, there are a few managers or coaches who will keep score on their lineup card during a game.

How to Read a Lineup Card

Lineup cards perform an important function before and during a game. Before the game, they let managers, coaches, players and umpires know which players from each team are eligible to play, which are starting, what each team's batting order is and what position each starter is playing.

Additionally, most current MLB lineup cards, and many minor league cards as well, indicate which players are righties, lefties or switch-hitters.

Once a game starts, additional information from the game is written onto the card by the umpires and often by a coach or manager, too.

Following are examples of different types of lineup cards as they look before and after a game.

Example #1

This is what a "clean" dugout or bullpen lineup card looks like before it gets marked up during a game. At the top is the MLB logo, team names and location. Below that are the names of the umpires for the game.

This was Oakland's card as indicated by the green and gold used for the trim and the watermark center-bottom celebrating the 50th anniversary of A's baseball in Oakland during the 2018 season. The card includes each team's starting lineup listed in the order the players batted. The player positions are listed by number in the "Pos." column.

Below the starting lineups are the eligible position players on the bench, and finally the available relief pitchers. There are more available players than normal because this game was played in September, when MLB rosters are expanded. On this card, starting pitchers not expected to pitch in a game, while eligible, are not listed.

Player names in black are right-handed hitters or right-handed pitchers, names in red are left-handed hitters/pitchers, and names in blue are switch-hitters.

Finally, there is a manager's signature line at the bottom. Managers are not required to sign dugout or bullpen lineup cards as they are only used by the team, not the umpires. Some managers sign dugout lineup cards knowing it is an added feature for someone being given or buying the card, but some do not. Bullpen lineup cards are rarely signed by the manager.

OAKLAND ATHLETICS at BALTIMORE ORIOLES
ORIOLE PARK AT CAMDEN YARDS • BALTIMORE, MD • SEPTEMBER 12, 2018

HP - Bill Miller 1B - Angel Hernandez 2B - Todd Tichenor 3B - Chad Whitson

OAKLAND ATHLETICS

#	ORIGINAL	POS.	CHANGE
1	LAUREANO	8	
2	CHAPMAN	5	
3	LOWRIE	4	
4	DAVIS	DH	
5	OLSON	3	
6	PISCOTTY	9	
7	SEMIEN	6	
8	MARTINI	7	
9	LUCROY	2	
P	HENDRIKS	1	

AVAILABLE POSITION PLAYERS

LEFT-HANDED	SWITCH	RIGHT-HANDED
FOWLER		PHEGLEY
JOYCE		BARRETO
TAYLOR		CANHA
		PINDER

AVAILABLE PITCHERS

LEFT-HANDED	RIGHT-HANDED
BUCHTER	WENDELKEN/MONTAS
KIEKHEFER	KELLEY/PAGAN/DULL
	PETIT/RODNEY
	TRIVINO/HATCHER
	FAMILIA/GEARRIN
MENGDEN/BASSITT	TREINEN/BROOKS

BALTIMORE ORIOLES

#	ORIGINAL	POS.	CHANGE
1	MULLINS	8	
2	VILLAR	4	
3	MANCINI	DH	
4	JONES	9	
5	DAVIS	3	
6	BECKHAM	6	
7	STEWART	7	
8	WYNNS	2	
9	PETERSON	5	
P	CASHNER	1	

AVAILABLE POSITION PLAYERS

LEFT-HANDED	SWITCH	RIGHT-HANDED
JOSEPH, CO.	WILKERSON	ANDREOLI
SISCO	VALERA	JOSEPH, CA
		NUNEZ
		RICKARD

AVAILABLE PITCHERS

LEFT-HANDED	RIGHT-HANDED
FRY	HESS/WRIGHT
SCOTT	CARROLL
GILMARTIN	MEISINGER
ROGERS	YACABONIS
	CASTRO
	GIVENS

MANAGER SIGNATURE _____

Oakland A's at Baltimore Orioles, September 12, 2018.

Example #2

These were the batting order cards kept by the Mariners. They did not mark up the cards during the game, so the cards look as they would when they were exchanged at home plate before the game.

How to Read a Lineup Card 27

OFFICIAL BATTING ORDER
Seattle Mariners
A
Thursday, May 19, 2022

	ORIGINAL	POS.	CHANGE	ALSO ELIGIBLE
				POSITION PLAYERS
1	Frazier, A	7	B	Crawford, J
			C	Ford, M
2	France, T	3	B	Raleigh, C
			C	**PITCHERS**
3	Rodriguez, J	8	B	1. Gonzales, M
			C	2. Misiewicz, A
4	Winker, J	DH	B	3. Ray, R
			C	4. Young, D
5	Suarez, E	5	B	5. Castillo, D
			C	6. Flexen, C
6	Torrens, L	2	B	7. Gilbert, L
			C	8. Mills, W
7	Toro-Hernandez, A	4	B	9. Munoz, A
			C	10. Murfee, P
8	Moore, D	6	B	11. Romo, S
			C	12. Sewald, P
9	Souza, S	9	B	13. Steckenrider, D
			C	14. Kirby, G (SP)
P	Kirby, G	SP	B	
			C	
			D	
			E	

Version 1 - 5/19/2022 at 5:58 PM

MANAGER'S SIGNATURE

OFFICIAL BATTING ORDER
Boston Red Sox
H
Thursday, May 19, 2022

	ORIGINAL	POS.	CHANGE	ALSO ELIGIBLE
				POSITION PLAYERS
1	Hernandez, E	8	B	Cordero, F
			C	Arroyo, C
2	Devers, R	5	B	Plawecki, K
			C	**PITCHERS**
3	Martinez, J	DH	B	1. Davis, A
			C	2. Diekman, J
4	Bogaerts, X	6	B	3. Strahm, M
			C	4. Barnes, M
5	Verdugo, A	7	B	5. Brasier, R
			C	6. Danish, T
6	Story, T	4	B	7. Eovaldi, N
			C	8. Houck, T
7	Dalbec, B	3	B	9. Pivetta, N
			C	10. Robles, H
8	Vazquez, C	2	B	11. Sawamura, H
			C	12. Schreiber, J
9	Bradley, J	9	B	13. Whitlock, G
			C	14. Hill, R (SP)
P	Hill, R	SP	B	
			C	
			D	
			E	

Version 1 - 5/19/2022 at 5:04 PM

MANAGER'S SIGNATURE

Seattle Mariners at Boston Red Sox, May 19, 2022. Of note, Trevor Story hit three home runs and knocked in seven RBI for the Red Sox, while 2022 AL Rookie of the Year Julio Rodriguez hit his third career home run.

The cards are both computer printed as has become the norm for MLB batting order cards. The date of the game is top-center on each card.

Boston was the home team, indicated by the card's white color and the large "H" in the upper right-hand corner. Seattle is the visiting team as noted by the light-blue

MINNESOTA TWINS at CHICAGO WHITE SOX
U.S. CELLULAR FIELD • CHICAGO, IL • APRIL 9, 2017

HP. DeMUTH. 1B. NAUERT. 2B. GUCCIONE. 3B. TORRES.
DANA-CC PAUL CHRIS CARLOS

MINNESOTA TWINS

#	ORIGINAL	POS.	CHANGE
1	DOZIER	4	
2	GROSSMAN	DH	
3	MAUER	3	
4	SANO	5	
5	CASTRO	2	
6	POLANCO	6	
7	ROSARIO	7	
8	BUXTON	8	
9	KEPLER	9	
SP	E. SANTANA	1	①②③④

CHICAGO WHITE SOX

#	ORIGINAL	POS.	CHANGE
1	CABRERA	7	
2	ANDERSON	6	
3	ABREU	3	
4	FRAZIER	5	
5	ASCHE	DH	DAVIDSON
6	GARCIA. A.	9	
7	SANCHEZ	4	
8	NARVAEZ	2	SOTO
9	MAY	8	GARCIA. L
SP	QUINTANA	1	①②③

AVAILABLE POSITION PLAYERS

LEFT-HANDED	SWITCH	RIGHT-HANDED
	ESCOBAR	GIMENEZ
	D. SANTANA	

LEFT-HANDED	SWITCH	RIGHT-HANDED
GARCIA. L.		DAVIDSON
		SOTO
		SALADINO

AVAILABLE PITCHERS

LEFT-HANDED	RIGHT-HANDED
BRESLOW	DUFFEY
ROGERS ①	TONKIN
	HALEY
	PRESSLY ②
	BELISLE ③
	KINTZLER ④

LEFT-HANDED	RIGHT-HANDED
JENNINGS ②	ROBERTSON ③
	JONES ①
	PUTNAM
	SWARZAK
	YNOA
	KAHNLE

MANAGER SIGNATURE _____

Minnesota Twins at Chicago White Sox, April 9, 2017.

color and "A" in the upper right-hand corner. Similar to the Oakland card, black, red and blue ink is used to indicate righties, lefties and switch-hitters, respectively.

Example #3

This example is a dugout lineup card from a game played between the Minnesota Twins and Chicago White Sox. On this card from 2017, the names are handwritten onto the card, rather than computer printed. As of 2022, it has become extremely rare for dugout lineup cards to be handwritten.

The card was in Minnesota's dugout, and the Twins wrote in notes and changes on the card during the game. The small circles to the left of the player names are used to indicate who made the last out each half-inning so the Twins knew who was leading off the next inning for each team.

Using a play-by-play recap of the game found on the Internet to retrace how the card was filled out, one finds that Joe Mauer made the last out of the top of the first inning.[1] Therefore, the manager or coach wrote the number "1" to the left of Mauer's name.

In the top of the second inning, Byron Buxton made the last out. The manager or coach would have colored in Mauer's circle, and then written "2" next to Buxton's game and circled it.

That process went on for the entire game. The Twins manager or coach did not bother to color in the "9" next to Buxton's name because the game ended. Buxton made the last out four times for Minnesota based on the four circles next to his name (the box score confirms that Buxton went 0-for-4 in the game).

MLB authentication hologram on top left of the lineup card.

The notes to the right of the starting player names indicate lineup changes made during the game. For the Twins, the only changes made were pitchers. Ervin Santana started the game, Taylor Rogers relieved him, then Ryan Pressly, etc. The White Sox made two non-pitcher changes: Matt Davidson came on to pinch-hit for Cody Asche and stayed in the game as DH, and Geovany Soto came on as a pinch-hitter and stayed in the game at catcher.

Finally, note the small hologram sticker in the upper right-hand corner of the card. Here is a closeup.

If you go to MLB's authentication lookup page, https://www.mlb.com/official-information/authentication, and enter the hologram number HZ324292, the website will confirm that this was Minnesota's game-used lineup card from its April 19, 2017, game against the White Sox.[2]

The MLB authentication program is designed to help fans avoid buying counterfeit memorabilia, including lineup cards. Since the program started in 2001, most dugout lineup cards have an authentication sticker.

Example #4

This is an official batting order card written by then–Montreal manager Felipe Alou. The card is a carbon copy that would have either been kept by Alou or given to Los Angeles manager Tommy Lasorda. The original (top) copy would have gone to the home plate umpire.

Alou neatly printed the names of his starters, their positions, and his eligible reserves, including starting pitchers that are not expected to play but are still eligible. Unlike dugout lineup cards, official batting order cards only include one team.

While official batting order cards are used by the home team. Home batting order cards used to include the home stadium's ground rules on the back, as this card does.

Montreal Expos official batting order card, April 21, 1993 (front)

OLYMPIC PARK

GROUND RULES

Ball hitting roof on outfield side of yellow line is a HOME RUN.

Everything in play --

    EXCEPT: Ball going beyond or on lines in front of dugout and camera pits - BOOK RULE.

                  Popup or fly ball hit into any one of four designated camera areas is out of play.

                  If ball hits overhanging speakers in fair territory, it is a homerun.

                  If ball hits overhanging speakers in foul territory, it is a dead ball.

                  Ball caught in padding of OF fence is ground rule double.

Montreal Expos official batting order card, April 21, 1993 (back)

Example #5

This is an example of a pair of batting order cards used by home plate umpire Alex Tosi. The home plate umpire's batting order cards are the official lineup cards for a game.

There is no required way for an umpire to track changes and keep notes on his set of lineup cards. In this case, Tosi presumably marked "A" through "E" for each reserve position player before the game. When Cincinnati's TJ Friedl left the game before the fourth inning due to injury and was replaced by Stuart Fairchild, Tosi simply wrote the letter "B" in Friedl's spot.

The reserve pitchers are numbered, so as each team replaced a pitcher, Tosi wrote the corresponding number in the "Change" column, then crossed the number out when they left.

Both teams used black print to designate righties, red for lefties and blue for switch-hitters. Managers David Bell and David Ross each signed their respective lineup cards.

Since relief pitchers in 2022 needed to pitch to at least three batters or end the inning (unless they are injured), Tosi kept track of what number in the batting order the relievers started and finished against.

There were likely no mound visits for Tosi to track, as those typically would be noted on the back of one of the cards.

The Lineup Card

OFFICIAL BATTING ORDER — Chicago Cubs (A)
Monday, October 03, 2022

ORIGINAL	POS.	CHANGE	ALSO ELIGIBLE POSITION PLAYERS
1. McKinstry, Z	5 B		A. Bote, D
	C		B. Contreras, W
2. Quiroz, E	4 B		C. Higgins, P
	C		D. Velazquez, N
3. Suzuki, S	9 B		E. Wisdom, P
	C		**PITCHERS**
4. Happ, I	7 B		1. Hughes, B
	C		2. Miley, W
5. Hoerner, N	6 B		3. Smyly, D
	C		4. Alzolay, A
6. Reyes, F	DH B		5. Assad, J
	C		6. Leiter Jr., M
7. Rivas, A	3 B		7. Rodriguez, M 8-1
	C		8. Rucker, M 7-7
8. Gomes, Y	2 B		9. Sampson, A
	C		10. Stroman, M
9. Morel, C	8 B		11. Thompson, K
	C		12. Uelmen, E 8-6
P. Wesneski, H	SP B	8-7-2	13. Wick, R
	C		14. Wesneski, H (SP)
	D		
	E		

Version 1 - 10/03/2022 at 5:18 PM

MANAGER'S SIGNATURE

OFFICIAL BATTING ORDER — Cincinnati Reds (H)
Monday, October 03, 2022

ORIGINAL	POS.	CHANGE	ALSO ELIGIBLE POSITION PLAYERS
1. Friedl, Jr.	8 B	B	A. Siani, M
	C		B. Fairchild, S
2. India, J	DH B		C. Reynolds, M
	C		D. Robinson, C
3. Farmer, K	5 B		E. Lopez, A
	C		**PITCHERS**
4. Fraley, J	7 B		1. Lodolo, N
	C		2. Sanmartin, R
5. Solano, D	3 B		3. Anderson, C
	C		4. Ashcraft, G
6. Steer, S	4 B		5. Cessa, L
	C		6. Cruz, F
7. Aquino, A	9 B		7. Diaz, A 9-2
	C		8. Farmer, B 8-7
8. Barrero, J	6 B		9. Gibaut, I
	C		10. Kuhnel, J
9. Romine, A	2 B		11. Law, D 7-4
	C		12. Overton, C
P. Greene, H	SP B	4-8-7	13. Strickland, H
	C		14. Greene, H (SP)
	D		
	E		

Version 1 - 10/03/2022 at 2:38 PM

MANAGER'S SIGNATURE

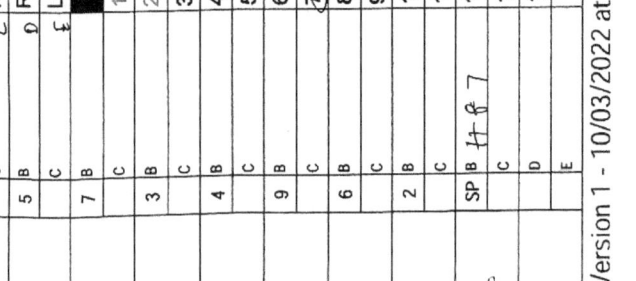

Chicago Cubs at Cincinnati Reds, October 3, 2022

How to Read a Lineup Card   33

OFFICIAL BATTING ORDER — New York Mets (A)

Tuesday, August 02, 2022

#	ORIGINAL	POS.	CHANGE	ALSO ELIGIBLE
				POSITION PLAYERS
1	Nimmo, B	8 (C)	B / C	Mazeika, P
2	Marte, S	9	B / C	Canha, M
3	Lindor, F	6 (A)	B / C	Robertson, K
				~~Escobar, E~~
4	Alonso, P	3	B / C	PITCHERS
5	Vogelbach, D	DH (D)	B / C	1. ~~Rodríguez, J~~
6	McNeil, J	4	B / C	2. Bassitt, C
7	Naquin, T	7 (B)	B / C	3. Carrasco, C
8	Guillorme, L	5	B / C	4. Díaz, E
9	Nido, T	2	B / C	5. Hunter, T (C) 2,3,4
P	deGrom, J	SP	B (A)(B)(C) / C / D / E	6. ~~López, Y~~ (B) 4,5
				7. Lugo, S
				8. ~~Nogosek, S~~ (A) 9+
				9. Ottavino, A
				10. Scherzer, M
				11. Walker, T
				12. Williams, T
				13. ~~deGrom, J~~ (SP)

Version 1 - 8/02/2022 at 6:15 PM

MANAGER'S SIGNATURE

OFFICIAL BATTING ORDER — Washington Nationals (H)

Tuesday, August 02, 2022

#	ORIGINAL	POS.	CHANGE	ALSO ELIGIBLE
				POSITION PLAYERS
1	Robles, V	8	B / C	Barrera, T
2	García, L	6 (C)	B / C	Escobar, A
3	Hernández, Y	7	B (1) / C	Thomas, L
				~~Vargas, I~~
4	Cruz, N	DH	B / C	PITCHERS
5	Ruiz, K	2 (A)	B / C	1. ~~Corbin, P~~
6	Meneses, J	3 (B)	B / C	2. Arano, V (A) 3,4,5
7	~~Palacios, J~~	9	B / C	3. Cishek, S
8	Hernández, C	4	B / C	4. Edwards, C (D) 5,6
9	Franco, M	5 (A)	B / C	5. Espino, P
P	Abbott, C	SP	B (A)(B)(C)(D) / C / D / E	6. Finnegan, K (C) 7,8,9
				7. Gray, J
				8. Harvey, H
				9. Machado, A
				10. ~~Ramírez, E~~ (B) 7,8,9
				11. Sánchez, A
				12. Weems, J
				13. ~~Abbott, C~~ (SP)

Version 1 - 8/02/2022 at 6:16 PM

MANAGER'S SIGNATURE

New York Mets at Washington Nationals, August 2, 2022 (fronts)

Example #6

As mentioned above, MLB umpires can track changes and take notes the way they want to. In this Mets at Nationals game, Jeremy Riggs was the second base umpire and kept changes and notes on his cards.

There was only one position player change in the game, with Washington's Lane Thomas replacing Yadiel Hernandez in left field in the top of the eighth inning. Riggs uses the number "1" to mark the change on the Nationals card.

New York Mets at Washington Nationals, August 2, 2022 (backs)

Riggs used letters to track the pitching changes, and also wrote the letter next to the first batter the relief pitcher faced. For example, when Stephen Nogosek replaced Jacob deGrom to start the sixth inning, Riggs wrote the letter "A" next to Nogosek's name, and also next to Maikel Franco on Washington's card as Franco was the first batter Nogosek faced.

Unlike Tosi in the previous example, who tracked the starting and ending point in the hitting team's order when a relief pitcher came in, Riggs only tracked the first three batters to face the relief pitcher, satisfying the rule.

On the back of his Washington card, Riggs tracked each team's mound visits; each team made one during the game.

Example #7

Équipe Québec was a one-year travel team that played in the independent Frontier League in 2019 due to Canadian COVID-19 restrictions. This was Équipe Québec's dugout card for the first game of a doubleheader against the Sussex County Miners played in Augusta, NJ. "GAME 1" is written atop the card.

Unique features of this card include:

- The Équipe Québec manager or coach only indicated righties/lefties/switch-hitters for his opponent, presumably because he knew his own players. He did this by writing "R," "L," or "S" in different-colored markers to the right of each opposing player's name.
- But for his team, the manager or coach kept score for each batter, and also tracked the number of pitches thrown per inning for his pitchers in the space under the name "Paiva."

How to Read a Lineup Card 35

GAME 1

FRONTIER League DATE: July 27th '21

ÉQUIPE QUÉBEC | **Sussex**

#	ORIGINAL	POSITION
1	Pelletier — 1B 5-3 out out	7
2	Glaude — F5 3u 1B 1B	4
3	Castro — 1B F8 out out	2
4	Pacca — 1B 5-3 HBP out	DH
5	Panas — 6u3 2B 1B out	3
6	Hodges — 2B F6 1B DB	5
7	Lacroix — 1B 43 2B 53	8
8	Rainey — F5 K out	9
9	Whatley — 3u 1B out	6
	Paiva	
	14 29 42 62 75	

#	ORIGINAL	POSITION
1	Jenkins L	8
2	Taylor S	7
3	Figueroa S	4
4	Ciriaco R	3
5	Johnson R	DH
6	Culver S	6
7	Rose R	5
8	Herrera S	2
9	Knapp L	9
	D. Marshall / Johnny	RHP

AVAILABLE POSITION PLAYERS

LEFT-HANDED	RIGHT-HANDED
Pittman	
Gauthier	
	Horvath

AVAILABLE POSITION PLAYERS

LEFT-HANDED	RIGHT-HANDED

AVAILABLE PITCHERS

LEFT-HANDED	RIGHT-HANDED
Ruel	Knapp
	Shill
Rutckyj	Moscatiello

AVAILABLE PITCHERS

LEFT-HANDED	RIGHT-HANDED

Équipe Québec at Sussex County Miners, Game 1, July 27, 2021

Normally, there is not this level of in-game detail on a lineup card, but when there is, it adds to the story the lineup card tells about the game after it is over.

Example #8

This is a Minor League (MiLB) dugout card used by the Greensboro Grasshoppers, the Pittsburgh Pirates High-A East affiliate during the 2021 season. The card

The Lineup Card

DATE: 9/14 TUES.

TEAM	1	2	3	4	5	6	7	8	9	10	11	12	R	H	E	LOB
THE BORO	X	X	1	4	1	X	1	3	X							
RENEGADES	X	1	X	X	X	X	X	X	X							

#				#			
1	PEGUERO	SS		1	VOLPE (R)	SS	
					INF:3 OF:SP		
2	GONZALES	2B		2	PEREIRA (R)	CF	
					INF:1 OF:SP		
3	TRIOLO	3B		3	WELLS (R)	C	
					INF:2 OF:SU		
4	SANCHEZ	LF		4	CHAPARRO (R)	1B	
					INF:3 OF:SU		
5	MATTHIESSEN	1B		5	DUNHAM (R)	LF	
					INF:3 OF:SO 2K:SU		
6	SABOL	C		6	NARVAEZ	DH	
					INF:1 OF:SU		
7	GORSKI	RF		7	SANFORD	RF	
					INF:2 OF:SO 2K:SU		
8	SHACKELFORD	DH		8	NELSON (R)	3B	
					INF:1 OF:SP 2K:SU		
9	DAVIS, J	CF		9	TORREALBA (R)	2B	
					INF:1 OF:SU		

SP	BURROWS			SP	SPENCE		
LH		SW	RH	LH		SW	RH
FAJARDO			ALVAREZ	CUEVAS			DEMARCO
			JARVIS				SANTOS
			WILKIE				TORRES
			WILSON				WAGAMAN

LH	PITCHERS	RH	LH	PITCHERS	RH
		BELLOMY	BARCLAY		ALVAREZ
		CAREY	MINICK		CORREA
		GARCIA			CRAFT
		GONZALEZ			ESPINAL
		MEJIA			HOLLOWAY
		MILIANO			PEREZ
		ROBERTS			RUEGGER
		SELBY			VALDEZ

High-A East South Division

 Believe 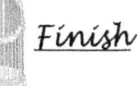 _Finish_ *Pittsburgh*

Greensboro Grasshoppers at Hudson Valley Renegades, September 14, 2021

is from a game against the Hudson Valley Renegades, a New York Yankees farm team.

There are two key differences between this card and the MLB dugout card examples above. The first is that the card includes the line score, which the Greensboro manager or coach filled in as the game went on. The Grasshoppers won the game, 10–1.

The second difference is that Greensboro included scouting notes for each of the Hudson Valley batters. For example, for Hudson Valley's leadoff hitter Anthony Volpe (one of the top MiLB prospects at the time), it reads "INF: 3 OF: SP." That is shorthand for how Greensboro wanted to position its infielders and outfielders when Volpe was at the plate.

The History of Lineup Cards

Much as the game itself, lineup cards have evolved since their first usage, believed to be in the late 19th century. This chapter charts their progression to how we know them today.

The beginning of baseball in America until 1900

Americans began playing the game of baseball as we know it in the mid–19th century, but there are no cards to be found, or even pictures of cards, for the first few decades. While it is not certain exactly when lineup cards were first used, there is evidence that different leagues required that a declaration of lineups had to be made in games by the 1880s. However, it is not clear whether those lineups were provided orally or in writing.

The earliest reference to the declaration of a batting order is found in an April 1881 article in *The New York Clipper* about a rule change coming to the National League for the 1881 season. The article states:

> A new rule adopted by the League requires the Captain of each nine to furnish the exact batting order by nine o'clock on the morning of each game and prohibits any change in order so furnished, except in cases of sickness or accident.[1]

It is not clear how lineups were handled before 1881. Could a team make its batting order as the game went on, or could it wait until closer to game time to declare it? One thing not specified by this rule is if the lineup had to be provided in writing.

There is also reference to an "official batting order" in a September 1887 *Saint Paul Daily Globe* article about a Northwestern League game the previous day between the Milwaukee Bulldozers and St. Paul Saints.

The article describes a debate over the St. Paul batting order, including:

> Manager Barnes claimed that he had notified the scorers of the change just before the game, but Hart insisted that such a fact had nothing to do with the case, as the official batting order was given him by Barnes in the morning and was printed on the scorecard.[2]

The phrase "given him" does not tell us if it is given orally or in writing.

Another article in 1887, in the November *Press and Daily Dakotaian*, summarizes an American Association rules meeting held in Pittsburgh.

Among the items discussed at the meeting included:

The rules were changed so that hereafter the official score card, with the batting order of both teams, shall be submitted to and approved by the umpire before the beginning of the game to avoid confusion and mistakes on the part of the spectators.[3]

This makes it sound like both teams had to provide their lineups to be put onto a score sheet to be approved by the umpire, but it is still not clear if the lineups had to be provided by the teams in writing, or if the "official score card" is a lineup card. More likely, the "official score card" is a score book.

Finally, Spalding's "Baseball Guide and Official League Book for 1889" included the following in the National League rules:

Rule 19 says that "Batsmen must take their position at the bat in the order in which they are named on the *score*." This *score* is not sufficiently defined in the rule, but it means the printed or written order of batting, which each captain of the contesting team presents the umpire prior to the commencement of the game; and such order, on approval from the umpire, should be copied verbatim in the score book of the official scorer of the home club, who alone is authorized to send a copy of the score of the game, as the official copy, to the secretary of the League or Association the club belongs to[4]

The way the National League rule is written, it sounds as though a written lineup had to be provided by each team, but there still is no definitive proof.

The 1900s: A picture

There was a picture posted on a public Facebook group called "Vintage Baseball" in November 2022 with the caption "Cleveland player manager Nap Lajoie reviews his lineup card before handing it to an umpire during a game in 1907."[5]

There is no provenance to prove that (1) the photo is from 1907, although Lajoie did manage the Cleveland Naps that year, and (2) more importantly, that it is in fact a lineup card that he is looking at. That said, it is believed that batting order cards were likely being used in the American League at that time, and it does look like it could be a batting order card.

If that is in fact a batting order card, it is the earliest visual evidence of one.

The 1910s: More rules and article references

An important distinction was added to the National League's rule book in 1910. Rule 39 states, in part:

The batting order of each team must be on the score card and must be delivered before the game by its captain to the umpire at home plate, who shall submit it to the inspection of the captain of the other side.[6]

The key difference starting in 1910 is the stipulation that the batting order must be provided in writing at home plate. This tradition, the pregame lineup card exchange at home plate, continues today.

There are a few references to written batting order cards during the decade, including:

- An April 1913 story in *The Chicago Daily Tribune* stating that "Umpire Brennan consulted his official batting order and talked with the rival manager" regarding a late-game lineup change in a Cubs-Reds game the day before[7]
- An article in *The Calumet News* indicating that an umpire "pulled out the official batting order" and declared a player out for batting out of order in a 1914 Washington–St. Louis game[8]

"The Reach Official American League Base Ball Guide, 1914" confirms that by at least 1914, and likely earlier, each American League was required to deliver a written copy of the order to home plate before the game:

> The batting order of each team must be on the score card and must be delivered before the game by its captain to the umpire at the home plate, who shall submit it to the inspection of the captain of the other side. The batting order delivered to the umpire must be followed throughout the game, unless a player be substituted for another, in which case the substitute must take the place in the batting order of the retired player.[9]

The 1920s: A second picture and another article reference

There continue to be examples of the usage of batting order cards, including a picture of Ty Cobb handing what is likely a Detroit Tiger batting order card to an umpire before a game, according to lineup card collector Jeffrey Lazarus. While there is no indication of when the picture was taken, Cobb managed the Tigers from 1921 to 1926.

A 1927 story in *The Sunday Star* talking about "chicanery in the conduct of the game" states:

> This official is handed cards bearing the batting order of each club before the game starts, yet they mean nothing to him unless a claim is made by one of the clubs that a batter is at the plate at the wrong time.[10]

Further into the story:

> When Joe Judge and George Sisler switched their batting position in the first two innings of the game here May 23, the Philadelphia management undoubtedly knew the men were going to bat in the wrong order. The A's bench knew that the line-up Manager Harris had handed Umpire McGowan called for Sisler to bat ahead of Judge, even though they had pasted a different line-up on the score board and telephone[d] a different line-up to the official scorer.

Aside from clearly stating that there were written batting order cards provided to the umpire in this time period, it is interesting that different versions of batting order cards are still an issue in the game to this day!

But without any actual cards or closeup pictures of cards from the 1920s, it is not clear what differences there may have been between cards used in the 1920s compared with lineup cards used in the 1930s. For example, was there a preprinted card template used by teams, or were the managers informally writing their lineups on a generic piece of paper?

The 1930s: The earliest lineup cards still in existence

The early 1930s is the era from which we start to see lineup cards still in existence. Possibly the earliest is a Washington Senators official batting order card, signed by manager and Hall of Famer Walter Johnson, that includes the names of fellow Hall members Heinie Manush and Joe Cronin.[11] While the card is undated, which was commonplace for cards of this era, research of the batting order and positions on the card reveals that the lineup was used by Johnson a handful of times during the 1931 season.

According to the description on WorthPoint, an online collectibles database, the card was sold on eBay after having been in the collection of a St. Louis Browns and St. Louis Cardinals fan. It is worth noting that two of the 1931 Washington box scores with a matching lineup were played against the Browns.

The first MLB All-Star Game was played on July 6, 1933, at Chicago's Comiskey Park, and the batting order cards for both the National and American Leagues survived thanks to Bill McKechnie, a coach who assisted National League manager John McGraw, including writing the cards.

McKechnie, a Hall of Famer, saved the cards, which were eventually sold at auction in 2007 for $138,000.[12]

The cards include a who's who of baseball names, including "Ruth," "Gehrig," "Gomez," "Grove" and "Frisch," to name just a few. Additionally, the American League card was signed by manager Connie Mack.

A picture of an official batting order card signed by Philadelphia Athletics manager Connie Mack and purported to be from 1934 was posted on Net54.com in 2018.[13] Research of the batting order written on the card finds the Athletics only used that lineup once, on May 25, 1934.

Some of the first cards include a stadium's ground rules on the back of the card, something commonplace on 20th-century batting order cards. It was handy to have

CHICAGO CUBS
Wrigley Field

HOME PLATE AREA
- Pitched or thrown ball lodges in or under grates on either side of home plate: Out of Play (Award by Book Rule).

OUTFIELD AREA
- Fair ball striking railing or screen above bleacher wall and rebounding onto playing field: In Play.
- Fair ball lodges in screen in front of bleachers: Two Bases.
- Fair ball lodges in vines on bleacher walls: Two Bases.
- Fair ball enters vines on bleacher walls and rebounds onto playing field: In Play.
- Batted ball in flight striking left or right field foul markers above painted mark: Home Run.
- Fair ball striking left or right field foul markers below painted mark: In Play.
- Fair ball lodges in or under grates in left or right field: Two Bases.

The ground rules for Wrigley Field, home of the Chicago Cubs, on the back of a batting order card (courtesy Zack Hample).

the ground rules on the back of the batting order cards exchanged at home plate before the game, as that is also when the umpires and managers went over the ground rules.

Other characteristics of cards dating from the 1930s include:

- They all use a general template, but there is some variation among teams
- Cards are one color, usually off-white, whether home or away
- Some cards include the year preprinted on the top of the card, and some do not; some cards include a line for the date to be written in, but it is not always done; because cards of this era typically only contain the starting lineup and do not indicate the team played, it can be difficult or even impossible to determine the exact date the game was played
- There usually is a dotted, slanted line in the bottom right-hand corner for the manager to sign

Hall of Famer Joe Cronin signed the card as manager and also penciled himself into the starting lineup for the Boston Red Sox in this 1935 game (courtesy Jeffrey Lazarus).

The 1940s and 1950s: Different-colored cards; signature and date lines

Different-colored home and away batting cards start to appear in the 1940s. Visiting batting order cards are a shade of light blue or blue-green and home batting order cards are off-white. Exactly why those colors were chosen is unclear, but sets of white and light-blue cards continue to be used in MLB games today.

The different colors "allows us that when we are looking at them at home plate, when we have a change, that we're not getting confused about which lineup card is which," said former MLB umpire Jim Reynolds.

But some cards in the 1940s and even into the 1950s continue to resemble the cards of the 1930s with the slanted manager's signature line and off-white color even for away cards. For example, the batting order cards below are from Game 4 of the 1944 all–St. Louis World Series between the Cardinals and Browns.

The Cardinals card, on the left, includes a line for the date to be entered, and

Hall of Famer Stan Musial hit his only postseason home run in Game 4 of the 1944 World Series (courtesy Jeffrey Lazarus).

Yogi Berra and Moose Skowron were among the starters for manager Casey Stengel's squad in a 1955 exhibition game played in Hawaii (courtesy Jeffrey Lazarus).

The Brooklyn Dodgers featured stars including Pee Wee Reese, Duke Snider, Gil Hodges, Jackie Robinson and Don Newcombe in 1955 (courtesy Jeffrey Lazarus).

Hank Aaron was a rookie in 1954 (courtesy Jeffrey Lazarus).

Roberto Clemente began his career with 121 hits in his rookie season (courtesy Jeffrey Lazarus).

does not include a manager's signature line. The Browns card, on the right, only includes the preprinted year and includes a manager's signature line.

Meanwhile, a batting order card used for a 1955 exhibition game the Yankees played in Hawaii, pictured on previous page, still has the preprinted year and slanted manager's signature line.

A Brooklyn Dodgers batting order card from Game 1 of the 1955 World Series is light blue, indicating the Dodgers were the visiting team against the New York Yankees. The card includes a line for the date to be entered but does not designate anywhere for the manager to sign the card.

Visiting team batting order cards from Hank Aaron and Roberto Clemente's respective rookie seasons in 1954 and 1955 are identical to the Dodgers card, save for the different team names.

Dugout lineup cards and carbon copies

The first dugout lineup cards begin to appear around 1960. Initially, some teams would tape or pin a batting order card on the dugout wall. For example, this 1961 Red Sox spring training card was believed to have been taped to the wall of Boston's dugout.

Around the same time, some teams begin using lineup cards specifically meant for dugout use.

The picture below is of a Milwaukee Braves dugout lineup card from the Braves' July 21, 1960, game against the St. Louis Cardinals. It is believed to be one of the first dedicated dugout cards.

This early dugout card looks little like the dugout cards of today, however. The card is similar in size to a batting order card, only includes Milwaukee's starting lineup and does not provide space to write in lineup changes during a game. But it is clearly a dugout lineup card given that the top of the card states: "For Dugout Use Only," and there is a hole at the top of the card for it to be pinned on a board or wall.

The dugout lineup cards that follow quickly evolved. Within just a

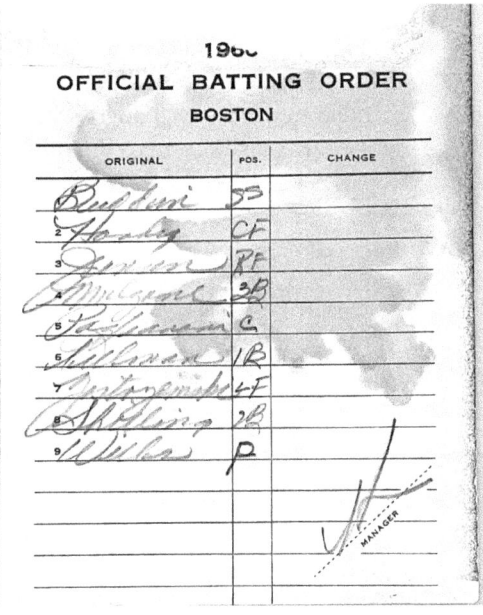

Tape marks are still visible on the top of this Boston batting order card (courtesy Jeffrey Lazarus).

This Milwaukee Braves card is one of the earliest dedicated dugout lineup cards still in existence (courtesy Jeffrey Lazarus).

The ticket stub provides reference as to how small this 1970 Baltimore dugout lineup card was (courtesy Bill Haelig).

few years, most dugout lineup cards increased significantly in size, generally measuring 8.5" × 14", although there was no uniform size.

The Baltimore Orioles were a noticeable exception to the larger cards. The Orioles continued to use a small dugout lineup card until the mid–1990s.

Dugout cards also began to include the starting lineups and other eligible players

A 1975 White Sox dugout lineup card (courtesy Jeff Garfinkel).

This 1978 Kansas City Royals dugout lineup card still has masking tape along the top of the card.

of both teams, making it much different than a batting order card, which at that time still only includes the starting lineup for one team.

Per the name "dugout lineup card," the card is posted in the dugout, where it is easier for the manager, coaches and even players to see and use it during the game. Some are pinned to a dugout wall while others are taped.

Dugout lineup cards from the 1960s until at least the 1990s are generally plain, usually just one printed color on a white or off-white card with no logos. Because they are only used in the dugout, dugout cards from the period are rarely signed by the manager.

Some American League teams did not include the pitcher on their dugout lineup card because they were not in the batting order. An interesting historical example is a lineup card from an August 10, 1977, game between the Milwaukee Brewers and Detroit Tigers. Despite the game being Hall of Famer Jack Morris's first career win, his name was not written on the lineup card. The lineup card was signed and inscribed by Morris roughly 45 years after the game.

Meanwhile, carbon copy batting order cards also start to appear around 1960. Carbon copies allow a manager or coach to handwrite a card once while

Jack Morris earned his first victory, but his name was not included on Milwaukee's dugout lineup card (courtesy Jeffrey Lazarus).

Batting order cards from Game 3 of the 1963 World Series. Space is provided at the bottom for the manager's signature. Also note the staple holes at the top of each card, likely indicating the cards were posted in the dugout (courtesy Rick Levy).

simultaneously making two or three copies along with the handwritten original. Generally, the top copy goes to the umpire, and the managers get carbon copies.

The first carbon copies continued to only include a team's starting lineup.

The diagonal line for the manager to sign disappears altogether in the 1960s, replaced with space at the bottom of the card for the manager's signature.

One of the more unique carbon copies of the time was Casey Stengel's batting order card for Game 7 of the 1960 World Series between the Pittsburgh Pirates and New York Yankees. Interestingly, both Stengel's top copy and a carbon copy reached the market, with both originating from manager Casey Stengel's personal collection.[14] Besides being from a significant game, which featured Bill Mazeroski's walk-off home run to capture the title for the Pirates, the carbon copy is noteworthy because it includes all the substitutions that Stengel made during the game, matching the handwritten copy.

This means that rather than giving the carbon copy to the umpire or opposing manager, Stengel used the carbon pad for himself with another copy or copies underneath. Eventually they got separated and were each sold at auction.

It seems reasonable to think that Stengel, who had managed since the 1930s and likely wrote out thousands of lineups on lineup cards that were not carbon pads, simply did not pay attention to the carbon pad.

1970s and 1980s: Carbon pad examples; full roster batting order cards; AL introduces the DH

Examples of full carbon copy pads used for lineup cards are not often found, since the carbons were normally separated for use during a game, though on occasion they

A draft Texas Rangers lineup card pad from a 1972 game. The card, which was not used because of a lineup change, is signed by Hall of Famer Ted Williams (courtesy Jeffrey Lazarus).

Carbon copy Yankees batting order card from the final game of the 1960 World Series (imaged by Heritage Auctions, HA.com).

do pop up, such as in instances where the manager filled out a lineup card and realized he had made a mistake, or just decided to change it.

A lineup card pad from the Texas Rangers' inaugural 1972 season is an example. Dated August 31, 1972, and written and signed by manager Ted Williams, the lineup card pad was ripped in half, likely due to Williams deciding to change the order. The rips are most visible on the carbon paper which shows half a sheet for each. The actual lineup cards were likely taped back together by an individual who recognized that it was an item worth saving, even if it was not going to be used in the game.

Looking closely at the lineup card,

The History of Lineup Cards 51

The lineup card pad was ripped, likely by Ted Williams (courtesy Jeffrey Lazarus).

A carbon copy from the lineup drafted by Ted Williams, pieced back together (courtesy Jeffrey Lazarus).

Top copy of a lineup card pad for Chuck Tanner's 1978 Pittsburgh Pirates (courtesy Jeffrey Lazarus).

Williams initially had rookie Tom Mason in the eighth slot, before deciding to play veteran Marty Martinez instead. Williams wrote the change on the lineup card, but then seems to have decided to move Martinez up to bat seventh and move Joe Lovitto to eighth. Lovitto was near the end of a rookie season that saw him bat .224, while Martinez had been acquired just a couple of weeks earlier, and had two hits, including a triple, the day before. Ultimately the changes did not help as Martinez went 0-for-4 and the Rangers lost the game to the Yankees, 7–0.

Another example of a lineup card pad is one written by longtime Pirates manager Chuck Tanner. While it is not dated, the lineup card is from 1978, the only season Will McEnaney played for the Pirates. McEnaney is listed as the starter, but never actually started a game in his MLB career.[15]

52   The Lineup Card

A piece of carbon paper in between the lineup card copies (courtesy Jeffrey Lazarus).

Will McEnaney was penned in as the starting pitcher on this lineup card draft, but McEnaney never started an MLB game in his career (courtesy Jeffrey Lazarus).

The Cleveland Indians listed just the starters on their 1988 batting order cards, but the full roster a year later (courtesy Jeffrey Lazarus).

The Baltimore Orioles also included all of their eligible players on their 1989 batting order cards. Also note the additional row "P" toward the bottom of the cards for the pitcher now that the American League is using a DH (courtesy Jeffrey Lazarus).

It is not clear why Tanner wrote in McEnaney as a starting pitcher given that he had never previously started an MLB game, nor would he the rest of his career. Regardless, it is a rare example of a lineup card carbon pad that is intact.

At least some National League teams begin populating batting order cards with their full eligible roster, as opposed to just the starting lineup, in the early 1970s.

There is evidence of the St. Louis Cardinals including their full roster on a batting order card in 1971,[16] and the Mets in 1972,[17] but it is unclear exactly when the National League began to require all teams to include their full roster on the card. American League teams do not follow suit until 1989.

The addition of the designated hitter (DH) rule in the American League means that an extra row has been added toward the bottom of American League batting order cards for the pitcher position, since the pitcher no longer takes up one of the nine spots in the batting order as they do not bat. This can be seen in the batting order card pictures above, which are American League teams.

1990s: A hint of what is to come

Only relatively minor changes are made to batting order and dugout lineup cards in the 1990s. Some teams begin to add a little creativity to their dugout lineup cards. For example, the Diamondbacks add a logo to their card.

ARIZONA DIAMONDBACKS

DATE 5-2-98

Diamondbacks

L or S	#	A / B	Name	C / D	POS.
S	1	A	WHITE ③ ⑨	C	CF
	2	A	BELL	C	SS
L	3	A	LEE ⑤ ⑧ ⑫	C	1B
	4	A	WILLIAMS ②	C	3B
	5	A	~~BENITEZ~~ ④	C	LF
		B	DELLUCCI ⑩	D	
	6	A	~~MEULENS~~ ~~FOX~~	D PITCHER	RF
		B	~~PITCHER~~		
	7	A	STINNETT ⑦ ⑧	C	C
	8	A	STANKIEWICZ ⑩	C	2B
L	9	A	~~BENES~~	C	P
		B	BREDE	D	
	10	A		C	

HITTERS

LH	S	RH
~~BREDE~~		BATISTA
~~DELLUCCI~~		
FABREGAS		
~~FOX~~		

RELIEVERS

PICKETT	BROW	
	MANUEL	
	OLSON	
	~~RODRIGUEZ~~	
	~~SODOWSKI~~	
	~~SPRINGER~~	

Expos

L or S	#	A / B	Name	C / D	POS.
S	1	A	SANTANGELO	C	2B
	2	A	GRUDZIELANEK ⑨	C	SS
S	3	A	~~FULLMER~~ ③ ⑤ ⑦ ~~STOVALL~~	C	1B
		B	~~PITCHER~~ ~~LIVINGSTONE~~ ⑪	D	
	4	A	WHITE	C	CF
	5	A	~~MAY~~	C	LF
		B	MORDECAI	D	
	6	A	GUERRERO ⑧	C	RF
	7	A	ANDREWS ②	C	3B
	8	A	WIDGER ④ ⑥ ⑩	C	C
	9	A	~~PEREZ~~	C	P
		B	~~VIDRO~~	D	
L	10	A	McGUIRE	C	

HITTERS

LH	S	RH
~~LIVINGSTONE~~ STOVALL		HUBBARD
~~McGUIRE~~ ~~VIDRO~~		~~MORDECAI~~

RELIEVERS

~~KLINE~~		~~BENNETT~~
		~~MADDUX~~
		~~TELFORD~~
		URBINA
		~~VALDES~~

The Diamondbacks put their logo on their 1998 dugout lineup cards (courtesy Jeff Garfinkel).

COLORADO ROCKIES
WORK SCHEDULE

DATE: April 5, 1993

_____ : Pre-Game Practice Stretching
_____ : Pre-Game Practice
_____
_____
_____
_____
11:50 : Stretching
12:10 : Batting Practice
    Extra Men 12:10 – 12:22
    Starters 12:22 – 36   12:36 – 12:50
1:05 : Infield Practice
_____
_____
_____ : Outfield Fungos

LINE-UP	POS
1. E. YOUNG	2B
2. COLE	CF
3. BICHETTE	RF
4. GALARRAGA	1B
5. CLARK	LF
6. HAYES	3B
7. GIRARDI	C
8. BENAVIDES	SS
9. NIED	P
P.	

1. _____ 2. _____ 3. _____ 4. _____

TENTATIVE ROTATIONS: SIDE OR BP PITCHERS:
WED   RUFFIN   _____   _____
_____   _____   _____
_____   _____   _____
_____   _____   _____

TOMORROW'S SCHEDULE: Players Report at BUS FOR WORKOUT 11:30

PRE-GAME WORK:
_____
_____
_____

TRAVEL/DEPARTURE PLANS: TOMORROW BUS 11:30

A Rockies today's lineup card for their first ever game, April 5, 1993 (courtesy Jeff Garfinkel).

Also, the Oakland A's use a card that is yellow.[18]

An early version of a today's lineup card shows up in 1993, used by the Colorado Rockies in their first-ever game. The card was likely posted in Colorado's clubhouse and included the starters as well as the pregame schedule and notes for the next two days.

The Lineup Card

Turn of the 21st century brings big changes to dugout, batting order cards

MLB lineup cards, both dugout and batting order, begin to change dramatically around the year 2000.

For batting order cards, some teams start to use computer-printed cards as a replacement for carbon copies. The change was not mandated, and teams adopted it on their own schedule.

OFFICIAL BATTING ORDER
(VISITING CLUB)

CLUB: CLEVELAND INDIANS DATE: 5/09/2003

#	ORIGINAL	POS.		CHANGE	ALSO ELIGIBLE
1	LAWTON	7	B	B	SELBY
			C		GERUT
2	VIZQUEL	6	B		BARD
			C	A	McDONALD
3	BRADLEY	8	B		
			C	F	MULHOLLAND
4	BURKS	DH	B	B	TRABER
			C	C	SADLER
5	SPENCER	9	B		
			C		BOYD
6	HAFNER	3	B	A D	ELDER
			C	E	RISKE
7	LAKER	2	B		BAEZ
			C		
8	BLAKE	5	B		SABATHIA
			C		RODRIGUEZ
9	PHILLIPS	4	B		ANDERSON
			C		DAVIS
P	WESTBROOK	1	B	C D E	
			C	F	
			D		
			E		

Manager's Signature

The Indians were likely one of the first teams to digitally print their batting order cards (courtesy Jeffrey Lazarus).

The History of Lineup Cards 57

Los Angeles Dodgers batting order cards from the 2003 and 2004 seasons (courtesy Jeffrey Lazarus).

The Indians made the change in early 2003, and the Reds made the change in the middle of 2003. Other teams, such as the Red Sox made the change sometime between the beginning of 2003 and the middle of 2004.

The Dodgers used computer-printed cards in 2003, then at least temporarily switched back to a handwritten card in 2004.

One of the last handwritten batting order card holdouts was the Detroit Tigers. Manager Jim Leyland was still writing out his lineup cards by hand in 2013.

It is easier for the manager or

Manager Jim Leyland handwrote this 2013 Tigers batting order card that included the likes of Miguel Cabrera, Max Scherzer and Justin Verlander on it (courtesy Jeffrey Lazarus).

	OFFICIAL BATTING ORDER MINNESOTA			
				DATE 03 / 30 / 2004
	ORIGINAL	POS.	CHANGE	ALSO ELIGIBLE
1	STEWART	7	B	RYAN
			C	MARSTERS
2	OFFERMAN	3	B	MORALES
			C	DAVIDSON
3	JONES	9	B	SANDOVAL
			C	SCANLAN
4	HUNTER	8	B	WEST
			C	
5	KOSKIE	5	B	
			C	
6	PUNTO	6	B	
			C	
7	BLANCO	2	B	BALFOUR
			C	RINCON
8	RODRIGUEZ	4	B	ROA
			C	MUNRO
9	THOMAS	1	B	LORRAINE
			C	HODGE
P			B	
			C	
			D	
			E	

Minnesota Twins manager Ron Gardenhire's signature was digitally copied and pasted onto these 2004 batting order cards (courtesy Jeffrey Lazarus).

coach to type cards out on a computer and indicate righties, lefties and switch-hitters with black, red and blue ink, respectively (if a team chooses to do so), and computer-printed cards are easier for the home plate umpire and other manager to read.

For the most part, managers continue to hand-sign their batting order cards. The Minnesota Twins are believed to be one of the first to use digital signatures on cards, as far back as 2004.

The Atlanta Braves got creative by adding their logo as a watermark on a 2018 batting order card (courtesy Jeffrey Lazarus).

The Mets printed Citi Field's inaugural season logo on the back of their 2009 batting order cards (courtesy Jeffrey Lazarus).

For the first few years of computer-printed batting order cards, teams are given some leeway regarding what they can print on their cards. Some examples of their creativity are above and on the following page.

It is also worth noting that the stadium ground rules written on the back of the home team's batting order cards for so long, begin to disappear early in the 21st century. There is nothing preprinted on the back of current MLB batting order cards.

Dugout cards, meanwhile, start to get a major face lift. Again, not every team jumps on board at the outset, but the changeover is fairly quick and dramatic.

Gone are the vanilla, 8.5" × 14" (or thereabout), one-color cards. The new dugout card is larger (11" × 17"), more modern looking with a colorful design and typically has the logos of both teams and MLB as watermarks.

The new design fits with the efforts of MLB and teams to sell more game-used memorabilia. Whereas dugout lineup cards were only marginally a collectible in the 20th century, they become one of the pieces in modern baseball's effort to sell virtually anything associated with a game, whether it be uniforms, bats, bases, even pitching rubbers.

Interestingly, batting order cards are one of the few items not generally sold by either teams or MLB itself, although a couple of teams began offering batting order cards for sale in 2022.

The Lineup Card

	OFFICIAL BATTING ORDER (VISITING CLUB)			
CLUB				
	ORIGINAL	POS.	CHANGE	DATE 05 / 15 / 06 ALSO ELIGIBLE
1	PODSEDNIK	7	B	JENKS
			C	MONTERO
2	CINTRON	4	B	POLITTE
			C	COTTS
3	THOME	DH	B	LOGAN
			C	THORNTON
4	KONERKO	3	B	
			C	
5	CREDE	5	B	PIERZYNSKI
			C	GLOAD
6	MACKOWIAK	9	B	IGUCHI
			C	DYE
7	URIBE	6	B	OZUNA
			C	
8	WIDGER	2	B	
			C	McCARTHY
9	ANDERSON	8	B	GARLAND
			C	VAZQUEZ
P	GARCIA	1	B	BUEHRLE
			C	
			D	
			E	

Manager's Signature *Ozzie Guillen*

DATE 08 / 05 / 06 ALSO ELIGIBLE: JENKS, McDOUGAL, RISKE, COTTS, THORNTON, GLOAD, MACKOWIAK, LOMAR, OZUNA, URIBE, CONTRERAS, BUEHRLE, GARCIA, GARLAND

DATE 05 / 10 / 07
ALSO ELIGIBLE
LOGAN
SISCO
THORNTON
AaRDSMA
MASSET
MacDOUGAL
JENKS

TERRERO
CREDE
MOLINA
CINTRON

GARLAND
BUEHRLE
VAZQUEZ
DANKS

Ozzie G.

8/18/2011
ALSO ELIGIBLE
THORNTON
SALE
OHMAN

CRAIN
SANTOS
FRASOR
STEWART

QUENTIN
LUCY
MOREL
LILLIBRIDGE

PEAVY
DANKS
FLOYD
BUEHRLE

The White Sox had some fun by including different pictures of Ozzie Guillen on their batting order cards in the years he managed the team (courtesy Jeffrey Lazarus).

OAKLAND ATHLETICS at BOSTON RED SOX
FENWAY PARK • BOSTON, MA • MAY 14, 2018

HP - BEN MAY   1B - MARK WEGNER   2B - JOHN TUMPANE   3B - JIM REYNOLDS

OAKLAND ATHLETICS

#	ORIGINAL	POS.	CHANGE
1	SEMIEN	6	
2	JOYCE	7	
3	LOWRIE	4	
4	DAVIS	DH	
5	OLSON	3	
6	CHAPMAN	5	
7	CANHA	9	
8	LUCROY	2	
9	FOWLER	8	
P	MANAEA	1	

BOSTON RED SOX

#	ORIGINAL	POS.	CHANGE
1	BETTS	9	
2	BENINTENDI	8	
3	RAMIREZ	3	
4	MARTINEZ	7	
5	BOGAERTS	6	
6	NUNEZ	4	
7	SWIHART	DH	
8	DEVERS	5	
9	LEON	2	
P	PORCELLO	1	

AVAILABLE POSITION PLAYERS (Oakland)

LEFT-HANDED	SWITCH	RIGHT-HANDED
MAXWELL		PINDER
	SMOLINSKI	

AVAILABLE POSITION PLAYERS (Boston)

LEFT-HANDED	SWITCH	RIGHT-HANDED
BRADLEY		VAZQUEZ
HOLT		~~RUSTIS~~
MORELAND		

AVAILABLE PITCHERS (Oakland)

LEFT-HANDED	RIGHT-HANDED
COULOMBE	CASILLA
	DULL/FONT
	HATCHER
	PETIT
	TRIVINO
	TREINEN

AVAILABLE PITCHERS (Boston)

LEFT-HANDED	RIGHT-HANDED
JOHNSON	WRIGHT
	KELLY
	BARNES
	HEMBREE
	SMITH
	KIMBREL

MANAGER SIGNATURE _____

Twenty-first-century MLB dugout cards are both larger and more colorful.

2018–2021: The perfect storm of more rule changes and COVID-19

A combination of MLB implementing a few rules changes to try and help improve pace of play and the subsequent onset of COVID-19 two years later created a perfect storm of sorts for changes in the use of official batting order cards during games from 2018 through 2021.

- Starting in 2018, teams have a limited number of times they can visit their pitcher on the mound over the course of a game. The home plate umpire must keep track of the number of mound visits for each team.[19]
- An MLB-instituted "minimum number of batters for pitchers" rule is adopted in 2019. It requires that starting and relief pitchers must pitch to either a minimum of three batters or the end of a half-inning, with some exceptions. The home plate umpire must make sure teams adhere to the rule.[20]
- For the first time, in 2020, a runner is placed on second at the start of every extra half-inning. Further, the runner placed on second is the player in the batting order immediately preceding that half-inning's leadoff hitter. The home plate umpire must keep track of who the runner on second should be.[21]
- The same year, roster size from Opening Day through August 31 is increased by one player, from 25 to 26. From September 1 through the end of the regular season, MLB teams can carry up to 28 players for a game.[22]
- Also in 2020, the National League temporarily adds the Designated Hitter rule for the COVID-19-shortened season, before adding it permanently in 2022.[23]

"The responsibility of the umpire now, especially the home plate umpire, has gone way beyond just calling balls and strikes, safe and out," said MLB umpire Jim Reynolds in an interview after the 2021 season. "We have to keep mound visits. We have to keep the lineup. We have to make sure there's 26 guys [on each batting order card]. We have to make sure this guy is actually on the lineup card. Now it's how many batters, also, that this reliever has faced."

"And as we get to extra innings, we also have to make sure we make a note of who made the last out so he goes to second," continued Reynolds.

As a result of the rule changes and added responsibilities, all MLB umpire crews started to have at least one other umpire, in addition to the home plate umpire, track all of this beginning in 2021.

Reynolds said that for his and most umpire

An example of notes written by an umpire on the back of a batting order card during a 2022 game (courtesy Tony Voda).

crews, the umpire at third also tracks changes and other pertinent info such as mound visits on his cards.

"Almost every crew is having the third base guy do it," said Reynolds. "The reason for that is he's got immediate access to the plate guy between innings. He doesn't have to run across the field. And then he's got access, in our case, to a dugout with a phone."

"On some crews, all four guys keep a lineup card," continued Reynolds. "On our crew, it's the plate guy and the third base guy. A lot of times as crew chief, I'll keep a set, too, just so if we get together, I don't have to be educated on everything, so it saves a little bit of time. But every crew does it differently."

Notes written by an umpire on the back of a batting order card during a 2021 game (courtesy Tony Voda).

So while there would almost always be just three sets of batting order cards for an MLB game before 2021—a set for each of the two teams and a set for the home plate umpire—now there could potentially be as many as six sets for a regular season game, and eight sets for a playoff game, although Reynolds thought it unlikely that more than four umpires would keep a set of cards.

One positive from all the changes, from Reynolds's perspective, is that getting the batting order cards in the locker room during 2020 and 2021 gave him and other umpires more time to check the cards. Traditionally, the home plate umpire would not first see the cards until the exchange at home plate minutes before first pitch.

Due to COVID-19 protocols, during 2020 and 2021 lineups were exchanged electronically using an MLB mobile application approximately a couple of hours before a game, and then sent back to the stadium where the official batting order cards were computer printed. The umpires and managers still met at home plate before the game, but received their copies of the batting order cards before they left the locker room.

"What used to happen prior to 2020, they'd hand me three sets at the plate," he said. "And I would make sure they are all identical there, make sure that we have one-through-nine, make sure that if there are two Robinsons on the card that they are designated by their first initial, and then I'd hand them back and keep one."

"It's one less thing we have to worry about that we've already crossed off before we go out there, in an environment that's not as stressful," Reynolds continued in the 2021 interview. "It allows us a lot more thoroughness. It's a lot better for us to knock that out prior to us going out [to the field]."

MLB also introduced a version number and time stamp to batting order cards to help the umpire and managers avoid using the wrong version if any last-minute lineup changes were made. Managers and the home plate umpire confirmed at home plate that everyone has the correct version of the card. This means that the managers

OFFICIAL BATTING ORDER
Cleveland Indians

Wednesday, May 26, 2021

#	ORIGINAL	POS.	CHANGE		ALSO ELIGIBLE
1	Hernandez, C	4	B		**POSITION PLAYERS**
			C		Chang, Y
2	Luplow, J	8	B		Hedges, A
			C		Rosario, A
3	Ramírez, J	5	B		**PITCHERS**
			C		1. Hentges, S
4	Rosario, E	7	B		2. Nelson, K
			C		3. Bieber, S
5	Ramirez, H	9	B		4. Civale, A
			C		5. Clase, E
6	Naylor, J	DH	B		6. Karinchak, J
			C		7. Maton, P
7	Miller, O	6	B		8. Mejía, J
			C		9. Quantrill, C
8	Bauers, J	3	B		10. Sandlin, N
			C		11. Shaw, B
9	Rivera, R	2	B		12. Stephan, T
			C		13. Wittgren, N
P	McKenzie, T	SP	B		14. McKenzie, T (SP)
			C		
			D		
			E		

Version 1 - 5/26/2021 at 4:51 PM

There was no manager signature line, and therefore no signature, on this 2021 Cleveland Indians batting order card.

no longer needed to sign their cards. In fact, they could not sign the opposing team's card or home plate umpire's card in 2020 or 2021 because they did not touch them. As an example, the 2021 Cleveland batting order card above does not even have a manager's signature line on it.

While the away cards continue to be light blue, and home cards white, there is now an "A" in the upper right-hand corner of the card for the away team's card, and an "H" on the home team's card.

The cardboard and templates for MLB batting order cards are now provided by the league, so the size and designs are all the same. In the past, card sizes and designs fluctuated a little bit by team.

2022: Back to the new normal, sort of

Some aspects of batting order cards go back to normal in 2022. For example, batting order cards are back to being exchanged at home plate before the game.

"We're back to the old school way, with more than two copies at home plate, which is why we are sticking with the version part," said Reynolds in a 2022 interview. "Now, because we need one [card] for me, one for another umpire on the field

OFFICIAL BATTING ORDER
Minnesota Twins **H**

Friday, May 13, 2022

	ORIGINAL	POS.	CHANGE	ALSO ELIGIBLE
				POSITION PLAYERS
1	Buxton, B	8	B	
			C	Contreras, M
2	Arraez, L	3	B	Kiriloff, A
			C	Celestino, G
3	Polanco, J	4	B	Miranda, J
			C	**PITCHERS**
4	Kepler-Rozycki, M	9	B	1. Thielbar, C
			C	2. Archer, C
5	Sanchez, G	DH	B	3. Cano, Y
			C	4. Cotton, J
6	Urshela, G	5	B	5. Duffey, T
			C	6. Duran, J C
7	Gordon, N	7	B	7. Jax, G A
			C	8. Pagan, E D
8	Jeffers, R	2	B	9. Ryan, J
			C	10. Smith, J B
9	Lewis, R	6	B	11. Stashak, C
			C	12. Winder, J
P	Gray, S	SP	B ABCD	13. Gray, S (SP)
			C	
			D	
			E	

Version 1 - 5/13/2022 at 5:09 PM

MANAGER'S SIGNATURE _____

2022 Twins batting order card signed by manager Rocco Baldelli (courtesy Tony Voda).

and one for the opposing manager, they're bringing three or four out. The version [number] allows us not to have to authenticate that they're all the same. As long as they all say 'Version 1,' we can assume that they are all the same. That's the reason they're doing that at least from our end.

"I think it's pretty universal now, that somebody [in the field] does it," continued Reynolds. "Some crew chiefs like keeping it and have another guy keep it. On my crew, I have the third base guy keep it because he's got the easiest access to the plate guy if there's an issue."

There is no hard-and-fast rule, though. "A lot of crews have moved to having the second base guy keep it because they're having either the third base guy or the first base guy do the substance checks," said Reynolds.

Managers have the option of hand-signing or copying and pasting a digital signature on their cards. At least one field umpire continues to keep a set of cards along with the home plate umpire, but whereas team batting order cards have varied a bit in size and design since computer-printed cards were introduced, they have now been standardized.

The Use of Lineup Cards in Other Sports

Lineup cards are not exclusive to baseball. In fact, virtually all professional team sports require the formal submission or declaration of some type of lineup or eligible player list for a game or event. In some cases, it is or was done with a lineup card or something similar.

Like baseball, COVID-19 has had a significant impact on how lineups are submitted for other sports. At certain levels in some sports, including the National Hockey League (NHL) and National Basketball Association (NBA), COVID-19 has led to a permanent change from hard copy lineup cards to electronic roster submission.

For sports that have in the past used, or continue to use, some form of lineup card, there is much less collectability than in baseball, if any.

A look at different levels of some of the most popular team sports to see which have, and still use, a lineup card or something similar follows.

Hockey

Based on research and input from those in or close to the game, hockey has long had a process that closely resembles baseball in that the head coach must submit his signed lineup—referred to as the "Club Playing Roster" on NHL cards—before a game.

But the NHL, professional hockey's highest level, changed its process for declaring lineups before a game after the outset of COVID-19.

According to an NHL team spokesperson, "due to COVID, lineups are entered online only now. [The] visiting team enters [its] lineup first. Everyone once in a while, if [the] NHL system is down, teams still submit a written copy to off ice officials."

Before COVID-19, the visiting team created and submitted four copies of its roster first: one each to the official scorer, referee, opposing coach and one for itself. The home team was given the opportunity to review the visiting team's lineup, then went through the same submission process.

The NHL lineup cards were four-part carbon copies like the carbon copy cards used by MLB two to three decades ago, with the original copy going to the official scorer.

As of the 2021–2022 season, at least one of hockey's minor leagues, the ECHL, was still using lineup cards to determine eligible rosters for its games.

Like the NHL, the ECHL uses four-part carbon pads dubbed the "Official Lineup Card."

A pair of 2022 ECHL lineup card carbon copies.

There is evidence of collectability of past NHL lineup cards, but it is nominal compared to MLB.

An informal June 2022 eBay search found a handful of NHL lineup cards for sale or recently sold.

Those that had sold—they were all pairs of cards—went for between $30 to $50. Those still for sale ranged in price from $40 to $100. The cards were all handwritten, signed by the coaches and appear to be the top carbon copy.

The NHL itself sold or auctioned off at least some cards, although based on an old page on the NHL Auctions website, it appears to have been infrequent. An example of a card available at that time was from the 2010 NHL Winter Classic game.[1] No final price was available.

A separate web page for framed lineup cards from Game 6 of the 2019 Stanley Cup Finals indicates the item sold for $180.[2]

Another web page shows a framed pair of lineup cards from "Patrice Bergeron 3rd NHL Hat Trick" sold for $330 in 2018.[3]

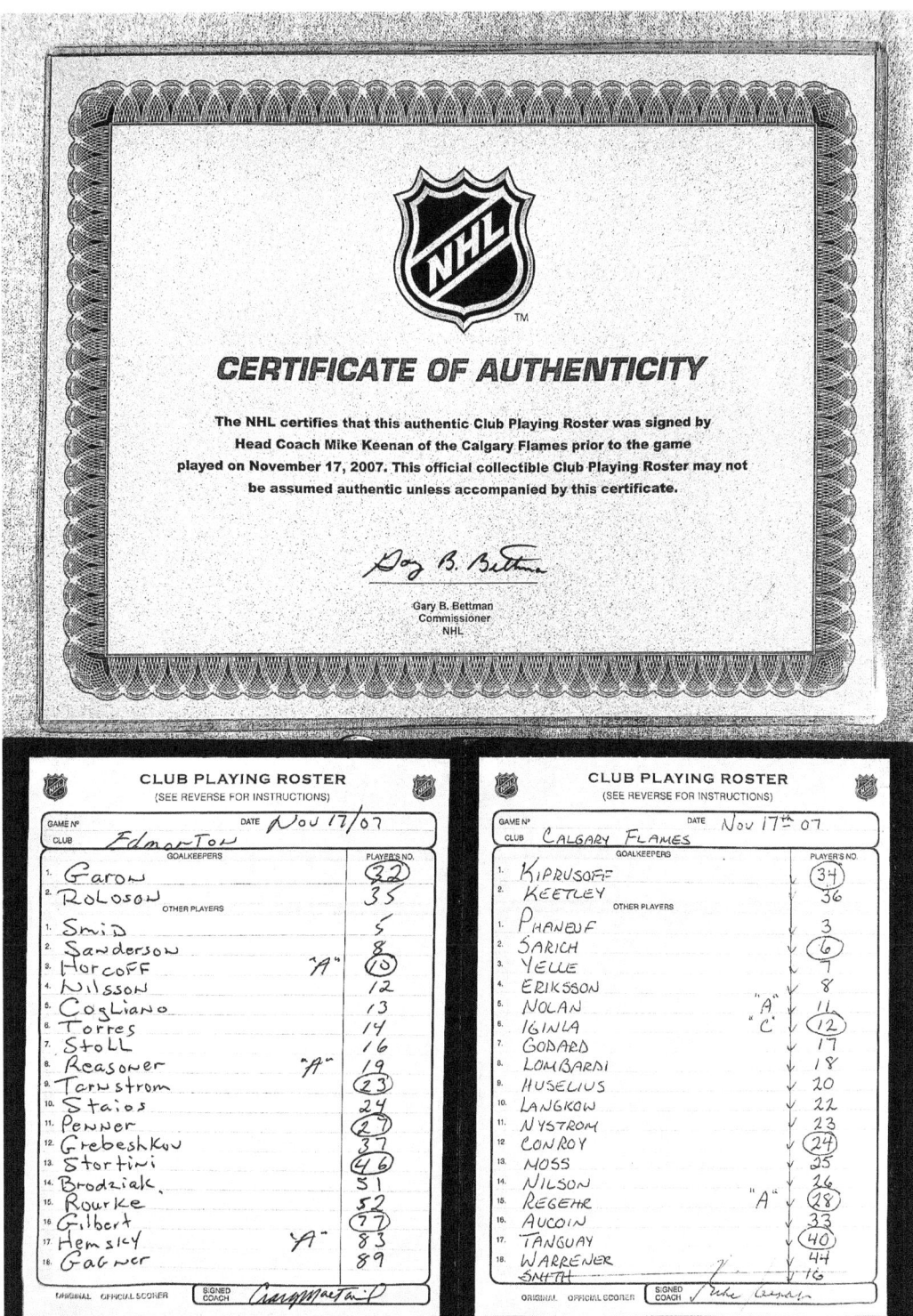

The lineup cards from an Edmonton-Calgary game along with the "Certificate Of Authenticity" included by the NHL (courtesy Ian Meadows).

70   The Lineup Card

Dallas Stars — Game N° 1202, Date 4·8·15

#	Goalkeepers	Player #
1.	ENROTH	1
2.	LEHTONEN	32

#	Other Players	Player #
1.	JOKIPAKKA	2
2.	KLINGBERG	3
3.	DEMERS	4
4.	DALEY "A"	6
5.	HORCOFF "C"	10
6.	BENN	14
7.	GARBUTT	16
8.	EAVES	18
9.	EAKIN	20
10.	ROUSSEL	21
11.	SCEVIOUR	22
12.	BENN	24
13.	GOLIGOSKI	33
14.	NEMETH	37
15.	FIDDLER "A"	38
16.	NICHUSHKIN	43
17.	HEMSKY	83
18.	SPEZZA	90
	SEGUIN	91

Anaheim — Date APR 9/15

#	Goalkeepers	Player #
1.	ANDERSEN	31
2.	GIBSON	36

#	Other Players	Player #
1.	STONER	3
2.	FOWLER	4
3.	COGLIANO	7
4.	PERRY A	10
5.	GETZLAF	15
6.	KESLER	17
7.	SACEMAN	18
8.	MAROON	19
9.	PALMIERI	21
10.	BEAUCHEMIN A	23
11.	DESPRES	24
12.	SILFVERBERG	33
13.	BELESKEY	39
14.	THOMPSON	44
15.	VATANEN	45
16.	SEKAC	46
17.	LINDHOLM	47
18.	RAKELL	67
	WAGNER	62

A pair of lineup cards from a 2015 Dallas Stars–Anaheim Ducks game (courtesy Aaron Goldstein).

The picture on previous page is of a pair of cards the NHL auctioned off from a 2007 Calgary Flames–Edmonton Oilers game. The cards came with a "Certificate of Authenticity."

As of October 2022, there were no lineup cards available for sale on the NHL Auctions website.

Aaron Goldstein owns a pair of NHL lineup cards from an April 8, 2015, game between the Dallas Stars and Anaheim Ducks. His favorite hockey player to collect memorabilia for, goaltender Jhonas Enroth, pitched a shutout in a 4–0 Stars win.

Goldstein won the cards in an auction for about $20 and was happy to add them to his Enroth collection.

"I remember seeing an NHL auction with some lineup cards available a few years ago, and I thought people adding them to their collections was a pretty unique idea to expand a collection," he said. "[The Enroth card] fits into my collection because it marked a game in which Enroth not only played, but earned his fifth career NHL shutout."

Goldstein would be interested in more Enroth lineup cards if the price was right, but he has never seen any others available.

Football

The National Football League does not have a traditional lineup card or paper roster submission, according to a spokesperson for the New York Giants.

"That information is usually provided 90 minutes before a game is scheduled to start," the Giants spokesperson said. "Team officials, along with game officials, meet and exchange that information. It's submitted electronically."

Based on both a review of the 2021 NCAA Football Rules and Interpretations as well as input from college football media relations staff, there are no lineup cards or anything similar in college football.[4] The closest thing college football has to a lineup card is what they refer to as flip cards, which typically include rosters and starting lineups.

Flip cards are used by media, other off-the-field staff and are sometimes made available to fans. There is some collectability of college football flip cards, as evidenced by a couple dozen available for sale on eBay in mid–2022. Prices ranged from $15–$25 per card.

Basketball

While both the men's and women's NCAA basketball rule books, respectively, state that lineups must be provided to the official scorer, there is no mention of it needing to be in writing:

> Before the 10-minute mark is reached on the game clock that is counting down the time before the start of the game, each team shall supply the scorers with names and uniform numbers of team members who may participate, and those of the five starting players.[5]

College basketball media relations staff confirmed that it does not need to be provided on paper, and there are no lineup cards along the lines of those used in baseball. Like college football, some teams make flip cards available to media and fans.

Teams in the NBA G League, the NBA's minor league, trade lineups well before tip-off, but not on a formal lineup card according to a spokesperson for the Sioux Falls Skyforce.

"We use a pretty generic way of getting lineups in," the spokesperson said via email. "It has to be completed within 90 minutes of tip-off, but most teams get them in two hours before. [The] home team's PR person will get their team's lineup and inactives from their [head coach] and bring to [the] opposing team. They share the same, go to [the head coach] with [the] info and input into our stat system."

The NBA had a "Team Roster—Active List" that served a similar purpose as baseball's official batting order cards. The active list was a black-and-white, 11" × 8.5" paper form including the active players for that day's game and was signed and dated by the team coach.

But the NBA recently switched to digital lineup submission, according to an NBA spokesperson. "The first time that the available player list was electronic rather than on paper was in the Summer of 2020 when we restarted the season in the 'bubble' in Orlando during the COVID-19 Pandemic," the spokesperson said.

Internet searches in mid–2022 did not show any NBA active lists for sale, and it did not appear that they were made available to the public with any regularity.

But there is at least one collector of NBA active lists.

Tyler Stocking was a student at Union University in Jackson, Tennessee in the mid–2010s. He and some friends would make the 75-minute drive to and from Memphis to see the Grizzlies play.

"We got season tickets for probably the worst seats in the house just to go to all the Grizzlies games we could go to," Stocking said. "Just by chance, the statistician for the Memphis Grizzlies, who is probably the absolute source on Memphis sports history, started a conversation with a friend of mine and I before one of the games. He showed me, 'this is what I'm doing now, I'm heading to the locker room to get this signed by the opposing coach.'"

"This" was the active list, which Stocking refers to as a lineup card.

"I said to him, 'what do you do with those after the fact?'" Stocking recalled. "He said, 'most of the time, we throw them away.' So at that point, I was in shock and said, 'could I ever get some of those?'"

The official statistician is responsible for going to both teams' locker rooms a couple of hours before a game and getting the coaches to sign the official active lists, one for each team, then "make photocopies of those and then that's distributed to the other coaches and all of the media members," explained Stocking. "But there's only one original copy. And that's the ones that I'm collecting, the ones signed by the coaches for each respective team."

Stocking built a relationship with the Memphis statistician and got 59 lineup cards over a three-year period, all from Grizzlies home games. Because the statistician needed the cards during the game, getting the cards involved some logistics.

"I always attempted to meet the statistician courtside, near the scorer's table after the game," Stocking said. "For games that I purchased lower bowl tickets, it was never an issue, but when I sat in the season tickets in the upper deck, sometimes I would be unable to meet him after the game, especially for high security games, for example, Kobe's last game in Memphis, Warriors games, Cavs games and playoff games. The statistician was always part of the post-game meeting with the referees, so I had to quickly meet him after the game or wait until a later game. In those situations, I would text the statistician and ask him to hold those sheets for the next game, and I would meet him before the game started."

National Basketball Association
Team Roster – Active List

Team: Cleveland Cavaliers
Date: 10-28-15 **Game:** Cleveland @ Memphis
                         Visiting Team   Home Team

The Head or Assistant Coach must designate its active players by circling the 11, 12 or 13 players to be included on the team's Active List for today's game.

Player Name

1. Cunningham, Jared
2. Dellavedova, Matthew
3. Harris, Joe
4. Irving, Kyrie – Inactive
5. James, LeBron
6. Jefferson, Richard
7. Jones, James
8. Kaun, Sasha
9. Love, Kevin
10. Mozgov, Timofey
11. Shumpert, Iman – Inactive
12. Smith, JR
13. Thompson, Tristan
14. Varejao, Anderson
15. Williams, Mo

Updated Roster Additions

16. _____
17. _____
18. _____
19. _____

Head Coach: David Blatt   Signature   10-28-15

Official Scorer: JOHN GUINOZZO   Signature   Oct. 28, 2015

The 2015–2016 Cleveland Cavaliers, led by LeBron James, would go on to win the NBA Championship that year (courtesy Tyler Stocking).

Stocking assumes the statistician told others about the lineup cards, but they probably did not see them the way Stocking does.

"I'm very analytical and I see the story behind the piece," Stocking said. "A lot of people would say, 'that's just a piece of paper signed in blue pen by a coach.' To me, I see that as that's what's authorizing those players to play in this big game. If something big happens in that game, this is the sheet that authorizes that player to play in that game."

Stocking points to a 2016 game when guard C. J. McCollum was inadvertently

The Stephen Curry–led Golden State Warriors won the 2016–2017 NBA Championship (courtesy Tyler Stocking).

left off the Portland Trail Blazers' lineup card, and therefore was ineligible to play. McCollum was the teams' second leading scorer at the time.

"That nailed home the significance to me [of the lineup cards] in that a minor error such as circling the wrong name could truly hold an All-Star caliber player out of an NBA game," he said.

The fact Stocking went to all the games he has lineup cards for makes the cards even more valuable to him. "That's kind of what makes it cool to me as well is that I was at those games. I can remember a certain play," he said.

About half of the cards in Stocking's collection are from the home team Grizzlies, and the rest from other NBA teams, including the Lakers, Celtics, Bulls, Spurs and Warriors. All the cards are the original, hand-signed documents.

Stocking already has one lineup card signed by a Hall of Fame coach, George Karl, and others likely to eventually join, including Gregg Popovich and Steve Kerr.

NBA Hall of Famer Kobe Bryant played his final season for the Lakers in 2015–2016 (courtesy Tyler Stocking).

In terms of players listed on the cards, he has the likes of Hall of Famer Kobe Bryant, Dwyane Wade, Tim Duncan, Stephen Curry and LeBron James, to name just a few.

Stocking has only seen a few other NBA cards other than those in his collection. He remembers seeing a card from the 2013 NBA Finals between San Antonio and Miami that was auctioned off by the NBA. A few of his friends also have a handful of cards.

"The Memphis ones, for the most part, were probably thrown in the trash before I showed interest in them," Stocking said. "They're probably [others] out there ... but pretty rare."

What does he think the NBA lineup cards are worth? He remembers the 2013 NBA Finals card being sold for around $1,000. As to the cards he and his friends owns, "A regular season one could probably not fetch anywhere near that, but it definitely shows there would be a market out there."

In fact, Stocking has been approached by people wanting to buy one or more of his cards, but he has politely declined.

"When I was in college getting these lineup cards, those brought a lot of joy to me and they're memories for those games," he said.

Almost all his cards are stored, save for the first two he ever got.

"The first one I ever got, it was the set, it was the Miami Heat versus Memphis Grizzlies," Stocking said. "I got [those] framed with a picture from the game. A friend and I actually sat pretty near to Justin Timberlake, so we got a picture with him. I framed those two lineup cards with that photo. That's something that hangs up in my basement."

Stocking has not been to a Memphis game since 2019 and was not aware that NBA team lineups are now submitted digitally rather than by lineup card.

"Thinking that other individuals won't be able to have that piece of history in the future is a little bit sad, but it does enhance the value of the ones that are out there," he said.

Soccer

For college soccer, according to the 2022 and 2023 NCAA Men's and Women's Soccer Rules book:

> An official NCAA game roster, including the names, numbers and total number of cautions and ejections of all players, coaches and other bench personnel, shall be submitted to the official scorekeeper not later than 30 minutes before game time. In addition, the roster shall include the name(s) and number(s) of the suspended player(s) and date(s) of the suspension(s).[6]

Said Jim Wojtkun, head coach of the NCAA Division III Baldwin Wallace University women's soccer team, "From an NCAA perspective, we have to submit our game day roster with our starting 11 highlighted." Wojtkun has an 11" × 8.5" template that he creates before the season with player names and roster numbers preprinted. He prints one out for each game, and indicates any cautions and ejections as directed by the rules.

England's Premier League, considered the world's top professional soccer league and perhaps the most recognizable league in all of professional sports, has "team sheets."

The Premier League Handbook for the 2021/2022 season states:

At least 75 minutes before the time fixed for the kick-off of a League Match, a representative of each participating club shall submit a team sheet by method as approved by the Board containing the following particulars: (1) the shirt numbers and names of its Players (including substitute Players) who are to take part in that League Match; (2) the colour of the Strip to be worn by its Players, including the goalkeeper; and (3) the names and job titles of up to seven Officials who will occupy the trainer's bench during that League Match[7]

Like baseball's official batting order cards, Premier League teams sheets are signed by the manager. Once the rosters and lineups have been set, the home team mass-produces a version of the team sheet with the rosters and starting lineups of both teams for media and fans.

Teams in the United Soccer League (USL) use what is called the "Official Game Day Lineup," which we will call a lineup card for short. The USL includes multiple divisions which sit under Major League Soccer, the top level of soccer in the United States.

The USL's lineup card includes the same information as the Premier League's team sheet. The cards are carbon copies like MLB batting order cards used to be.

Research finds little collectability of the Premier League's team sheet—not including the mass-produced versions sold to fans at the

An FC Cincinnati lineup card from a 2017 game (courtesy Todd Osborne).

78   The Lineup Card

stadium as there are several of those for sale or recently sold on eBay—but there is one very notable soccer team sheet that was kept by a fan and sold for a significant amount of money.

That team sheet was from Sir Alex Ferguson's 1986 Premier League debut as manager of Manchester United and is signed by Ferguson. Ferguson is considered one of soccer's all-time great managers.

According to a 2013 ESPN article, the card was given to an Oxford fan as a

The first soccer lineup cards Todd Osborne ever scored, from a 2010 game (courtesy Todd Osborne).

souvenir by Peter Rhoades-Brown, an Oxford player.[8] How Rhoades-Brown got the team sheet is unclear.

The Oxford fan put the Ferguson debut team sheet up for auction in 2013, and it was expected to sell for about £3,000. However, it ended up selling to an undisclosed buyer for £19,500 (worth about $30,000 at the time).[9]

7/7/2017					Game Day Roster			
National Premier Soccer League					🌐 npsl.bonzidev.com ✉ director@npslsoccer.net 📞 (555) 555-5555			
~~Dayton Dynamo~~								GAME DAY ROSTER

	DATE	TIME	LOCATION	GAME ID	EVENT / LEAGUE	REGION/CONFERENCE	ESTIMATED ATTENDANCE
GAME	07/07/2017	07:30 PM	Roger Glass Stadium	4033977	2017 NPSL Season	East Conference	

	TEAM NAME	SCORE	TEAM INITIALS	CONTACT NAME	CONTACT PHONE
HOME	Dayton Dynamo			Dan Griest	(937) 207-9833 (cell)
AWAY	Erie Commodores			John Melody	(814) 490-5121 (cell)

	FULL NAME	ROLE	RED CARDS	YELLOW CARDS	COACH SIGNATURE
STAFF	Catherine Gordon	Assistant Coach			
	Dan Griest	Head Coach			
	Jeff Monbeck	Assistant Coach			
	James Thomas	Assistant Coach			

	#	FULL NAME	DATE OF BIRTH	POSITION	STARTER	RESERVE	NOT ROSTERED	MINUTE IN	MINUTE OUT	GOALS	GOAL MINUTES	ASSISTS	CAUTION (CODE)	CAUTION MINUTE	SEND OFF (CODE)	SEND OFF MINUTE
ROS	20	Christian Alexander	09/30/1993	D		X										
	21	Michael Deyhle	07/14/1989	D		X										
	4	Nick Hagenkord	06/05/1996	M		X										
	13	Conner Hughes	11/26/1996	M	X											
	0	Ryan Hulings	07/19/1991	GK	X											
	5	Eric Hutton	09/17/1996	M		X										
	24	David Janusz	02/27/1995	M		X										
	3	Baye Ali Kebe	12/24/1978	D		X										
	9	Matthew Kinkopf	06/02/1995	F	X											
	26	Austin Kinley	12/29/1996	D	X											
	12	Tristan Lyle	10/03/1996	F	X											
		Kristian Moore-Cowell	10/28/1996	M		X										
	16	Peyton Mowery	07/16/1997	D	X											
	23	Krzysztof Rapacz	07/10/1994	D		X										
	10	Tate Robertson	05/31/1997	M	X											
	18	Bradley Schluter	11/16/1994	M	X											
	28	Angelo Willi	06/10/1994	M		X										

A 2017 Dayton Dynamo (NPSL) game day roster (courtesy Todd Osborne).

In the United States, Todd Osborne collects both baseball and soccer lineup cards.

"I started collecting baseball lineup cards first.... I wish I had thought about asking for [soccer lineup cards] when I was stationed in England (1982–1995), but the thought never crossed my mind," he said.

"I got my first soccer lineup card at a Dayton Dutch Lions game in 2010," Osborne continued. "Dayton had a team in the USL Pro, and they played at Bellbrook High School in Bellbrook, Ohio. I got both teams' lineup cards from the Dutch Lions' coach."

Osborne estimates he has between 75 and 100 soccer lineup cards, primarily from USL division teams, but also the National Premier Soccer League. He has gotten them primarily from coaches, but also the press box. "Referees typically keep them and turn them in to the league office," he said.

He is not aware of anyone else that collects soccer cards. "I've never met anyone else who has asked for these," he said.

Softball

Softball is considered a direct descendant of baseball, and as such, it is not surprising that softball's use of lineup cards is more like baseball than any other sport.

Similar to baseball, softball teams exchange batting order cards and provide a copy to the home plate umpire.

A key difference between baseball and softball is the Designated Player (DP)/ Flexible Player (Flex) rule used in softball.

"The DP/Flex rule in softball has no counterpart in baseball," said high school and college softball umpire Kenneth Miller. "It is a modified version of the DH rule, which allows for a designated hitter to bat for any player, not just the pitcher. It becomes complicated when the player designated as the Flex—whom we used to call the 'DEFO,' for 'defense only'—goes into the batting order."

A team using a DP/Flex player will always have 10 starters, with the 10th position on the lineup card going to the Flex player, like the starting pitcher being listed as the 10th position on a baseball lineup card.

Some levels of softball offer more flexibility than baseball regarding player re-entry, which means umpires must keep meticulous notes on the batting order cards during a game.

"The penalties for batting out of order are the same, and the requirement for all substitutions to be announced and recorded are identical, too," said Miller. "However, softball codes at various levels seem to be more forgiving with respect to allowing starters to re-enter the game than I remember about baseball rules. For example, in college ball, any starter may be replaced by a sub, but then may re-enter in the same spot in the order at any time. High school rules are even more liberal in this respect. So we have to record re-entries such as these on our lineup cards."

There appears to be little if any collectability of softball lineup cards.

For example, the 2021 and 2022 national champion University of Oklahoma (OU) women's softball team typically disposes of its batting order cards after games, according to an OU spokesperson.

The Use of Lineup Cards in Other Sports 81

SOFTBALL

Date: 6/9/22
VS: Texas

#	NAME	POS	SUB	INN
24	1 Jayda Coleman	8		
78	2 Jocelyn Alo	DP		
23	3 Tiare Jennings	4		
3	4 Grace Lyons	6		
33	5 Alyssa Brito	7		
9	6 Kinzie Hansen	2		
5	7 Taylon Snow	3		
20	8 Jana Johns	5		
0	9 Rylie Boone	9		
98	10 Jordyn Bahl	1	flex	

0 Rylie Boone	17 Sophia Nugent	27 Hannah Coor
3 Grace Lyons	19 Nicole May	33 Alyssa Brito
5 Taylon Snow	20 Jana Johns	42 Turiya Coleman
7 Hope Trautwein	21 Grace Green	43 Quincee Lilio
9 Kinzie Hansen	22 Lynnsie Elam	78 Jocelyn Alo
12 Mackenzie Donihoo	23 Tiare Jennings	88 Emmy Guthrie
13 Macy McAdoo	24 Jayda Coleman	98 Jordyn Bahl

Head Coach: Patty Gasso
Associate Head Coach: Jennifer Rocha
Assistant Coach: JT Gasso

The University of Oklahoma women's softball team captured the 2022 national championship with a win over the University of Texas (courtesy The University of Oklahoma).

OU does, however, keeps image of some of its batting order cards, including the 2022 national championship clincher.

Why are only baseball's lineup cards truly collectible?

It has been established that most major sports have, or had, something similar to baseball's lineup card.

Why, then, are baseball lineup cards far more collectable than other sports' cards? There are likely a few reasons.

No other sport has anything like MLB's dugout lineup card, and that is the card

The Lineup Card

MINNESOTA TWINS AT DETROIT TIGERS
COMERICA PARK • DETROIT, MI • OCTOBER 2, 2022

HP -   1B -   2B -   3B -

MINNESOTA TWINS

#	ORIGINAL	POS.	CHANGE
1	Miranda, J	3	
2	Correa, C●	6	
3	Gordon, N●	4	
4	Urshela, G●●	5	
5	Cave, J	7	
6	Sanchez, G●⑧	DH	
7	Jeffers, R●	2	
8	Wallner, M●	9	
9	Celestino, G	8	Contreras
P	Woods Richardson, S	1	Ⓐ Ⓑ Ⓒ Ⓓ

DETROIT TIGERS

#	ORIGINAL	POS.	CHANGE
1	Baddoo, A	7	
2	Greene, R●	8	
3	Haase, E	2	
4	Cabrera, M●	DH	
5	Schoop, J●●	4	
6	Candelario, J⑧	5	
7	Torkelson, S	3	
8	Kreidler, R●●	6	
9	Reyes, V●	9	
P	Wentz, J	1	Ⓐ Ⓑ Ⓒ Ⓓ Ⓔ

AVAILABLE POSITION PLAYERS (Twins)

LEFT-HANDED	SWITCH	RIGHT-HANDED
Arraez, L	Hamilton, B	Hamilton, B
Contreras, M	Hamilton, C	
	Palacios, J	

AVAILABLE POSITION PLAYERS (Tigers)

LEFT-HANDED	SWITCH	RIGHT-HANDED
Castro, H	Barnhart, T	Baez, J
Clemens, K		Davis, B

AVAILABLE PITCHERS (Twins)

LEFT-HANDED	RIGHT-HANDED
Moran, J	Bundy, D / Duran, J
Thielbar, C	Ⓓ Fulmer, M / Jax, G ②
	Ⓒ Lopez, J / Megill, T Ⓑ
	Ober, B / Pagan, E
	Ryan, J / Varland, L
	Winder, J

AVAILABLE PITCHERS (Tigers)

LEFT-HANDED	RIGHT-HANDED
Alexander, T	Cisnero, J / De Jesus, A
Chaflin, A	Diaz, M / Foley, J Ⓒ
Norris, D Ⓑ	Hill, G / Hutchison, D
Rodriguez, E	Ⓓ Lange, A / Vest, W Ⓐ
Soto, G Ⓔ	

MANAGER SIGNATURE _____

No other sport has a lineup card remotely as nice-looking as MLB's dugout lineup card.

that is currently most visible, marketed and collected among current and recent baseball lineup cards.

The uniqueness of baseball's lineup structure, particularly its no reentry rule, is also a factor, as is the history of baseball's pregame lineup card exchange.

"I think lineups can be so strategically important in baseball perhaps compared to other sports, so the lineup cards represent a manager's plan of action more than they might in other sports," said Brian Dwyer, president of Robert Edward Auctions (REA). "The exchanging of the cards prior to the game may also bring them into the forefront of collectors' minds more."

Perhaps the most important factor was MLB's decision around the turn of the 21st century to start monetizing its game-used items, including dugout lineup cards.

In and of themselves, MLB lineup cards do not generate much revenue; low five-figures per team, per season in most cases. But they are almost pure profit, and when combined with the other game-used items sold, the overall number becomes more significant.

Other sports likely have not seen enough revenue in their lineup cards to sell them, save for a unique circumstance such as the card from the 2013 NBA Finals that Stocking mentioned above and the handful of NHL cards from noteworthy games that sold for only $100–$300.

And for those trying to get lineup cards given to them after a game, accessibility is a key factor. "I think baseball lineup cards are more collectible because you can get down by the dugout after games," said Osborne. "Usually, you don't have that type of access at [other sports games]."

A Day in the Life of a 2022 Lineup Card

As we have seen, the process of producing baseball lineup cards for a game has changed significantly over the years. Some 90 years ago, official batting order cards were filled out by hand, only the starting lineup needed to be included and there were no dugout or bullpen lineup cards.

As of 2022, it was believed that the only MLB lineup card of any kind still being handwritten was the White Sox dugout card, written in calligraphy by bench coach Jerry Narron. The rest are all digitally printed.

Based on input from the Boston Red Sox as well as a couple of current and former MLB managers and coaches, here is a look at how MLB lineup cards are created and used before, during and after a game in 2022.

The life of MLB lineup cards—batting order, dugout and bullpen cards—starts with the light cardboard used to make them, as well as the format template for the printing of the cards. Both the light cardboard and format are provided by MLB. The standard MLB dugout card is 11" × 17", batting order card is 5.5" × 8.5" and bullpen card ranges from 8.5" × 14" to 11" × 17".

In the case of dugout cards, three are provided each team by MLB for every game. The Red Sox fill in two with each team's lineup, one to be used in the dugout and the other in the bullpen. While more and more MLB teams are doing the same, some teams create their own bullpen lineup card, and some (e.g., the 2022 Seattle Mariners) do not use one.

A Red Sox staff member fills out the lineup cards—dugout, batting order and bullpen—by typing the player names into the template and computer-prints them whether the team is home or on the road (host teams provide printers for visiting teams, but the Red Sox bring their own printers). The same staffer is responsible for distributing the cards to the appropriate coaches.

As to when the cards are printed out from game to game, "The timeline varies and is dependent upon when Alex Cora finalizes that day's starting lineup," said a Red Sox spokesperson. "Sometimes, everything is done early in the afternoon (between 1:00 p.m. and 2:00 p.m.), and other times it is done closer to game time (6:30 p.m. or 7:00 p.m.). If, for example, the team is waiting until after batting practice to determine whether a player is healthy enough to play in that day's game, the lineup cards will not be printed until closer to game time. Most of the time, however, the process is complete by 3:00 p.m."

In the case of a last-minute lineup change, "the person responsible for printing the cards makes the change on his end and re-prints the cards."

A Day in the Life of a 2022 Lineup Card

KANSAS CITY ROYALS AT BOSTON RED SOX

Fenway Park • Boston MA • June 28, 2021

HP- PAT HOBERG   1B- RON KULPA   2B- BEN MAY   3B- CHRIS CONROY

KANSAS CITY ROYALS

#	ORIGINAL	POS	CHANGE
1	MERRIFIELD	2B	
2	SOLER	RF	
3	SANTANA	1B	
4	PEREZ	C	
5	~~O'HEARN~~	DH	ALBERTO
6	RIVERA	3B	
7	DOZIER	LF	
8	TAYLOR	CF	
9	LOPEZ	SS	
P	~~DUFFY~~	P	

BOSTON RED SOX

#	ORIGINAL	POS	CHANGE
1	E. HERNANDEZ	CF	
2	DEVERS	3B	
3	MARTINEZ	DH	
4	BOGAERTS	SS	
5	RENFROE	RF	
6	VAZQUEZ	C	
7	DALBEC	1B	
8	GONZALEZ	LF	
9	CHAVIS	2B	
P	~~RICHARDS~~	P	

AVAILABLE POSITION PLAYERS (Kansas City)

LEFT HANDED	SWITCH	RIGHT HANDED
DYSON		~~ALBERTO~~
		RIVERO

AVAILABLE POSITION PLAYERS (Boston)

LEFT HANDED	SWITCH	RIGHT HANDED
VERDUGO	SANTANA	WONG

AVAILABLE PITCHERS (Kansas City)

LEFT HANDED	RIGHT HANDED
BRENTZ	BARLOW/DAVIS
BUBIC	~~HERNANDEZ~~
	HOLLAND
	SANTANA
	~~STAUMONT~~
	SWARZAK/~~ZIMMER~~

AVAILABLE PITCHERS (Boston)

LEFT HANDED	RIGHT HANDED
D. HERNANDEZ	ANDRIESE
~~TAYLOR~~	~~BARNES~~
	OTTAVINO
	RIOS/~~SAWAMURA~~
	WHITLOCK
	WORKMAN

This Kansas City bullpen card is in the same format as a dugout card, but at 8.5" × 14", is smaller.

BOSTON RED SOX vs SEATTLE MARINERS

Saturday, May 27, 2017

#	BOSTON	Pos	#	SEATTLE MARINERS	Pos
1	BETTS	9	1	SEGURA 5	6
2	PEDROIA 2	4	2	VALENCIA 3 8	3
3	BOGAERTS 7	6	3	CANO	4
4	BENINTENDI 5	7	4	CRUZ 2 6	DH
5	RAMIREZ, H.	DH	5	SEAGER 4	5
6	MORELAND 3	3	6	MOTTER	7
7	BRADLEY JR.	8	7	HEREDIA 2	9
8	LEON 1	2	8	ZUNINO 7	2
9	MARRERO 4 6	5	9	DYSON	8
P	JOHNSON, B	1	P	WHALEN	1

EXTRA MEN		EXTRA MEN	
	RUTLEDGE	GAMEL	RUIZ
	TRAVIS	POWELL	
	VAZQUEZ		
	YOUNG		

LHP	PITCHERS	RHP	LHP	PITCHERS	RHP
ABAD	BARNES		RZEPCZYNSKI - 25		DIAZ - 39
SCOTT	HEMBREE		PAZOS - 47		ZYCH - 55
	KELLY				VINCENT - 50
	KIMBREL				LAWRENCE - 61
	WORKMAN				ALTAVILLA - 53
					CISHEK - 31

A bullpen card used by the Red Sox in 2017.

During the game, Boston bench coach Will Venable marks the dugout lineup card with changes and notes.

Dugout lineup cards are authenticated per MLB's Authentication Program immediately after a game. "Most of them are then given to the team store to sell. The exceptions are when Alex Cora presents them to a player, such as for a pitcher's first win or save," the Red Sox spokesperson said.

As for the batting order cards, some managers or coaches will keep the cards, some will occasionally give the batting order cards to a fan after the game, at least a couple of teams (the Cubs and Orioles) make batting order cards available for purchase after a game, and some teams discard them. In the case of the Red Sox, "the batting order cards are disposed of" after a game.

Bullpen lineup cards are either kept by the coach, given to a fan or thrown away.

Famous Lineup Cards

Introduction

A lineup card captures the history of a game that virtually no other game-used item can. It has the names of the starters listed in the order they batted, their positions, and may include the date, names of eligible reserves, manager's signature and changes made during the game.

Take the first-ever MLB All-Star Game in 1933, which included an incredible 27 players, managers, coaches and umpires combined who are now in baseball's Hall of Fame. Many of their names were written on the pair of batting order cards, and Connie Mack even signed his card.

Just looking at a picture of the cards exudes history.[1]

Sadly, most lineup cards from twentieth-century games no longer exist, given that lineup cards were rarely thought of as a collectible and were routinely thrown in the garbage after a game. But the cards that are left from the 20th century, along with a large number from the 21st century, paint a wonderful picture of the game's history.

Following are the stories of several cards from historic games that have survived, from that first All-Star Game in 1933, through a couple of milestones in 2022.

Not only are the cards themselves of interest, but the stories of how they have managed to survive and get to where they are now are just as intriguing.

1933 lineup cards: All-Star Game batting order cards; Averill's cycle

The batting order cards from MLB's first-ever All-Star Game in 1933 are not only a couple of the oldest cards still in existence, but also two of the most noteworthy.

The first MLB All-Star Game was played on July 6, 1933, at Chicago's Comiskey Park, and as noted earlier, batting order cards for both the National League and American League teams survived thanks to Bill McKechnie. McKechnie was a former player who then managed in the National League for 24 years. In 1933, he managed the Boston Braves.

As a player, McKechnie was good enough to play 11 seasons, batting .251. But as a manager, he earned himself a spot in the Hall of Fame with 1,896 wins, two World Series titles and four pennants.

Fellow Hall of Famer John McGraw managed the National League squad in the inaugural All-Star Game, and selected McKechnie as one of his assistant coaches. It was McKechnie who wrote out the National League card.[2]

At a time when virtually no one bothered to keep batting order cards after a game, McKechnie had the wherewithal to save the cards, which turned out to be great not only for the game of baseball itself, but also his descendants. The cards eventually sold at auction for $138,000 in 2007.[3]

More than half of the players in the 1933 All-Star Game, 20 of the 36, would eventually be inducted into the Hall of Fame, plus both managers (Connie Mack and McGraw), three of the four coaches (McKechnie, Eddie Collins and Max Carey) and two umpires (Bill Klem and Bill McGowan).

As was the tradition at the time, the cards only include the names of the nine starters for each team, but a few pitching changes were written onto both cards.

A few weeks later, the Philadelphia Athletics traveled to Cleveland to take on the Indians. About 7,000 fans were on hand at Cleveland Stadium as Cleveland's Earl Averill became one of eight players to hit for the cycle in 1933, the only cycle of his career. Philadelphia's Jimmie Foxx and Mickey Cochrane had two hits apiece, but Walter Johnson's Indians smacked 19 hits and bested Mack's A's, 15–4, in a game that took one hour and 52 minutes to play.

Averill, Foxx, Cochrane, Johnson and Mack are all in the Hall of Fame.

It is not clear who saved the cards, but they were in a scrapbook before being sold at auction in 2020 for $1,500. Interestingly, there is no mention of Averill's cycle in the item description, nor is the date of the game listed other than that it was played in 1933.[4]

The Indians beat the A's, 15–4, behind Earl Averill's only career cycle. These batting order cards are two of the oldest still in existence (courtesy Jeffrey Lazarus).

The Lineup Card

Lineup cards from Ripken's 2,131st game have stories to tell

Lineup cards from Cal Ripken's record-breaking 2,131st consecutive game, breaking Lou Gehrig's long-standing record, are among the most notable and storied lineup cards still in existence today.

Not only is Ripken's streak one of the greatest in all of sports—he would go on to play in 2,632 straight games, a record considered to be one of the most unbreakable records in all of professional sports—but the streak is synonymous with lineup cards because his name was written onto all 2,632 Baltimore lineup cards for that stretch of more than 16 years.

It should go as no surprise that the batting order cards from the 2,131st game were in high demand, so much so that Phil Regan, the Orioles manager at the time, reportedly penned an original batting order card plus five carbon copies for the game.[5]

While it is not known exactly how many lineup cards were used during the historic game, here is what is known about some of them:

- What is purported to be a Baltimore dugout card, along with a pitching chart from the September 6, 1995, game, were sold in 2014 for $15,405.[6] They were sold by the family of Mike Flanagan. Flanagan was a former Oriole who served as the team's pitching coach in 1995. He passed away in 2011. However, in November 2022, Hunt Auctions sold a lot of dugout lineup cards from former Orioles bench coach Chuck Cottier for $3,080.[7] The lot included what

A pair of carbon copy batting order cards from Cal Ripken Jr.'s 2,131st consecutive game (courtesy Bill Haelig).

also claimed to be a Baltimore dugout lineup card from the 2,131st game, and it is different than the Flanagan card. More on this shortly.
- The original batting order card (i.e., the top copy) was sent to the National Baseball Hall of Fame and Museum in Cooperstown, New York.[8]
- A carbon copy was given to Ripken.[9]
- Home plate umpire Larry Barnett donated his copy to Bowling Green State University. That card and other memorabilia were initially put on the market for $1 million, but went unsold at that price.[10] The items were eventually sold by Bowling Green to Baltimore businessman James Ancel for $20,000.[11]
- One of the carbon copies was donated to the Babe Ruth Birthplace and Museum in Baltimore.[12]
- A copy went to opposing manager Marcel Lachemann, who reportedly gave the card away, but it is not clear who he gave it to.[13]
- There is also no indication as to what happened to California's dugout lineup card from the game.
- Phil Regan kept a copy along with the pen he used to fill out the batting order card. Regan gave his copy and the pen used to fill out the cards to his daughter.[14]

The fun starts with the lineup card carbon copy and pen Regan gave his daughter. She in turn decided to sell the items in late 1998.[15]

According to a 1998 Associated Press article, the 2,131st-game card, along with the 2,130th-game card for the game in which Ripken tied Gehrig, and the pen used to fill out the two cards, were put up for auction. Ancel was reportedly the high bidder, willing to pay more than $35,000 for the items.[16]

Not so fast, said the Baltimore Orioles organization, which did not like the idea of Regan's daughter selling the famous cards, believing the team owned the cards and pen. The Orioles went so far as to obtain a court order blocking Regan's daughter from going forward with auctioning the items off.[17]

The parties reached an out-of-court settlement roughly a year later that allowed Regan's daughter to sell the cards. No terms were disclosed.[18]

Ancel at this point had already gone ahead and paid $20,000 for the carbon copy of the lineup card that Barnett had given to Bowling Green State University, as well as some Angels batting order cards and a few other items.[19] Therefore, he was no longer interested in the card being sold by Regan's daughter.

An Alexandria, Virginia, man named Warren Fitzgibbon ended up buying the 2,131st game batting order card and pen owned by Regan and his daughter, along with a batting order card from Ripken's 2,030th game, for more than $40,000 (an exact price was not given).[20]

Sadly, Fitzgibbon did not get to enjoy the cards for long. He passed away in March 2005 at the age of 43. His obituary mentioned the 2,131 lineup card.[21]

There is no further indication as to what happened to the historic lineup cards and pen owned by Fitzgibbon.

2022 developments

There were a pair of new developments in 2022.

First, noted Cal Ripken Jr. collector Bill Haelig revealed in a 2022 interview that he had been gifted carbon copies of the Orioles and Angels batting order cards from the 2,131st game.

There was one stipulation tied to the gift: the person who gave the cards to Haelig wished to remain anonymous.

"It was given to me maybe two or three years ago by someone who is familiar with my collection, and knew it was something that my collection had to include, and I was very happy to accept it," said Haelig.

Second, as noted earlier, Hunt Auctions listed for sale a couple of auction lots from Cottier in late 2022. Jeffrey Lazarus purchased both collections.

The first lot included Baltimore batting order cards from the record-tying 2,130th game as well as the record-breaking 2,131st game. While they are noteworthy pieces, the lot description acknowledges the likelihood that the cards for sale were draft copies of Baltimore's lineup for those games and were not used in either game. Lazarus purchased the lot for $743.[22]

The second lot included the Orioles dugout lineup card from the 2,131st game.[23] But it is not the same 2,131st dugout lineup card sold by Flanagan's family in 2014 for $15,405, as referenced earlier. The base card, the information and changes on the card and the handwriting are the same. There are, however, subtle differences in some of the letters, and there is not the staining on this card that is visible on the card sold by Flanagan's family. Clearly, it is a different card.

Lazarus, who bought this lot for $3,080, used a photo matching service to confirm that the Cottier 2,131 dugout card was in fact posted on the dugout wall during the game.

It makes sense that the Cottier 2,131 card was the dugout card because the bench coach (Cottier) is more typically responsible for keeping the dugout card

Orioles dugout batting order card from Cal Ripken Jr.'s 2,131st consecutive game, per the Chuck Cottier collection (courtesy Jeffrey Lazarus).

than the pitching coach (Flanagan), and Cottier's collection included many other dugout lineup cards from that season.

It is not clear how or even if the Flanagan card was used during the game. Because the coaching staff knew it would be a record-setting game, a second card might also have been kept in the dugout, or it may have been written after the game; it does appear that both cards are written in Cottier's hand. But without more information from one of the coaches, it is impossible to know for sure.

Ritual trumps Pujols 703rd home run bullpen lineup card

Rituals have long been a part of baseball, whether it is singing "Take me out to the ball game" during the seventh inning stretch, playoff beards or not stepping on the foul lines coming on or off the field. The 2022 St. Louis Cardinals' bullpen had a ritual whereby they would tear up the bullpen lineup card after a loss.

So, despite the enormity and historical significance of Albert Pujols hitting his 703rd and final career home run and subsequently moving past Babe Ruth into second place on the all-time runs batted in (RBI) list in an October 3, 2022, game against the Pittsburgh Pirates, one of the Cardinals' bullpen staff tore the bullpen card into four pieces because the visiting Cards lost the game to the Pirates, 3–2.

The pieces of the card remained in the St. Louis bullpen until

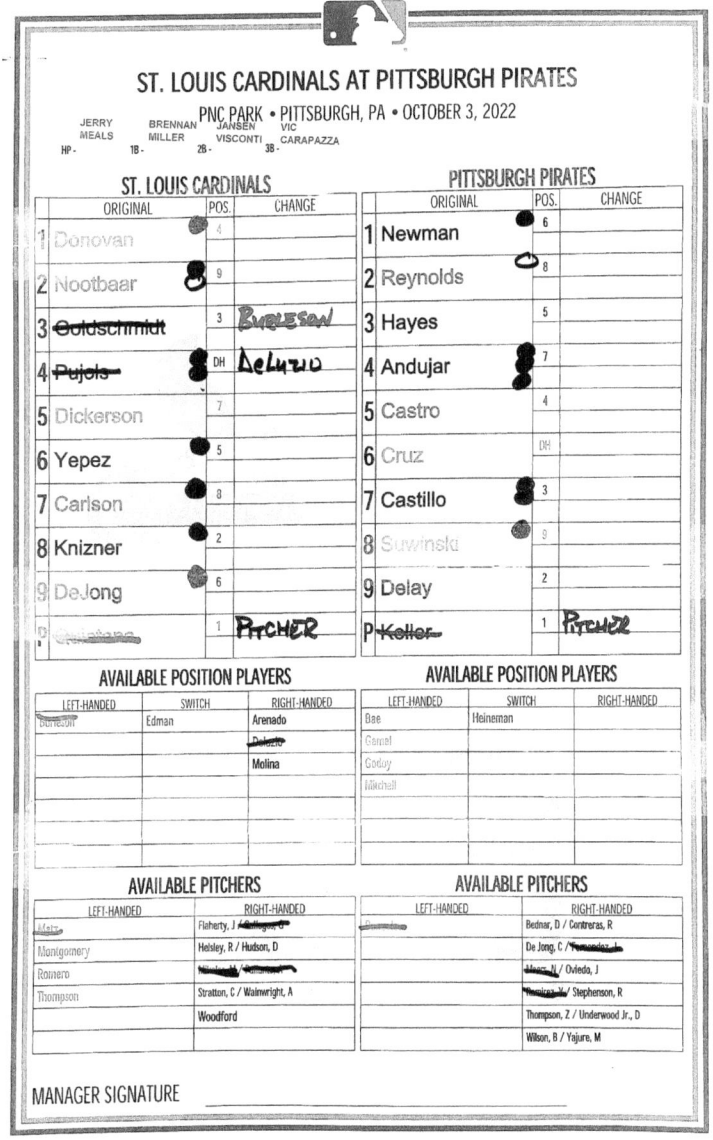

The four pieces of the St. Louis bullpen lineup card from Albert Pujols's final career home run after being taped back together.

they were asked for and given to a fan before the next day's game. On the previous page is the historic card after the pieces were taped together.

It is hard to say what the card is worth in its current form, given that is torn and not authenticated by MLB, but it would likely be worth something given the significance of Pujols' final career home run and passing Ruth on the career RBI list, and the large number of Cardinals and Pujols fans.

The next night, October 4, Pujols played in his final career game, recording the last hit and RBI of his career. (Author's Note: While Pujols went on to play in two 2022 playoff games and recorded two hits, MLB does not count playoff statistics as part of a player's career stats.)

The St. Louis bullpen lineup card from Pujols's final regular season game found a better fate than the previous night's card. Pujols was pulled in the middle of the third inning after going 1-for-2 with a two-run single. The Cardinals, down 7–3 through six innings, rallied to send the game into extra innings and won in the 10th inning, 8–7.

So rather than getting torn up, the winning card got a large "W" written onto it by one of the bullpen staffers, remained in one piece and was given to a fan.

There is less certainty about what happened, or will happen, to both teams' dugout cards for the two games. The Pirates confirmed in early November 2022 that they have the cards but would only say that they "haven't decided what we'll do with those just yet," per a team spokesperson.

A St. Louis spokesperson said that he was not sure what happened with their lineup cards. Cardinals Authentics, which sells the team's game-used merchandise, said via email that they "do not get lineup cards."

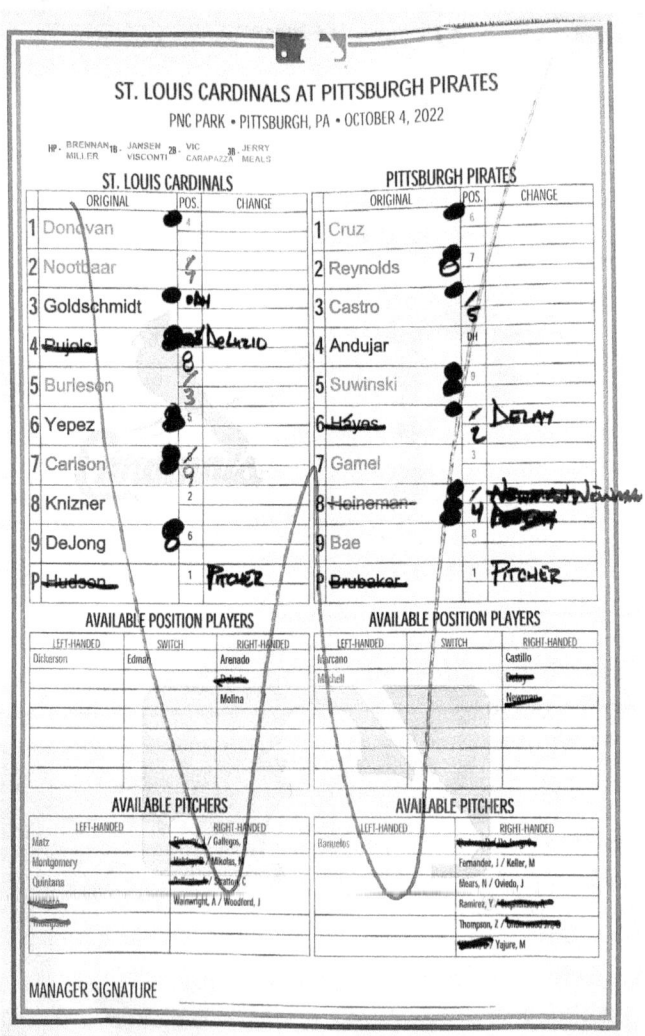

The Cardinals' bullpen lineup card from Albert Pujols's final regular season game.

The lineup card that captures both baseball and American history

Lineup card collector Jeffrey Lazarus has many cards in his collection that speak both loudly and meaningfully of the history of baseball.

Lazarus has cards from George Brett's 3,000th-hit game, four World Series-clinching games, Carl Yastrzemski's final home run, Mike Piazza's first career home run, Tom Glavine's first victory and all four Atlanta cards from the Yankees' sweep of the Braves in the 1999 World Series, to name just a few.

Yet the card that speaks more powerfully to Lazarus than any other card in his collection does not have a single player's name printed on it.

The card is a Baltimore Orioles pre-printed dugout card that would have been used on September 11, 2001. The

Atlanta's batting order card from Tom Glavine's first career win, signed and inscribed by Glavine (courtesy Jeffrey Lazarus).

Batting order carbon copy cards from Mike Piazza's first career home run game. The writing on the Dodgers card appears to have been traced over in ink (courtesy Jeffrey Lazarus).

A blank September 11, 2001, Blue Jays–Orioles dugout lineup card. The game was canceled due to the terrorist attacks of that day (courtesy Jeffrey Lazarus).

Orioles were to host the Toronto Blue Jays that evening, and the preprinted card had the team names and logos, and location of the game to be played.

The card also has a Cal Ripken Jr. watermark on it as Ripken had announced that he would retire at the end of the season.

The game, of course, was not played due to the terrorist attacks that took place that morning in New York City, at the Pentagon and on a plane that was headed toward Washington, D.C., but instead crashed in Pennsylvania.

MLB canceled all games that day as well as the next five days as America mourned.

The unused lineup card says everything about what went on in America that day without a single word or name written onto it.

"I'm comfortable saying that that is the most meaningful lineup card I have," Lazarus said.

Batting order card used by the Twins on 9/11/19 with a watermark commemorating the September 11, 2001, terrorist attacks.

Lazarus, a New York City–based lineup card collector, owns the card pictured above. There is an identical blank card in the National Baseball Hall of Fame's collection. Those are the only two known MLB lineup cards from 9/11/01.

"The blank lineup card, to me just captures that everything shut down. You couldn't escape it. I remember, you turn on the TV, and I was desperate to find some distraction," recalled Lazarus, who aside from living near Ground Zero in New York City at the time, also had family in Baltimore, just 40 miles from the Pentagon.

"So that was an enormously significant game from a personal perspective," continued Lazarus. "To have the lineup card from that game … there may not be a game in history that will carry more weight than having a blank lineup card from 9/11."

Deal, or no deal

How the Orioles 9/11 card got to Lazarus is also an interesting story.

A friend owned it and decided to sell it in late 2019 to help fund an expensive vacation. The card had a letter of authenticity from Mark Wiley, the Baltimore pitching coach for the 2001 season.

The problem for Lazarus? The friend did not want to sell just the 9/11 card. He wanted to package it with a couple of other lineup cards that Lazarus was not really interested in. Lazarus tried to convince the friend to just sell him the 9/11 card.

After some back and forth, "ultimately, he decided he was going to either sell them all as a lot, or just not sell them," said Lazarus. "It took a couple of weeks, and I was like, you know what, I am not going to get another chance at this and ended up just buying all three."

A deal was made, and Lazarus owned the 9/11 card.

"I remember walking away thinking that I probably overpaid, but I've found with all the things, especially the collectible that you won't have another shot at, is that you either get them when they're available … or you have to be comfortable with not having them," he said.

Two-plus years later, Lazarus is very happy with his decision to buy such an important piece of not only baseball history, but also American history. "That was one that I definitely felt like I was happy I didn't let pass," he said.

The most expensive card ever: Boston's 2004 World Series Game 4 dugout card

Sky Lucas, a partner at a hedge fund company, New Hampshire native and lifelong Red Sox fan, along with his lawyer and friend David Campbell, were two of the many Red Sox fans still celebrating their team's memorable 2004 World Series title a few weeks after Boston ended 86 years of heartbreak with a four-game sweep of the St. Louis Cardinals.

And on an early December day that year, the pair were able to acquire a key piece of memorabilia from the historic event's deciding game. It did not come easily, or inexpensively, though.

The whirlwind day for Lucas and Campbell started that morning when Campbell went online and saw that MLB's auction site had Boston's dugout lineup card from Game 4 up for sale, and the highest bid was only $10,000 with the auction ending that night.

Campbell called Lucas who was in New York City on a business trip. "I told him, 'jeez, Sky, it's only 10 grand. That's a pretty good deal,'" recalled Campbell in late 2021.

Lucas agreed and the mission to acquire the card was on.

The two initially planned to split the cost. But the high bid did not stay at $10,000 for long.

"When it was at $10k, $20k, $30k, I was in for half," said Campbell. "I was getting nauseous the entire time it was going up and up and up. It's kind of amusing that I was a partner until the bid started going over $25k or $30k, and I said, 'I can't do this.'"

Lucas decided he would fund the purchase on his own and take Campbell off the hook financially, but he still needed Campbell's help to track and make bids as Lucas headed to the airport to fly back to New Hampshire.

Long story short, the high bid continued to surge upward as the day went on.

"It goes up and up and up," recalled Campbell, eventually surpassing $160,000.

By this point, Lucas had gotten back to New Hampshire and driven to Campbell's house.

The final few minutes of the auction were a flurry of action and confusion, according to Campbell. Lucas's final bid was $165,010, but Campbell and Lucas initially thought he had lost.

"We thought we were out, and all of a sudden we get notified, 'you're the winner at $165,010.00,'" Campbell said.

Campbell paid on his American Express card, with Lucas reimbursing him, and with that, Lucas officially owned the historic Red Sox lineup card.

The Red Sox World Series Game 4 lineup card is historical not only for the game it was used

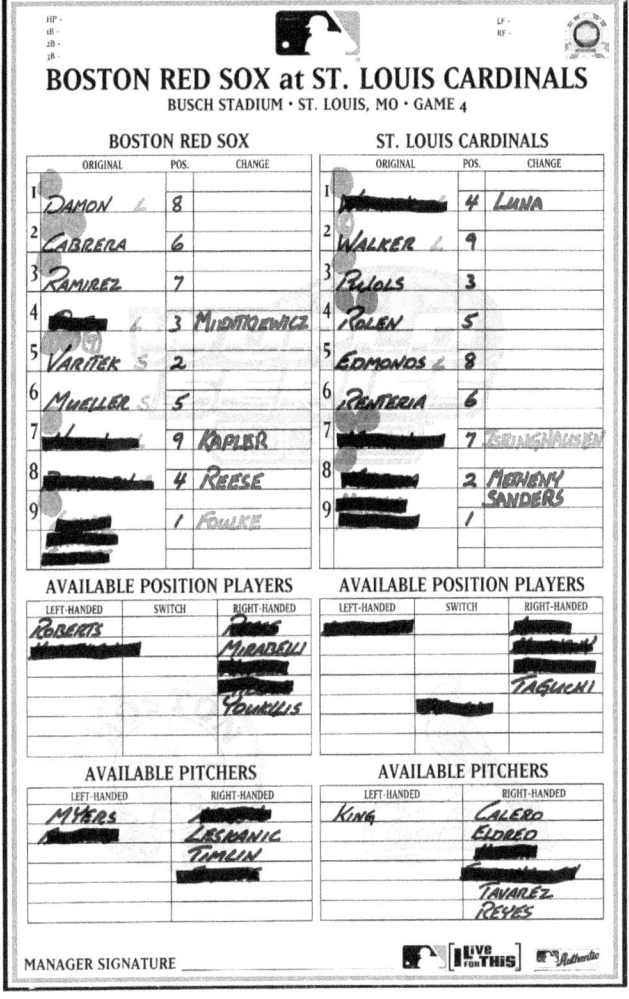

Dugout lineup card from the game the Red Sox won to capture their first World Series title in 86 years (courtesy Sky Lucas/David Campbell.

in, but also because the $165,010 paid by Lucas is the most ever spent on a lineup card, based on research and input from collectors and those who sell high-end official batting order and dugout lineup cards.

The next most expensive lineup card as of 2022 was the $138,000 spent in 2007 on a pair of batting order cards from the first-ever MLB All-Star Game held in 1933.

According to Campbell, at least at that time, the Red Sox World Series Game 4 lineup card was also the most expensive piece of baseball memorabilia ever sold on MLB Auctions.

Lucas wants to share the card with Red Sox Nation, although aside from showing it at private functions, his efforts to either lend it to the Red Sox to be seen by fans or sell high-resolution copies of the card to benefit a charitable organization such as the Jimmy Fund have not worked out for various reasons.

One of those reasons is what Lucas refers to as an ongoing "misunderstanding" between him and MLB as to who owns the rights to reproduce the card.

"I could make 100 prints, or 1,000 prints, whatever, and sell them through the Jimmy Fund, and [the Jimmy Fund] could keep all the proceeds, I don't care because I'm not trying to make money," Lucas said.

But Campbell and Lucas are optimistic that future efforts to make the card available for Red Sox fans to see and enjoy firsthand will ultimately work out.

"The 20th anniversary is coming up here in two years, and probably that's the best time to do it," said Campbell.

Other items of note related to the card:

Sky Lucas and his sons holding Boston's 2004 World Series-clinching dugout lineup card (courtesy Sky Lucas/David Campbell).

- Unfortunately, in the postgame excitement of the World Series victory, the lineup card was removed from the wall of the dugout wall before Red Sox manager Terry Francona signed the bottom of the card, as MLB managers sometimes do.
- Lucas and Campbell had a friend in the sports memorabilia business make a few high-resolution copies few years ago. One ended up in the hands of a scammer who pretended to own the card and tried to sell it on eBay.

The description on the listing read:

2004 Game 4 "reverse the curse" World Series Lineup Card. Authenticated by MLB Estate sale. This piece was a family members [sic] who recently passed and left behind. Purchased Dec 04. Custom made frame with "reverse the curse" at the bottom. Dimensions: 26.5 × 20.5. Immaculate condition. Please feel free to ask me any questions whatsoever.[24]

But Lucas and Campbell got wind of it and the fake was quickly removed from eBay.

Judge's historic 62nd home run lineup cards benefit charity

The short story is that Michael Klett temporarily owned both dugout lineup cards from Aaron Judge's historic 62nd home run game on October 4, 2022, the home run that pushed Judge past another Yankee great, Roger Maris, for the top spot on the American League's most home runs in a season list.

Klett, a 40-year-old consultant who lives in New York City, sold the pair of cards at auction in December for a total of $61,200, including the winning bid and buyer's premium.[25] Klett will donate the proceeds to charity.

How Klett ended up with both cards is a longer story. It starts in July of 2022 with Klett stuck at home with COVID-19 and looking at the MLB Auctions website.

"I was thinking of getting some items from MLB Auctions to donate to a charity auction," Klett said. "My uncle unfortunately passed away a couple years ago, and I wanted to support the charity golf tournament in his honor."

He noticed that MLB Auctions was offering late-season 2022 Yankees' dugout lineup cards for presale. "At the time, the Yankees were setting the world on fire, and there was the possibility they might eclipse 115 wins and Aaron Judge had an outside shot at Maris' record. As a fan I thought, regardless of what happens, that would be a really neat collectible to have."

Klett prepurchased lineup cards from New York's last four regular season games against the Texas Rangers: October 3, the October 4 double-header, and October 5 which also happens to be Klett's birthday.

He paid just over $1,100 combined after taxes and fees for the four cards. The items would be shipped six to eight weeks after the games.

Judge hit his 62nd HR of the season in the second game against the Rangers on October 4, one of the games Klett had chosen.

"Of course, I was excited," he said.

Not so fast

Klett recalled that there was some "fine print" on the sale confirmation back in July. It read:

> This is a presale. It is possible your order can be cancelled after the game has been played due to the availability of each item and possible requests made by players, MLB, MLB Hall of Fame and team archivists.

He also remembers having looked back a couple of weeks after he pre-bought the four cards thinking, "'maybe I should have gotten more games,' and it appeared they had taken down all of the presales for the rest of the year by that point."

Klett decided to check on his order. The response he received was simply that the lineup cards would ship in six to eight weeks.

Meanwhile, the Yankees' opponent from that historic game, the Texas Rangers, listed its dugout lineup card for auction on the MLB Auctions site on October 10.

"That made me feel terrible, because here I was not knowing if I was going to get the item I had purchased and paid for," Klett said. "The same site was auctioning off a nearly identical item."

"I thought not only is [the Texas Rangers card] an extremely unique and valuable collectible, but also it might be a way to improve my negotiating position on the other items I purchased," he continued. "Because ultimately, I made the decision to donate both items to charity, or at least the proceeds from the sale of the two items."

So Klett bid on the Rangers' card and ended up winning the auction with a high bid of $12,530 on October 14 and received it from the Rangers a couple of weeks later.

NEW YORK YANKEES AT TEXAS RANGERS
GLOBE LIFE FIELD • ARLINGTON, TX • OCTOBER 4, 2022

HP - Chris Segal 1B - Lew Williams 2B - Andy Fletcher 3B - Randy Rosenberg

TEXAS RANGERS

#	ORIGINAL	POS.	CHANGE
1	Semien, M	4	
2	Lowe, N	3	
3	Garcia, A	DH	
4	Jung, J	5	
5	Smith, J	6	
6	Huff, S	2	
7	Calhoun, K	9	
8	Taveras, L	8	
9	Thompson, B	7	
P	Tinoco, J	1	Allard Hearn Moore

NEW YORK YANKEES

#	ORIGINAL	POS.	CHANGE
1	Judge, A	9	Kiner-Falefa
2	Stanton, G	DH	
3	Cabrera, O	4	
4	Donaldson, J	5	
5	LeMahieu, D	3	
6	Peraza, O	6	
7	Bader, H	8	
8	Trevino, J	2	
9	Hicks, A	7	
P	Cole, G	1	Schmidt

AVAILABLE POSITION PLAYERS — TEXAS

LEFT-HANDED	SWITCH	RIGHT-HANDED
Seager, C	Heim, J	Culberson, C
		Mathias, M
		Plawecki, K

AVAILABLE POSITION PLAYERS — YANKEES

LEFT-HANDED	SWITCH	RIGHT-HANDED
Rizzo, A	Gonzalez, M	Higashioka, K
		Kiner-Falefa, I
		Torres, G

AVAILABLE PITCHERS — TEXAS

LEFT-HANDED	RIGHT-HANDED
Allard, K	Alexy, A / Barlow, J
Burke, B	Gray, J / Hernandez, J
Hearn, T	Leclerc, J / Otto, G
King, J	Rodriguez, Y / Santana, D
Moore, M	
Perez, M	

AVAILABLE PITCHERS — YANKEES

LEFT-HANDED	RIGHT-HANDED
Chapman, A	Abreu, A / Castro, M
Cortes, N	Effross, S / German, D
Luetge, L	Holmes, C / Loaisiga, J
	Schmidt, C / Severino, L
	Taillon, J / Trivino, L
	Weissert, G

MANAGER SIGNATURE

The Texas Rangers dugout lineup card from Aaron Judge's historic 62nd home run game in 2022 (courtesy Texas Rangers).

On October 19, Klett finally heard from Fanatics, which serves as the Yankees' game-used memorabilia arm.[26]

In short, Fanatics emailed Klett to let him know it had canceled his order for the milestone lineup card and refunded the money, per the fine print in the purchase agreement which it repeated in the email. Fanatics did not cancel Klett's purchase of the other three cards, nor did it give him the option to do so.

But for the "inconvenience," as Fanatics put it in the email, it instead offered Klett a Phil Rizzuto autographed baseball bat. Fanatics also stated: "We are also working with our Game-Used department to identify whether there are any other additional items from the remainder of the season we can provide for the inconvenience."

Klett declined the Rizzuto-signed bat in his response, and instead asked for something worn by Judge from the historic game that would be donated to charity or sold with the proceeds given to charity.

Michael Klett holding both dugout lineup cards from Aaron Judge's 62nd home run game, breaking Roger Maris's American League record (courtesy Michael Klett).

About four weeks and a few emails later, Klett finally spoke with a Fanatics' executive. Fanatics indeed had the game-used lineup card and had planned to gift it to Judge, according to the executive. But in subsequent conversations with Klett, the executive eventually agreed to send Klett the Judge #62 home run card, as well as refund his $1,100.

Klett's gamble in buying the cards and persistence in getting Fanatics to honor the prepurchase of the Yankees card ultimately paid off in the form of a sizable donation to charity.

"I think it's a great result, and in addition to doing some good, hopefully it helps affirm the significance of lineup cards as important pieces of baseball history and generates greater appreciation for them in the hobby," Klett said.

Koufax a little more perfect than Hendley

On paper, the prospects of the September 9, 1965, game between the visiting Chicago Cubs and Los Angeles Dodgers being a great game were not overwhelming.

Chicago starter Bob Hendley was a journeyman pitcher, and the Cubs were starting a pair of players, Don Young and Byron Browne, who were making their MLB debuts.

The Dodgers were countering with eventual Hall of Famer Sandy Koufax. That Koufax might pitch a gem would surprise no one, but by his standards, he had only been average at best in his previous five starts, suffering three losses and a pair of no-decisions.

And yet on that early September night, Hendley and Koufax would combine to pitch arguably the greatest MLB game ever, recording 51 outs with just one hit, one walk and one unearned run between them.

Koufax was perfect literally and figuratively, striking out 14 in throwing MLB's eighth-ever perfect game. And while Young and Browne were making their debuts, Koufax still had to face a Chicago lineup with three of the game's great hitters with eventual Hall of Famers Billy Williams, Ron Santo and Ernie Banks manning the middle of Chicago's order that night.

Hendley was nearly equal to the task. The only marks against him were a Lou Johnson base on balls in the fifth, and a Johnson double in the seventh. The Dodgers scored the game's lone run in the fifth when Johnson advanced to second on a sacrifice bunt, stole third and scored on the catcher's errant throw.

Almost as amazing as the pitching performance is the fact that both dugout lineup cards have survived in an era when they were typically thrown in the trash after a game.

The Dodgers' dugout card ended up in the hands of Los Angeles sportswriter and official scorer George Lederer. Lederer has since passed, but his family still has the Koufax perfect game lineup card.[27]

The Chicago Cubs dugout lineup card from Sandy Koufax's 1965 perfect game. The card is signed by both Vin Scully, who called the game, and Koufax (courtesy Rick Levy).

Famous Lineup Cards

Vintage sports memorabilia collector Rick Levy has the Cubs dugout card. He bought it about 15 years ago for $3,000 from someone who used to work at Dodger Stadium.

"He had worked his way through college as an usher at Dodger Stadium," said

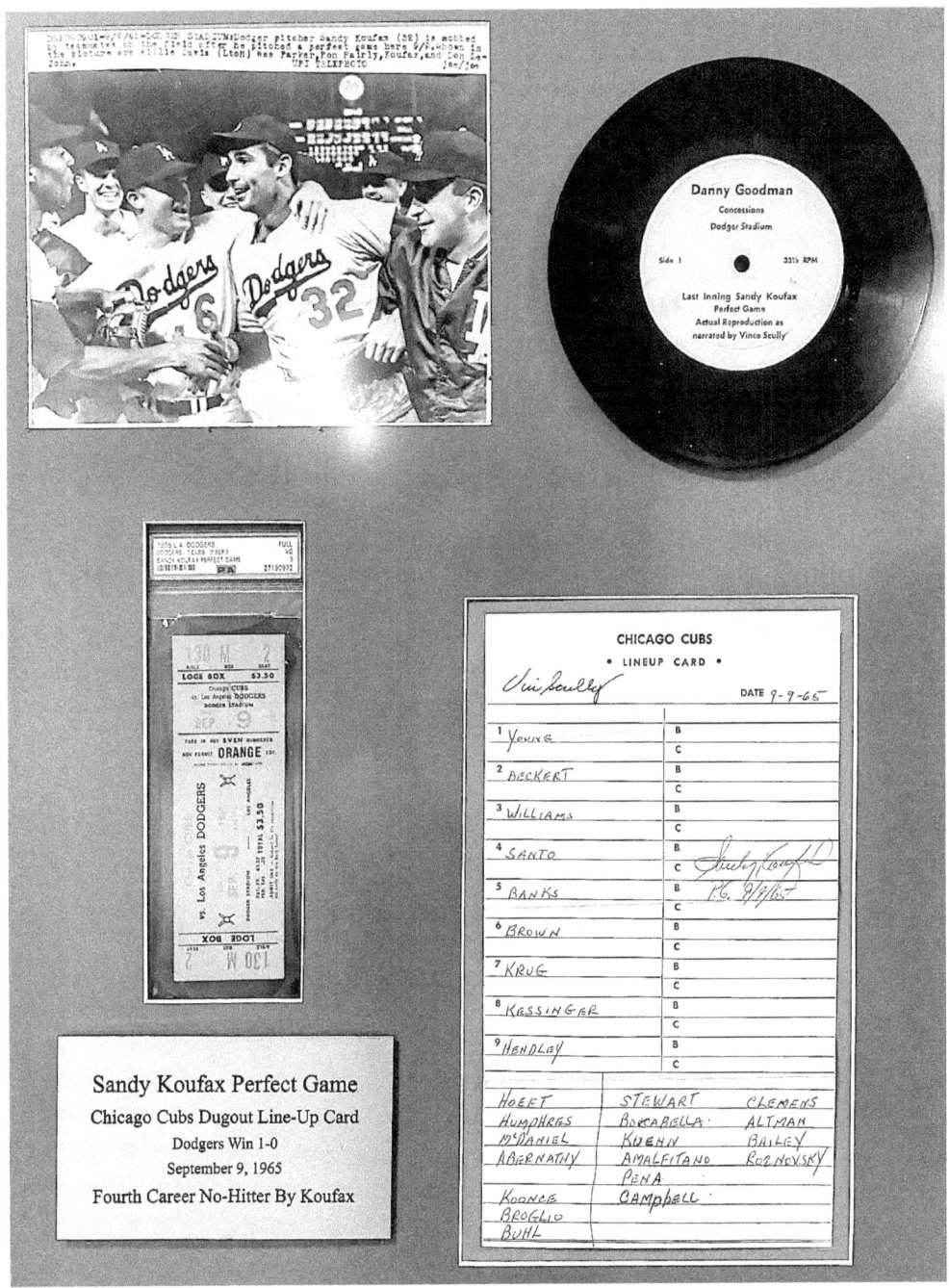

Rick Levy put the lineup card in a display with other items related to Sandy Koufax's perfect game (courtesy Rick Levy).

Levy of the person he bought the historic lineup card from. "His job at the end of the game, he would walk down to the playing field at the very end for the ninth inning, and when the game was over, he would have to jump onto the field and make sure nobody jumped onto the field except for him."

"He happened to look in the Cubs' dugout and saw the lineup card sitting there, so he grabbed it, folded it up and stuffed it into his pocket, and he hung onto it for pretty much 40 years until he decided to sell it," Levy continued.

At one point, the usher sent the card to the Dodgers to try and get Koufax to sign it. The Dodgers were unable to make that happen but did get iconic broadcaster Vin Scully to sign the card. Scully called Koufax's perfect game.

Levy has since gotten Koufax to sign and date the lineup card. He displays it with a picture of Koufax and his teammates celebrating after the game, a vinyl recording of Scully's call of the last inning and a ticket stub.

There are some interesting aspects to the card itself.

For starters, as noted earlier, dugout lineup cards were relatively new in the mid–1960s, and there was little uniformity in the cards themselves and how they were written.

The Cubs only included their roster on the card, which measures about 6" × 11", according to Levy.

"They actually misspelled Browne's name he was so new," said Levy. "There should be an 'e' at the end of his name."

There were a couple of Chicago substitutions in the top of the ninth inning—Joey Amalfitano pinch-hit for Don Kessinger, and Harvey Kuenn pinch-hit for Hendley—but the changes were not written onto the lineup card.

That the Cubs' lineup card was part of such a memorable night is meaningful to Levy. "I picture whoever the Cubs manager was that day looking at his lineup card saying, 'who can I put in there that can get a hit off this guy?'" rhetorically asked Levy. "To me, it really is a great representation of the game."

Lineup Card Artistry

Introduction

Major League Baseball has required teams to fill out and submit a batting order card before each game for more than 100 years. As we have seen, although not mandated by the league, teams have also filled out a dugout lineup card since the 1960s.

Digitally printed cards were introduced to MLB in the early 21st century, and by 2021, all batting order cards were done that way. As of 2022, the only MLB team believed to still fill out its dugout lineup card by hand was the Chicago White Sox, courtesy of bench coach Jerry Narron.

Barring a surprising change, the era of handwritten lineup cards at the MLB level will likely be done when Narron retires.

On one hand, it is sad because handwriting is charming and more personal than a typed document. A handwritten Earl Weaver batting order card has more personality than a typed and computer-printed Tony La Russa batting order card. There is no guarantee that La Russa even touched a typed card, other than to perhaps sign it.

But from a practical standpoint, the world is going digital, and typing and computer-printing lineup cards make sense.

"Today, everything is computerized," said Tom Runnells, a former MLB manager and coach who took pride in writing aesthetically pleasing cards. "I get it. It's a lot faster and easier."

This chapter celebrates three MLB managers and coaches—Runnells, Narron and Don Wakamatsu—who put the time and effort into eloquently handwriting dugout lineup cards, creating masterpieces in the process. There are distinct similarities between the three:

- They all had at least one or both parents impact their handwriting. For Runnells and Wakamatsu, it was at least one parent impressing on them to write neatly. For Narron, it was his parents' stressing to do his best at whatever task he undertook, large or small. It was also at his mother's house that he found a calligraphy pen to write his first calligraphy lineup card.
- All three are extremely meticulous. Runnells and Wakamatsu specifically referred to themselves as "anal-retentive" when it comes to neatness. All three, if time would permit, would rather rewrite a lineup card because of a lineup change instead of just crossing out the name and adding the change.
- All three created their own styles of calligraphy.
- None of the three kept many of the cards they wrote out over the years.

It was more important to them for the cards to go to players and umpires celebrating debuts or milestones, or to kids. But some of their cards ended up in the trash because lineup cards were not nearly as sought after in their earlier coaching years as later.

Each of their stories follows.

Tom Runnells: Combining art and baseball

Penmanship has always been important to Tom Runnells.

"When I was a young boy, I know that my mother used to always impress upon me to have perfect penmanship, and at some point, I took it to heart and was very prideful of my printing," he recalled. "I don't know that I was the greatest with cursive, but my printing was always pretty to the 'T.' I don't know why, it just always stuck with me. When I would read notes from people or try to read someone's letter, and I couldn't read it, I would get frustrated, so I always made sure that my printing was very legible, and I tried to just make it perfect."

Runnells enjoyed a 10-year professional career as a player, including 40 games played for the Cincinnati Reds spanning the 1985 and 1986 seasons.

From there, Runnells embarked on a 30-year career as a coach and manager, including 149 games as manager of the Montreal Expos spanning the 1991 and 1992 seasons, and four games filling in for Rockies manager Walt Weiss during the 2015 season.

Runnells filled out a lot of lineup cards over the years, not only as bench coach, but also as manager. Particularly in MLB, it is common for a manager to delegate filling out the batting order and dugout cards to a coach. But Runnells chose to do it himself.

"I still filled out the lineup cards. I cannot remember a time when I did not fill out the lineup cards," he said. "Back then, I was a young manager at 35, I think I was at the time. I didn't know any better, really. At that point, it was just something I did. I enjoyed doing it."

And he filled them out the only way he knew how, with precision and purpose.

"I felt very proud of any time that I did print a lineup, either for myself or someone else. It was very legible, very neat, very unified," Runnells said. "The columns were always straight and things like that. A lot of this was from my parents."

There was pressure to fill out the dugout lineup cards correctly, because there was not a lot of margin for error. "Every night, they'd give you, I think, three sheets for the dugout card. So that was always an issue, don't screw up more than two because then you're down to your last one, so you better not mess it up."

In the first half or so of Runnells's coaching and managing career, batting orders were usually written out on a carbon pad, where you would write out the top copy, and the carbon would duplicate the writing on the second and third sheets.

That did not work for Runnells.

"I didn't like the way that looked, so I would fill out three copies of the [batting order] card, one to hand to the umpire, one to hand to the other team, and one for the manager or myself," he said.

"It was painstaking. It would always irritate me if I had to do three lineup cards, and one of the players would back out of the game right before the lineups were turned in and I'd have to redo it," he laughed. "I was so anal about it that I would actually rip up all three and write all three again, instead of just crossing out the guy's name or whiting out a person's name and writing over it."

"Now, there were times when I had to do that because it was like five minutes before game time and I didn't have time to do it," Runnells continued.

Runnells did not name names, but suffice it to say, not all managers and coaches were as fastidious about the legibility of their lineup cards as he was.

"I would get irritated if we exchanged lineup cards at home plate and you couldn't read a player's name and you only had the numbers to go by," he said. "And even some of the numbers were so scratched that it was like, 'OK, what is that? Is that a six or is that a nine? What is that? I don't know what that is.'"

An example of how faded the writing on the last carbon copy can look (courtesy Jeff Garfinkel).

Evolution of Runnells's lineup cards

Runnells's initial style was to print the dugout cards simply and neatly. But that evolved over time, based on a few factors.

One was seeing cards written in calligraphy by Jerry Narron. "Narron is the one guy that I always looked at: 'This guy really goes beyond with his lineup cards.'

"I am not unique, and certainly not the best, necessarily," said Runnells, mentioning both Narron and Don Wakamatsu, another former MLB coach and manager who played for Runnells in the minors. "I've seen some of their cards, and they're pretty special."

Second was the feeling that if he was going to try and make the cards look as nice as he could, he may as well pull out all the stops and get creative.

"Yeah, I figured as long as I am doing it by hand, I figured I might as well add a little flare to it, I guess," he said.

The Lineup Card

COLORADO ROCKIES at SAN DIEGO PADRES
PETCO PARK • SAN DIEGO, CA • SEPTEMBER 4, 2011

COLORADO ROCKIES

#	ORIGINAL	POS.	CHANGE
1	FOWLER	8	
2	ELLIS	4	
3	GONZALEZ	9	
4	TULOWITZKI	6	
5	GIAMBI	3	
6	SMITH	7	
7	KOUZMANOFF	5	
8	ALFONZO	2	
9	~~COOK~~	1	

SAN DIEGO PADRES

#	ORIGINAL	POS.	CHANGE
1	VENABLE	8	
2	BARTLETT	6	
3	HUDSON	4	
4	~~GUZMAN~~	7	MAYBIN
5	HERMIDA	9	
6	~~RIZZO~~	3	BLANKS
7	PARRINO	5	
8	~~MARTINEZ~~	2	HUNDLEY
9	~~LATOS~~	1	

AVAILABLE POSITION PLAYERS (Colorado)

LEFT-HANDED	SWITCH	RIGHT-HANDED
HELTON	YOUNG	IANNETTA
	HERRERA	WIGGINTON
		~~SPILBORGHS~~

AVAILABLE POSITION PLAYERS (San Diego)

LEFT-HANDED	SWITCH	RIGHT-HANDED
		FORSYTHE
		CUNNINGHAM
		JOHNSON
		~~HUNDLEY~~
		DARNELL
		GONZALEZ
		~~BLANKS~~ MAYBIN

AVAILABLE PITCHERS (Colorado)

LEFT-HANDED	RIGHT-HANDED
~~REYNOLDS~~	ROENICKE
BROTHERS	~~BELISLE~~
	~~LINDSTROM~~
	STREET
	BETANCOURT

AVAILABLE PITCHERS (San Diego)

LEFT-HANDED	RIGHT-HANDED
~~THATCHER~~	FULCHINO
SPENCE	GREGERSON
	~~QUALLS~~
	FRIERI
	BRACH
	BELL / BASS
	CARPENTER

MANAGER SIGNATURE _____

A 2011 Colorado Rockies dugout lineup card written by Tom Runnells.

COLORADO ROCKIES
SPRING TRAINING 2013

COLORADO ROCKIES

#	ORIGINAL	POS.	CHANGE	#	ORIGINAL	POS.	CHANGE
1	~~Young~~	8	Blackmon	1	Crawford	7	
2	Brignac	4		2	Ellis	4	
3	Gonzalez	7	Pacheco	3	Kemp	8	
4	Cuddyer	3	Pitcher	4	Gonzalez	3	
5	Colvin	9		5	~~Ethier~~	9	Castellanos
6	Arenado	5		6	Cruz	6	
7	~~Hernandez~~	2	Torrealba	7	Uribe	5	
8	~~Herrera~~	6	LeMahieu	8	Ellis A.J.	2	
9	~~Garland~~	1	Irabarren	9	Harang	1	

AVAILABLE POSITION PLAYERS

LEFT-HANDED	SWITCH	RIGHT-HANDED
~~Blackmon~~		Pacheco
~~Irabarren~~		LeMahieu
		Torrealba
		Nelson
		Rosario
		Rutledge

LEFT-HANDED	SWITCH	RIGHT-HANDED

AVAILABLE PITCHERS

LEFT-HANDED	RIGHT-HANDED
	~~Corpas~~
	~~Betancourt~~
	Ottavino
	~~Volstad~~
	~~Kensing~~

LEFT-HANDED	RIGHT-HANDED

MANAGER SIGNATURE _____

By 2013, Runnells's handwriting had evolved to a more stylistic form.

Finally, there was the influence of his father.

"My dad ... he really enjoyed art, and kind of had some flare to his art, and when he wrote, I remember actually that he had a blotter ink pen on his desk at home," said Runnells. "He would practice calligraphy and do things like that. I was amazed at how cool it looked, even though some of the times I couldn't read what letters he was doing, but it was really neat."

"I just thought, I'm going to mess around with that a little bit, doing the lineup cards, and I would go buy calligraphy pens and doing that, and I liked it, I liked the way it looked," he continued. "You start getting comments from everybody about how great the lineup card looks, and 'Boy, that's cool,' and it just kind of took off from there."

Where did they all go?

Runnells meticulously filled out thousands of cards over the years. Sadly, he only kept a few cards for himself.

"Many, many nights, I remember walking into the clubhouse and it's still up there and everybody's gone and I just got it—maybe had a bad game—and ripped it up," laughed Runnells.

While MLB teams started selling the dugout lineup cards in recent years, earlier in Runnells's coaching career, he would give some of them away.

"At the end of the game, organizations would take them and give them to fans, or donate them. Or if a little kid would come down to the edge of the dugout after a game and say, 'Hey, can I have the lineup card?' Of course I'd hand it to him," Runnells said.

And some went to players, particularly over the last few years of his coaching career.

"My first year with the Rockies, every single time there was a player that had his debut, we were giving him that lineup card," Runnells said. "I'm sure it's much more prevalent now than it was back then."

And if there was a milestone, like Ubaldo Jiménez's 2010 no-hitter, or Ichiro Suzuki's 3,000th hit against Colorado in 2016, Runnells made sure those players got the card. He would even make duplicates.

"Any time I knew that there was big event or potential of a 1,000th hit, 2,000th hit, Todd Helton retirement night, whatever, I would go ahead and write two copies," he said. "That way, you could give one to the player and if you wanted to keep one for yourself or give one to the organization they could use, you could do that."

"For instance, the actual game card for Ichiro's 3,000th hit at Coors Field, obviously I made one, but I went ahead and made two other copies," Runnells continued. "Certainly, you don't have all the scratches from during game play, crossing out a player and writing in a substitute. You don't have all the crosses out of the bullpen. You don't have all the markings of when the innings ended. So, at the end of that game, I had multiple cards, I just had to go back and recreate the way the game played out. Certainly, the main card has been kept by the organization and I think given to Ichiro. The duplicates, I have one of them, Ichiro signed it and [MLB authenticated] it. Those are the things that I kind of relish."

That is one of a few cards Runnells still has. He has three lineup cards from his playing days, but not from his MLB debut for the Reds.

"It wasn't as common back then," said Runnells of the tradition of giving a player his MLB debut card. "Certainly, I wish I did have my playing debut card. I think I have the game ticket and [the ball from] my first hit."

He does not have many from his coaching and managing days, either.

"Probably only about half a dozen," Runnells said, although he added he did make it a point to collect three or four dozen batting order cards from other teams that he still has, including cards signed by Hall of Fame managers such as Tommy Lasorda, Tony La Russa and Sparky Anderson. Runnells wishes he had kept more, but it was not part of his thought process at the time.

"When I got called to the big leagues as a coach and a manager, I was still pretty young. I'm thinking to myself, I'm going to be here for the next 40, 50 years," Runnells said, adding that it took him 17 years to get back to MLB as a coach after being let go by the Expos in 1992.

"You don't think about collecting items when you are in it as much," he added. Now retired from baseball, Runnells has more time on his hands to think about— what else?— baseball and art.

He has combined his passion for both into creating art that honors baseball players past and present, using items including baseballs or even lineup cards. Runnells used both in a piece he created featuring Anderson.

"So, like with Sparky Anderson I have a piece where I have the lineup card, and I made the old English 'D' out of a leather baseball and the seams," he said.

Whether it's the artwork he's currently creating, or the lineup cards he painstakingly wrote during his coaching days, Runnells is proud of the legacy he has created.

"When someone texts me or sends me a picture and says, 'Look what's hanging in my man cave' or something," said Runnells, "and it happens to be my lineup card and their historic moment, it does give me a nice feeling."

Don Wakamatsu created artistic memories with his lineup cards

A few elements factored into Don Wakamatsu's decision to handwrite artistic dugout lineup cards.

"My grandfather had tremendous penmanship; my mom had great penmanship. So I think it's a code on one side of the family, I guess," said Wakamatsu, who retired from baseball after the 2021 season. "A lot of it had to do with my makeup, too. I was pretty anal about what things look like."

Then there was the impact of fellow MLB coach and manager Jerry Narron, a few years older than Wakamatsu, who led the way in using calligraphy or calligraphy-like printing on dugout lineup cards.

"Jerry is the one who influenced me by far," said Wakamatsu. "I saw his, I'd go, 'That's something that I'd like to do.'"

Finally, there was the fact that Wakamatsu received the lineup card from his MLB debut for the Chicago White Sox on May 22, 1991. He knows firsthand how special that card is to a player. He still has his debut card some 30 years later.

"I don't know when that tradition started, but when I got mine, that was pretty commonplace," said Wakamatsu, who made his major league debut for the Chicago

A 2018 Mother's Day lineup card written by Don Wakamatsu (courtesy Don Wakamatsu).

White Sox on May 22, 1991. "It was a courtesy from the manager, guys that had a feel for how special that is."

"The importance of knowing that it might be on the wall of somebody's house for the rest of their life, that whole thing kind of led me to try and get better doing it," he continued.

Wakamatsu said he never had any formal training in calligraphy. He created his own font that blends gothic and Japanese elements.

The "tortured artist" stereotype is true, according to Wakamatsu. While to almost everyone else his cards were things of beauty, he did not always see it that way. The more cards he wrote, the more he felt the need to improve.

"It's like painting a house," he related. "You see all the errors, but nobody else does. It's a never-ending quest to be better."

There were other challenges, too, like writing names such as "Saltalamacchia" into the lineup card's small, provided rectangle. And last-minute lineup changes could mean starting again from scratch.

"The All-Star Games were a challenge because you had so many guys [on each roster]," Wakamatsu said.

But the worst were doubleheaders.

"Doubleheaders were the ones that killed me because ... you only have 15 minutes in between [games]," said Wakamatsu. "To get the lineup from like Buck Showalter and then go up and do it in calligraphy was a pain in the butt."

Given that it could take Wakamatsu up to 30 minutes to write out a dugout lineup card, he had to draw a line in the sand on certain things.

He'd digitally print dugout cards during spring training, and he did not have the time to write cards for the seasons he managed the Seattle Mariners in 2009 and 2010. Ty Van Burkleo, Wakamatsu's bench coach, handled the dugout lineup card duty.

"He actually learned on the fly just to be able to do it to pay tribute to the lineup cards that I did," said Wakamatsu, who has Van Burkleo's first card framed. "And he did a nice job."

And Wakamatsu wouldn't handwrite batting order cards once digital printing became an option.

"It's kind of weird because one side of me is traditional, the other side is digital because Joe Maddon was the one who got me digitized into organizing schedules and everything else," he said. "Most of that stuff went digital."

The pen is mightier than the sword, but the computer printer...?

Handwritten dugout lineup cards were already on their way out before Wakamatsu retired.

"[2021] was the first year that I didn't do it, other than Opening Day and a couple special occasions, because they went electronic," said Wakamatsu of the Texas Rangers' decision to primarily use computer-printed cards in his final season as bench coach. "And that's kind of a sad deal, I think."

And while the handwritten dugout lineup card, with its personality and distinction, appears to be headed toward an unfortunate end, Wakamatsu's time and effort spent to painstakingly create thoughtful works of art will not soon be forgotten.

The Lineup Card

Don Wakamatsu was one of the American League's assistant coaches for the 2016 MLB All-Star Game. Not surprisingly, AL manager Ned Yost had Wakamatsu pen the AL's dugout lineup card (courtesy Don Wakamatsu).

There are the players on the teams he coached for who would be presented with Wakamatsu's card when they debuted or reached a milestone, even if it meant Wakamatsu had to write out multiple cards for a game. For special events like Opening Day and the World Series, he would make extra copies for the coaching staff.

And if a player on the opposing team unexpectedly reached a significant milestone during a game, Wakamatsu would do his best to hook the player up with a card he wrote.

"I know a couple of no-hitters, I've sent [the card] back over to pitchers," said Wakamatsu, specifically mentioning Justin Verlander's 2011 no-hitter.

"Unfortunately, it was against us," he laughed.

He also gave Dallas Keuchel a card for the 2015 All-Star Game he started. And Wakamatsu has given cards to umpires for their MLB debuts, too.

Especially in the last years of Wakamatsu's coaching career, it often became a race between coach or manager, MLB officials and the team's authentics department as to who could get the dugout lineup cards first, especially if it was a meaningful game.

"There are two different facets. One is MLB. I remember, the World Series one, it was off the dugout wall before we got back from celebrating on the field," Wakamatsu said. "MLB would take certain ones. They overrode everything."

"The other thing was, for years, the team store would take all of them from every game, and sometimes you'd have to steal them," laughed Wakamatsu. "It was a tug of war, whether you kept it or they kept it. For me, I always felt it was mine, obviously because it was handwritten."

Whoever got Wakamatsu's artistic lineup cards after a game, whether purchased or given, they will be treasured for years to come.

Jerry Narron takes his lineup card writing to the next level

Jerry Narron spent 16 years playing professional baseball and has put in another 30-some-odd years as a coach, and yet one of the things he has become most known for is his calligraphy on dugout lineup cards.

"It's probably not official calligraphy," admitted Narron in 2022. "It's kind of like a freelance, freehand calligraphy, but it just works for me, it looks kind of neat and I enjoy doing it."

Whatever you want to call it, Narron has gotten so good at it, some people do not believe his cards are handwritten. "A lot of people see mine, and they want to know how I got the letters on the computer like that," Narron laughed.

Wherever Narron has coached—he has coached or managed eight MLB teams through 2022—people have taken notice of his lineup cards. Narron and his lineup cards have been featured on newscasts and in publications such as CBS News Chicago, the *Boston Globe*, ESPN and *The Globe and Mail*.

He credits three people for getting him to start writing dugout lineup cards in calligraphy.

"I was fortunate to have a mom and dad that taught my brothers, sisters and I that whatever we do in life, do it to the very best of our ability, no matter how big or small. The lineup card's no big deal, but when I do it, I try to do it to the best of my ability," Narron said.

The Lineup Card

A 2019 dugout lineup card written by Jerry Narron.

The third person was Johnny Oates, another longtime baseball guy who hired Narron to be part of his Baltimore Orioles coaching staff for the 1993 season. One of Narron's responsibilities was to pen Baltimore's dugout lineup card.

"When [Oates] told me he wanted me to do the dugout lineup card, I knew that I was going to have to do something really neat for him, so I practiced a little bit," recalled Narron. "My mom had a calligraphy pen laying around the house and I went by their house one day and I just messed with it a little bit, and you know it came out OK."

That was the start of what has now become a 30-year labor of love.

"Since '93, that was my first year [coaching] in the big leagues, so I've been doing it for a while and it comes pretty easy now. It took me a little more time in '93 and '94 than it does in '21 and '22," said Narron, who said he now typically writes a dugout lineup card in about 10 minutes.

"It doesn't take me any longer than it would if I just took a Sharpie and printed it on there," he added. "It doesn't take me any more time. I can whip it out pretty quick."

Earn your vowels

One quirk of Narron's dugout cards is that the reserve names almost never include any lowercase vowels.

"The extra men, I take out the vowels," said Narron, "unless it's a bona fide, Hall of Famer ticket–punched guy. Like if Miguel Cabrera doesn't play this year when we play Detroit, if he's an extra man, I'll write 'Cabrera' completely out."

Another feature of Narron's cards is that for Asian players, he tries to write their name in their native language out of respect. That typically means getting help from a translator to make sure he gets it right.

And Narron tries to make the cards festive on holidays. "St. Patty's Day, I do it all in green," he said. "Memorial Day and the 4th of July, I'll do it in red, white and blue."

Narron did not use calligraphy when he used to handwrite the batting order cards. "I did it neat, but I wouldn't do it in calligraphy," he said.

Battle scars

Writing out lineup cards is not always as simple as one might think. For starters, Narron is proud of his work, so when there is a last-minute lineup change, he typically rewrites the card from scratch.

"Most of the time, I redo it," he said. "I've had people apologize to me, and I just tell them, 'I need the practice.' It doesn't really bother me."

Narron has also found that calligraphy pens can sometimes leave battle scars, of sorts.

"Sheaffer pens, they kind of kind of leak sometimes, especially if you go on a road trip and you've been flying," said Narron. "They'll leak all over my hands sometimes like I've been bleeding or something."

And then there was the time that Narron managed to find himself in hot water with one of baseball's greats for how he wrote the batting order cards, through no fault of his own.

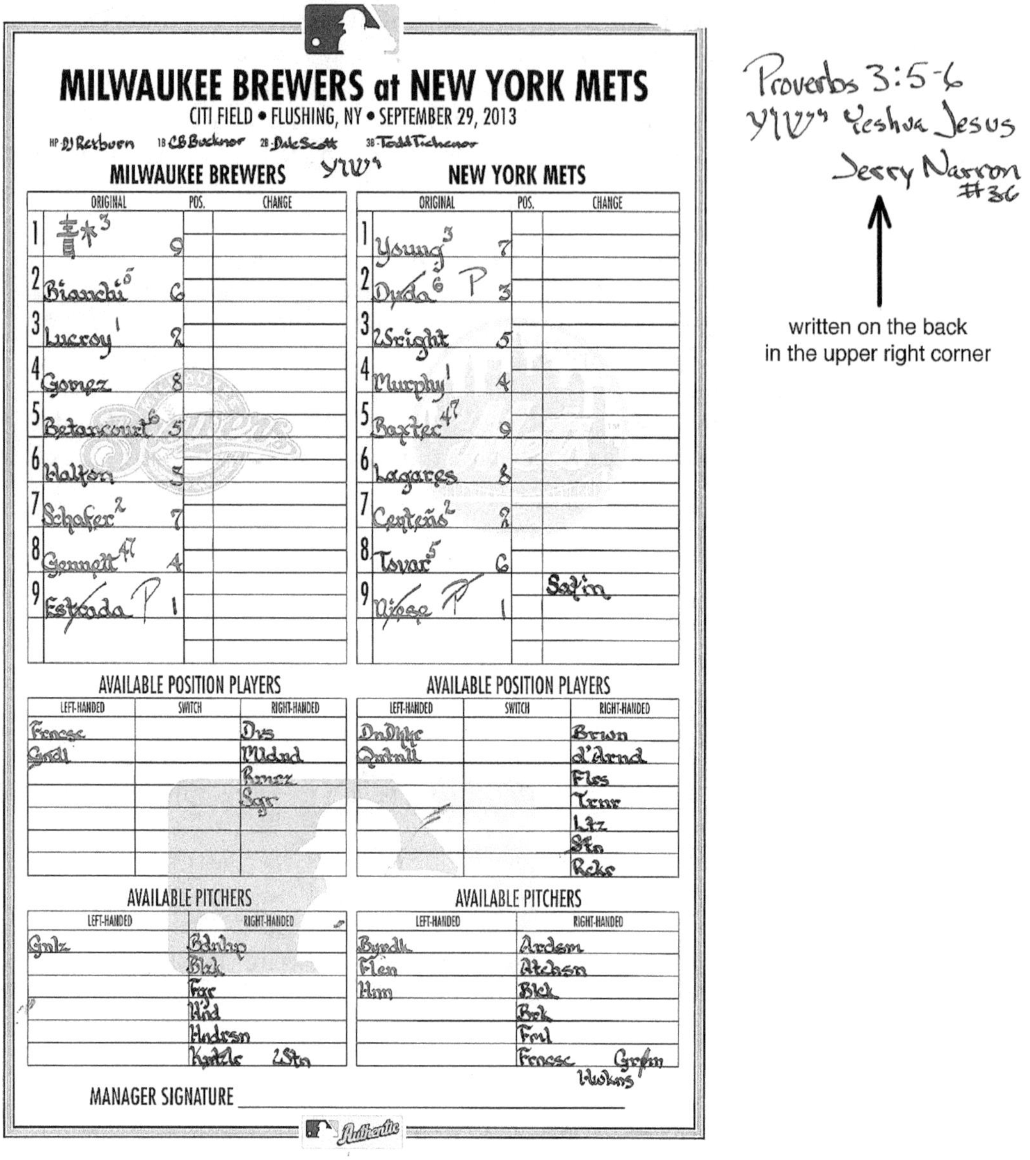

[Lineup card image with handwritten notes]

Jerry Narron wrote Nori Aoki's name in Japanese. Note that there are no lowercase vowels in the names of any of the reserves, a trademark of Narron's lineup cards (courtesy Zack Hample).

"Johnny Oates, when I was coaching for him, he wanted to have room underneath each name [on the batting order card] so he could put notes or kind of keep score on there … so I would write the name a little bit small so there would be room under there," Narron recalled. "We're playing Detroit, Sparky [Anderson] just got all over me at home plate one day. He could not see the guys' names because the writing was too small. The next day, I came out and I made sure for Sparky's card, I filled that blank up."

Better to give than to receive

Narron has filled out thousands of lineup cards, both batting order and dugout over the years, but has kept very few himself.

"I didn't even think about it at the time, and I could probably have gotten it," said Narron of his MLB debut with the New York Yankees in 1979. He does have at least one keepsake related to his debut, though.

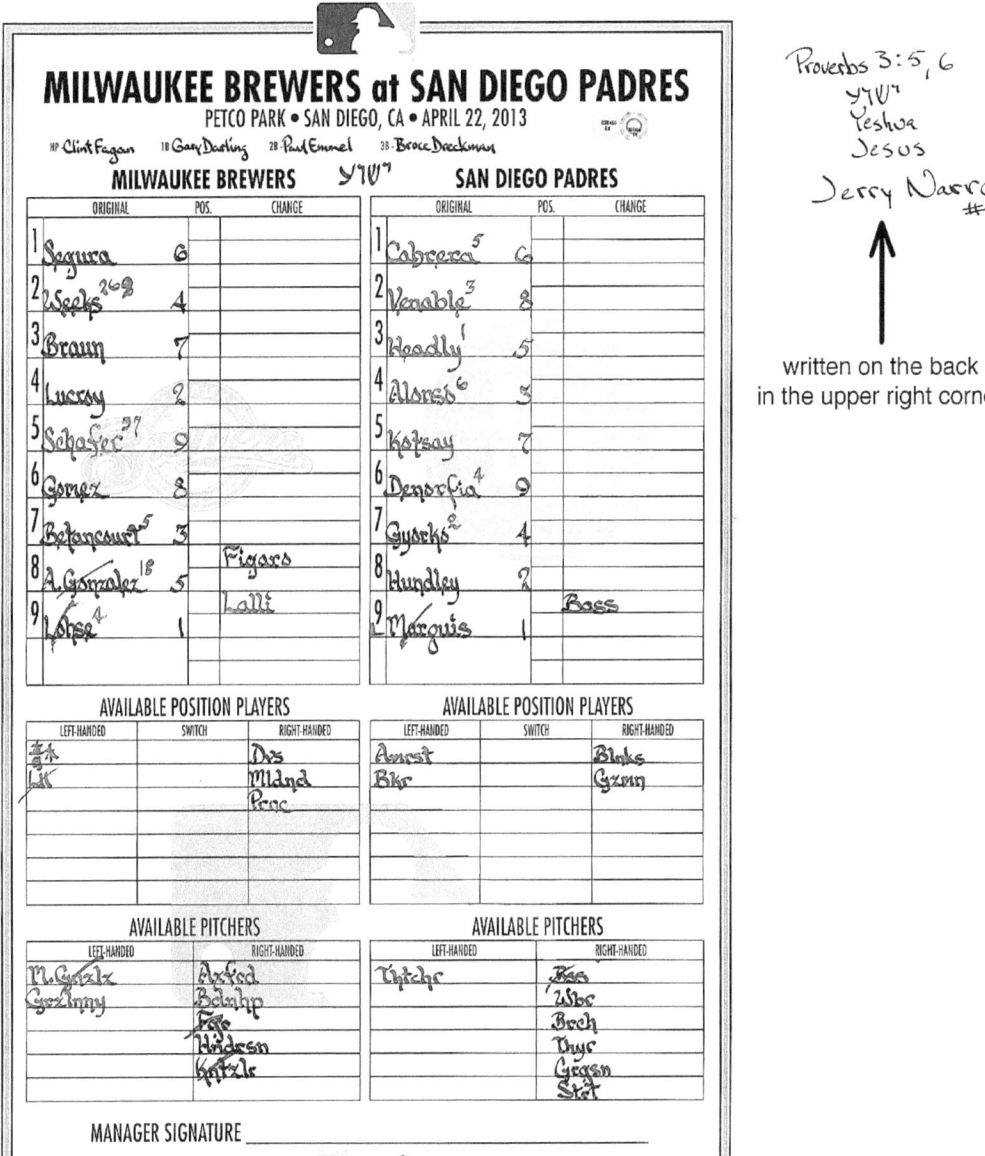

Jerry Narron also wrote Nori Aoki's name in Japanese on this 2013 dugout lineup card. To the right is a Bible reference that Narron often includes on the back of his lineup cards (courtesy Zack Hample).

"Mr. Steinbrenner sent me a nice note after I got my first hit," Narron said. "I've got that."

One card that he knows for sure that he has is from 2006 when he managed the Cincinnati Reds. "George Bush threw out the first ball in Cincinnati one year, and he signed my lineup for me," said Narron. "That was real nice of him."

"I've got that George Bush [signed] card, and I think I've got a card or two from when I managed. I think there was one year I brought a bunch home. I'd have to look in my attic to see what I've got. Over 48 years, I've got a lot of stuff in the attic," Narron laughed.

Before MLB and teams began selling dugout lineup cards, Narron said he "really used to enjoy, after a game, finding a kid by the dugout and giving him the card."

Some of Narron's cards have been given to players who made debuts or reached milestones.

"If someone does something special, I'll make sure our guy gets it or I'll reproduce something for him," he said.

As an example, Narron gave cards to the three White Sox players—Tanner Banks, Anderson Severino and Bennett Sousa—who made their MLB debuts in the first three weeks of the 2022 season.

"When Dallas Keuchel won his one-hundredth game [on April 13, 2022], he got the card after the game," Narron added.

Narron does not limit giving cards away to just players. "I try to look after the umpires a little bit, too."

Dan Iassogna is among the MLB umpires Narron has given a debut game card to. When Joe West set the record for most games umpired, in 2021, Narron wrote out cards for not only West, but also the other three umpires working with him that night.

Narron has also memorialized the passing of umpire's family members by copying and pasting a digital image of the loved one on batting order cards for games when John Hirschbeck and Hunter Wendlestedt were behind the plate.

"I did for John. I did that for people over the years like Hunter Wendlestedt, I put the picture of his dad on his card when he was working the plate," Narron said. "I've enjoyed doing that with guy's pictures."

"Michael [Hirschbeck] came around a lot," continued Narron. "Most people in baseball knew Michael as a batboy or just being around the clubhouse with John. I love John, I love his family. I'm just thankful that he and his wife appreciate it."

The future of handwritten lineup cards?

Narron sees the handwriting on the wall, so to speak, when it comes to written lineup cards.

At the MLB level, all batting order cards are currently produced using a computer printer.

"I want to say, about five or six years ago, everybody started doing it on computer, and it's easier," Narron said.

Even dugout cards are headed in that direction. While Narron is still handwriting them as of 2022, others like Runnells and Wakamatsu who also handwrote cards have retired.

"Not many guys are doing it anymore," said Narron. "It's so easy to computer-generate it."

Minor League Lineup Cards

As in Major League Baseball, lineup cards also play a role in telling the history of minor league baseball—including both affiliated (MiLB) and independent leagues—through the years.

Of course, the history of minor league baseball pales in comparison to its big brother, and far fewer minor league lineup cards have been kept, particularly the further back you go in time. That is despite the fact that there have been many more minor league teams than MLB teams over the years. In 2022, for example, there were 120 affiliated MiLB teams and another few dozen independent teams, compared with 30 MLB teams.

But most minor league cards were seen as worthless and thrown away after games.

Like MLB, however, there are still some older cards in existence that help tell minor league baseball's not-so-recent story.

For example, the batting order cards from the longest professional game ever played, a 33-inning affair between the Pawtucket Red Sox and Rochester Red Wings that featured eventual Hall of Famers Wade Boggs and Cal Ripken Jr., are in the National Baseball Hall of Fame's collection.[1]

A Minneapolis Millers batting order card from the late 1950s showing Elijah Jerry "Pumpsie" Green leading off still exists. Green would go on

Pumpsie Green batted leadoff for manager Gene Mauch's Minneapolis Millers (courtesy Jeffrey Lazarus).

to become the first black player to play for the Red Sox in 1959, the last pre-expansion MLB team to integrate.

MLB similarities

Like their parent clubs, minor league teams have a dugout card, and share batting order cards with the opposing manager and home plate umpire. Minor league

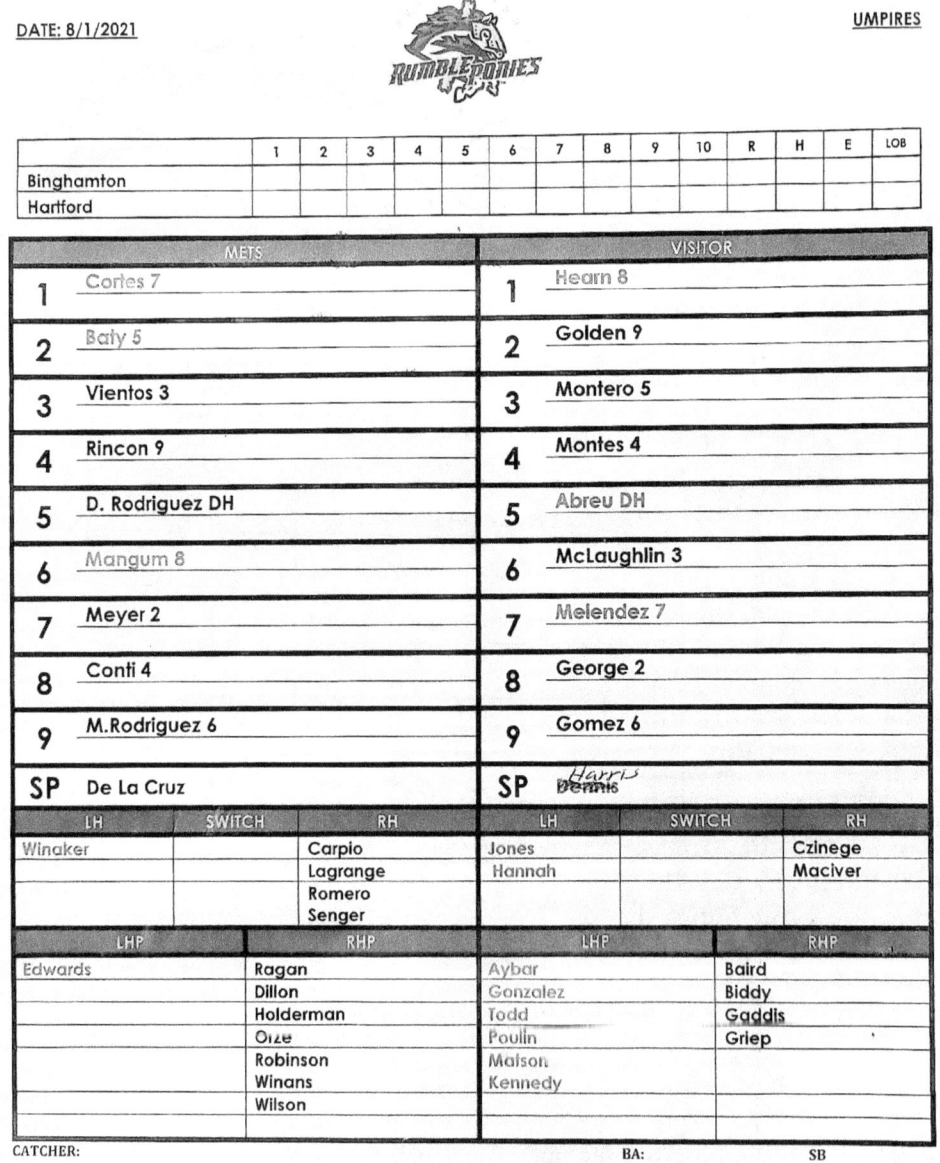

This smaller (8.5" × 11") paper card was posted in the Binghamton Rumble Ponies clubhouse before a 2021 game.

teams typically do not have a coach in the bullpen, and therefore rarely are there any bullpen cards.

Minor league teams also typically have some form of today's lineup card posted in the clubhouse, home or away.

"Our manager, Chris Denorfia, has a printed lineup card that he hangs in the clubhouse and the players can come in and see if they are playing that game," said a Hartford Yard Goats spokesperson in 2022. "It also has times for batting practice and stretch."

MLB differences

While MLB has recently had at least one field umpire join the home plate umpire in tracking lineup changes, mound visits, et cetera on extra sets of batting cards during a game, neither MiLB nor independent league baseball has followed suit, at least not yet.

"We will likely have two [umpires track game changes on batting order cards] next season," said Dusty Dellinger, MiLB Senior Manager, Umpire Development, referring to the 2023 season. "However, some crews [already] have the base umpire use a scratch

(Left) Almost all minor league batting order cards are white, sometimes with a place to check whether the team is "Home" or "Away." **(Right)** A rare example of a recent light blue "away" minor league batting order card.

sheet to track different aspects."

Although there are occasional exceptions, minor league baseball typically eschews the light blue for visiting team batting order cards.

For many years, the various affiliated minor leagues would provide teams with pre-printed batting order carbon copy pads to use for their lineup card exchange with the other team and home plate umpire.

"Until sometime in the late 2000s or early 2010s, the league printed and distributed triplicate carbon cards to each club," said Tom Kayser, president of the Texas League for 25 years.

Most MiLB teams now create and print their own batting order cards.

"Sometime in the 2010's we stopped having to do that as managers were using computer generated cards on which they had printed the league logo and, often, the logos of both their team and the visiting club," said Kayser.

The majority of independent teams continue to use handwritten batting order and dugout cards.

April 19, 2022

	BATTING ORDER	POS	R/L
1	Volpe, A - 7	SS	R
2	Dietrich, D - 16	2B	L
3	Breaux, J - 22	C	R
4	Chaparro, A - 24	3B	R
5	Dunham, E - 17	RF	L
6	Lockridge, B - 10	LF	R
7	Rosario, J - 33	CF	L
8	Beltre, M - 34	DH	L
9	Burt, M - 20	1B	R
SP	Brito, J - 31	RHP	

REMAINDER OF ROSTER	
LEFT	RIGHT
Bell, C - 23	Bastidas, J - 1

SWITCH	
Gasper, M - 12	Perkins, B - 5

RELIEF PITCHERS	
LEFT	RIGHT
Maciejewski, J - 15	Craft, D - 41
Minnick, M - 14	Ernst, N - 21
	Espinal, C - 2
	Jennings, S - 9
	Loseke, B - 4
	Ruegger, C - 32
	Vasquez, R - 8
	Zurak, K - 19

Many MiLB teams, including Yankees farm team the Somerset Patriots, have switched from handwritten to computer-printed cards.

Independent league teams still typically hand-write their batting order cards as of 2021.

Tales of minor league lineup cards

As noted above, not many minor league baseball lineup cards are still in existence, especially cards from the 20th century. But some do exist.

Former MiLB umpire Bob "Bino" Serino didn't necessarily plan on collecting

The Lineup Card

lineup cards from his umpiring days, but he did end up with a dozen or so sets of cards that he still has to this day.

"We were supposed to mail the lineup cards back into the league every seven days," said Serino, who was a full-time MiLB umpire for six years spanning the late 1970s into the 1980s, spent an additional season (1984) in Italy as an umpire/consultant, umpired the U.S. Olympic Festival in 1986, and was also a substitute umpire for South Atlantic League games hosted by the Lakewood BlueClaws from 2007 to 2018.

"The purpose behind that may have been that they wanted to see the lineup cards every now and then, that everybody listed on the lineup card was under contract," explained Serino. "Some leagues, like Class A ball, they had an age limit or veteran status, they could only carry so many [veterans] on the roster."

Serino points out that there was no Internet with almost instantaneous box scores in those days, unlike today. Some MiLB teams were in small cities or towns where there might not always be newspaper coverage of games. Communication was often limited.

"If somebody got ejected the night before, and then we move to that town ... we didn't know [they were ejected]," said Serino. "Or if there was a brawl or beanball incident."

Verifying player eligibility was exactly the reason the Texas League had umpires send in the batting order cards, confirmed Kayser, who started working in MiLB in 1976, and served as president of the Texas League from 1992 to 2017.

"The purpose for having umpires send lineup cards to the office was, as [Serino] surmised, to ensure that clubs had not used an ineligible player," said Kayser.

"I really had no idea that lineup cards were being mailed into league offices until I became a league president in 1992," continued Kayser. "I continued the practice throughout my 25 years. I did not have the time to monitor each of the eight clubs' transactions, so the cards were a backstop should a problem arise."

There ended up being exactly one such issue in the 25 years Kayser ran the Texas League.

"It was caught by someone in the MLB office and confirmed by the lineup card," Kayser recalled. "A club had put a player on an active roster before the paperwork had been received and approved by MLB."

"As I remember it, the offending club ... had lost the game in which the illegal player had been used, or else we would have had to declare a forfeit," continued Kayser. "I was happy not to have had to pull that trigger."

What did the league offices do with the lineup cards after reviewing them? Serino doesn't know. "I never did ask the [league] presidents what they did with them," he said.

In each of his 25 years running the Texas League, "I kept all 500-plus lineup cards until the end of the season, then tossed all but the few historically significant," said Kayser, adding that the kept cards included All-Star Games, no-hitters and big offensive games. Some of those cards were sent to the DeGolyer Library at Texas Christian University in Dallas as part of a Texas League collection.[2]

It should be noted that not all minor leagues required their umpires to send back

Opposite page: A lineup card from a game played in Italy in the 1980s. Names of note on the card include Jeff Hamilton, who would go on to play parts of six seasons with the Dodgers, and eventual Expos and Mets GM Omar Minaya (courtesy Bob Serino).

A pair of batting order cards from a 2007 South Atlantic League game (courtesy Bob Serino).

the cards. The independent Atlantic League of Professional Baseball (Atlantic League) did not, according to current president Rick White. Of course, the Atlantic League was not founded until 1998, when other resources were available to monitor player eligibility.

Dellinger confirmed that MiLB no longer requires its umpires to mail in their lineup cards. It is "really unnecessary now," wrote Dellinger in an email.

Back to Serino, who worked for New York–Penn League, Western Carolinas League, South Atlantic League, Carolina League, Southern League and the Eastern League.

Serino said that the leagues he worked for in the late 1970s and 1980s would provide stamped envelopes for the umpires to mail the cards back. "It was up to the crew chief to do that," he said.

Under Kayser's leadership, Texas League umpire crews "mailed them in then filed the expense of envelope and postage on regular expense reports," he said. "Later, after crews got a credit card, they simply charged the expense.

"It is possible that a card might have been omitted, but crew chiefs were pretty good about making sure that all the cards were sent in," continued Kayser.

For most of the MiLB leagues Serino worked for, "They didn't really bust our chops if we didn't send them," he said.

The Southern League was one that did.

"The [Southern] League president, he was on top of that stuff. He was the kind of league president that you'd get a phone call, 'where's the lineup cards?'" Serino reminisced.

So while Serino has a handful of cards from other leagues—"maybe two or three sets each year if for some reason we didn't mail them back to the league," he said—he has none from his time umpiring in the Southern League.

And that is a shame, considering how many eventual major leaguers came through the Southern League while Serino worked for the league.

"When I was in the Southern League in '81, it was loaded with people who went to the major leagues," he said, rattling off names like Don Mattingly, Buck Showalter, Frank Viola and Craig McMurtry, to name just a few. In fact, Serino's first Southern League game behind the plate was a Viola-McMurtry matchup. The two would go on to pitch parts of 23 seasons and earn 213 wins combined in the majors.

Serino does have a few sets of cards from working in the Eastern League in 1983. One set stands out above the others: a pair of cards from a mid–August game between the New Britain Red Sox and Albany A's.

TEXAS LEAGUE
OFFICIAL BATTING ORDER

CLUB   NWA NATURALS

DATE   JULY-11-2011

	NO.	LINE UP	POS	
1	9	ROBINSON	CF	
2	6	BIANCHI	SS	
3	12	MYERS	RF	
4	3	FRANCIS	LF	
5	2	SERATELLI	1B	
6	39	PEREZ	C	
7	8	NAVARRO	2B	
8	26	ROMAK	DH	
9	29	LISSON	3B	
SP	14	BAEZ	SP	(19) (35) (33)
11	19	BARRERA ✓	RP	
12	13	HERRERA	I	
13	35	KEATING ✓	I	
14	33	LEBRON ✓	I	
15	31	PAULINO	I	
16	36	HARDY	I	
17	32	CHAPMAN	I	
18	17	ODORIZZI	SP	
19	25	SMITH W.	I	
20	21	MINER	I	
21	28	DWYER	I	
22				
23	4	COLON	UTL	
24	16	EIGSTI	I	
25	23	THERIOT	I	

MANAGER *Bri. Pdlly*

Salvador Perez caught for the Texas League's Northwest Arkansas Naturals in 2011.

The starting pitcher for New Britain that night? None other than eventual seven-time MLB Cy Young winner Roger Clemens.

"The one with Clemens, that was his first year of pro ball," said Serino. "Texas won the national championship [that spring], he was the number 1 pick [1st round, 19th overall]. And it was an 18-inning game, that's another reason I kept it, too. I had like four or five of his starts that year."

Of the lineup cards Serino has held on to, the Clemens card attracts the most interest.

"I show people that, the Clemens card, and they like that, the people that follow baseball," he said.

Not anywhere near the same level as Clemens, but the Albany A's had a couple of future stars on their team, too, including Mike Gallego and Steve Ontiveros.

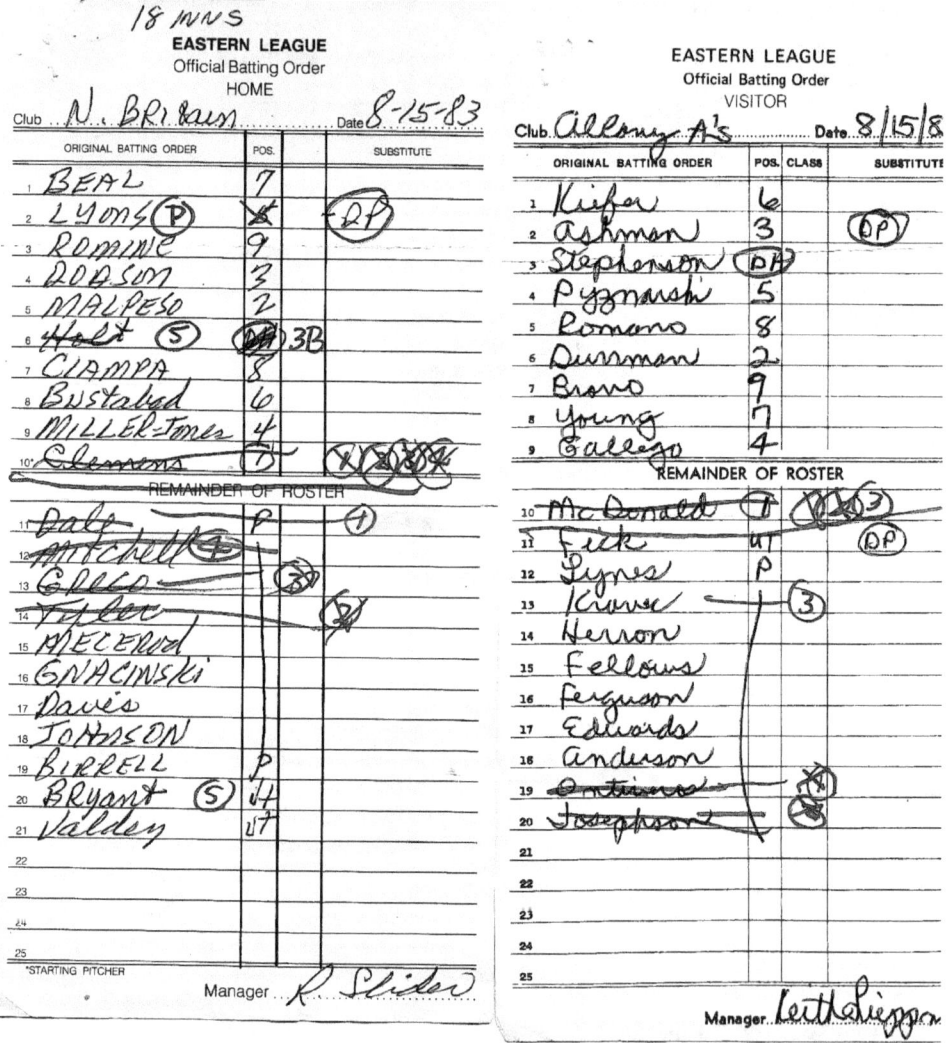

Roger Clemens started for the Eastern League's New Britain Red Sox in this 1983 game. He would be pitching for the Boston Red Sox less than a year later (courtesy Bob Serino).

Among some of the other minor league lineup cards that Serino still has from games including future MLB players are the following.

Eastern League

Serino was behind the plate for a Mike Maddux start when the Reading Phillies took on the Lynn Sailers late in 1983.

Rick Renteria and Mike Bielecki played for the Sailers. Bielecki went on to a lengthy MLB career, while Renteria played for parts of five seasons, and managed the White Sox for another five.

A few players on this pair of Eastern League batting order cards would go on to major league careers, including Mike Maddux and Mike Bielecki (courtesy Bob Serino).

Western Carolinas League

Serino umpired in the Western Carolinas League in 1979, which would be the league's last year under that name. It switched to the South Atlantic League in 1980.

Among the notable players included Gerald Perry of Greenwood and Gary Redus of Greensboro, who would each go on to play 13 years in the majors.

Gerald Perry and Gary Redus both made a stop in the Western Carolina League in 1979 on their way to lengthy major league careers (courtesy Bob Serino).

Florida Fall Instructional League

A fall 1982 Florida Instructional League game umpired by Serino included Bobby Bonilla, John Cangelosi and Ron Karkovice.

Minor League Lineup Cards

Bob Serino umpired an instructional league game that included eventual MLB players Bobby Bonilla, John Cangelosi and Ron Karkovice in 1982. Note the text at the bottom of the lineup cards, which asks the home plate umpire to mail the cards daily to the league president (courtesy Bob Serino).

South Atlantic League

A few eventual MLB players—including Tuffy Gosewisch, Quintin Berry and Hector Rondon—were on the lineup cards for a Lake County Captains at Lakewood BlueClaws South Atlantic League game Serino served as a substitute umpire for in late August 2007.

Bob Serino was still umpiring part-time in the South Atlantic League in 2007 (courtesy Bob Serino).

Back to school

Aside from occasionally substituting for the South Atlantic League, Serino primarily umpired high school games from the late–1980s on.

He still has a few of those lineup cards, too. "I used to just throw them in the bin when I was done in the back of my car," he said.

On a far more infrequent basis than when he umpired in the minor leagues, Serino still saw some good players at the high school level, including major leaguers Brad Brach, Todd Frazier, Jeff Frazier, Anthony Renaudo and Anthony

LINEUP CARD 8/13/11

	THUNDER	R/L		SENATORS	R/L
1	KRUM		1	KOMATSU	L
2	PIRELA	R	2	RAHL	R
3	KRUML	L	3	DAVIS	L
4	LYERLY	L	4	MOORE	R
5	MESA	R	5	HARPER	L
6	ALMONTE	S	6	PAHUTA	L
7	GIL	R	7	PEREZ	R
8	MUJICA	L	8	McCONNELL	R
9	MARUSZAK		9	JOHNSON	S
P	HEYER		P	PEREZ	

Thunder line score: 4 0 0 2 1 0 0 0 0
Senators line score: 0 0 3 0 0 0 0 0 0

AVAILABLE POSITION PLAYERS

LHH	SWITCH	RHH	LHH	SWITCH	RHH
JOSEPH		BAKER			FOX
SUBLETT					KING
					NORRIS

AVAILABLE PITCHERS

LHP	RHP	LHP	RHP
HALSEY	ARBISO	McCOY	BARTHMAIER
IGAWA	POPE	VAN ALLEN	MARTINEZ
	WHITLEY		MARTIN
	TEXEIRA		LEHMAN
VENDITTE			PENA

HP MATT 1B SHAUN 2B 3B SCOTT

Bryce Harper only played 37 games for the Double-A Harrisburg Senators on his way to the major leagues. The August 13, 2011, game was one of them (courtesy Jeff Garfinkel).

DeSclafani. Minor leaguers included Charlie Frazier and then–Red Sox prospect Jay Groome.

Minor league lineup cards today

As noted earlier, minor league lineup cards have gained more visibility in the last decade or so as some fans and collectors have realized they can ask managers and umpires for cards after a game and may get them, and some minor league cards with

New York Yankees

April /13/ 16

V	RAILRIDERS	1	2	3	4	5	6	7	8	9	10	11	R	H	E
H	PAWTUCKET														

RAILRIDERS

#	Player	Pos	R/L
1	GAMEL	CF	L
2	JUDGE	RF	
3	HEATHCOTT	LF	L
4	REFSNYDER	2B	
5	SOLANO	3B	
6	PUELLO	DH	
7	PARMELEE	1B	L
8	RODRIGUEZ	C	
9	KOZMA	SS	
10	~~HAYNES~~	P	

PAWTUCKET

#	Player	Pos	R/L
1	MARRERO. D	3B	
2	HERNANDEZ	SS	L
3	TRAVIS	1B	
4	MAXWELL	DH	
5	CRAIG / Marrero.C	RF	
6	DOMINGUEZ	7	
7	LaMARRE	SS	
8	BUTLER	C	
9	COYLE	2B	
10	~~OWENS~~	P	L

AVAILABLE POSITION PLAYERS (RAILRIDERS)

LHH	SWITCH	RHH
		DIAZ
		SANCHEZ

AVAILABLE POSITION PLAYERS (PAWTUCKET)

LHH	SWITCH	RHH
	LEON	MARRERO.C
		RUTLEDGE
		VAZQUEZ

AVAILABLE PITCHERS (RAILRIDERS)

LHP	RHP
PAZOS	GOODY
WEBB	MORENO
	MULLEE
	PESTANO
	~~PINDER~~

AVAILABLE PITCHERS (PAWTUCKET)

LHP	RHP
47 ESCOBAR	37 HEMBREE
36 SCOTT	28 LIGHT
	39 ~~MARBAN~~
	40 MARTIN
	41 MENDEZ
	24 VARVARO

| HP | · ROBERT | 1B | ERIK | 2B | MAXX | 3B | SHAN |

Aaron Judge would get called up to the New York Yankees a few months after this April game between the Scranton/Wilkes-Barre RailRiders and Pawtucket Red Sox.

the names of current MLB stars such as Mike Trout, Bryce Harper and Aaron Judge have proven to be worth something.

For example, a pair of 2011 Arkansas Travelers batting order cards listing Mike Trout sold for $110 and $164, respectively, on eBay in 2022.

Of course, not all umpires and managers give them away, for various reasons.

In the case of Yard Goats manager Denorfia, "[he] keeps the winning lineup cards and posts them on the wall in his office," the Yard Goats spokesperson said.

The Lineup Card Collectors

Introduction

Eleven lineup card collectors were interviewed for this book, in addition to a review of the lineup cards in the National Baseball Hall of Fame's collection. The 11 collectors interviewed are generally a diverse group, aside from gender, where just one is female.

Age-wise, the collectors span almost 50 years from youngest to oldest. Professions run the gamut, including a former MLB umpire, a YouTuber, songwriter and an insurance agent.

How they get their lineup cards also varies from collector to collector. Getting lineup cards was part of John Hirschbeck's job as an MLB umpire when he was behind the plate.

A few collectors, including Zack Hample, Tony Voda, Erynn Johnson and Todd Osborne, get the vast majority if not all their cards by asking managers, coaches and umpires for them after games. Others, such as Jeffrey Lazarus, Jeff Garfinkel, Scott Meza, Rick Levy, Bill Haelig and Seth Swirsky, have collected cards by purchasing them. And, of course, all of the cards in the Hall of Fame's collection are donated.

Another common trait among the collectors, save for Hirschbeck and Voda, was that they started collecting baseball items before knowing they could get lineup cards. They learned by seeing or hearing about someone else asking for a lineup card at a game, or seeing a lineup card for sale in an auction house catalog or otherwise.

Once they found out about the availability of lineup cards, they were hooked. The lineup card collector profiles follow.

The National Baseball Hall of Fame's lineup card collection

Only a very small number of the approximately 150 lineup cards in the Hall of Fame's collection are on display in the museum. Cards on display in November 2021 included Atlanta's batting order card used by the umpire during the game in which Hank Aaron hit his 715th career home run to surpass Babe Ruth, and the Detroit dugout card used in the first game ever played at Comerica Park in 2000.

The rest of the cards are kept in the museum's reference library, the Giamatti Research Center. Most are kept together and are available for researchers to search through the collection. There are some cards tied to other collections that are not routinely pulled as part of the lineup card collection.

Based on quantity alone, the Hall of Fame's collection is perhaps underwhelming. There are several if not many collectors who have more cards.

But what it lacks in quantity, the Hall of Fame's collection makes up in quality. There are very few collections that rival the Hall of Fame in capturing key historical moments from the game's history, some well-known, and some more obscure.

Here is a sampling of a few of the most notable cards in the Hall of Fame's collection:

- The original Angels and Orioles batting order cards from the games Cal Ripken Jr. tied and then broke Lou Gehrig's consecutive games played streak. A pair of carbon copies of the Orioles card from both games, along with the pen used to fill the cards out, sold for more than $40,000 in 2000, so the actual cards penned by Baltimore manager Phil Regan and California manager Marcel Lachemann would likely be worth six figures if they were for sale.
- The batting order cards from both teams in the longest professional baseball game ever played, a 33-inning, 8 hour and 25 minute affair between the International League's Pawtucket Red Sox and Rochester Red Wings that started on April 18, 1981. Two future Hall of Famers, Ripken and Wade Boggs, played in the game.
- The California Angels' dugout lineup card from their September 28, 1974, game against the Minnesota Twins in which Hall of Famer Nolan Ryan threw his third career no-hitter. The card, which also includes Hall of Famer Rod Carew, is signed and dated by Ryan.
- The Oakland dugout lineup card from Game 3 of the 1974 World Series. The A's won the game, 3–2, and would go on to win the World Series, 4-to-1.
- The Red Sox dugout lineup card from May 31, 2008, when the Red Sox played the Orioles in Baltimore. Manny Ramirez hit his 500th home run in the game, becoming just the 24th player to achieve the feat.

There are other lineup cards in the collection that are not as historic, but still hold significance:

- The Rays started the first all-left-handed lineup since at least 1901 in a September 11, 2020, game against the Red Sox. Even starting pitcher Blake Snell was a lefty. Because teams typically denote lefties in "red" ink, the lineup card indeed has a unique look to it. And the all-lefty strategy was not just a gimmick, as the Rays won the game, 11–1.[1]
- Without background, the fact that the Baseball Hall of Fame has a June 25, 2015, lineup card from the obscure independent Pacific Association is puzzling. But research shows that Sonoma Stompers starting pitcher on that day, Sean Conroy, was the first openly gay baseball player to play in a professional baseball game.[2]
- The Toronto and Miami batting order cards from their August 11, 2020, game played at Sahlen Field in Buffalo, New York. The game was played in Buffalo because of Canada's decision to not allow the Blue Jays to host games in Toronto due to COVID-19. Interestingly, it was not the first major league game played at Sahlen Field. The Federal League's Buffalo Blues played there in 1915. The Federal League was considered a "major" league at that time,

along with the American League and National League. The Federal League folded after the 1915 season.

The cards in the Hall of Fame's collection are kept in folders which are in turn kept in a box. There is usually a brief description written on the folder, but it is not always clear what the significance of the cards is.

One such example is a Florida State University dugout lineup card. There was no indication of what the card's importance was on the folder, and the card only indicated that the game was played in 2018. There was nothing as to who the other team was, just Florida State's starting lineup and a few relief pitcher names crossed because they had played in the game.

Based on the lineup and a lot of digging, the game took place on May 5, 2018, against Clemson, with the Seminoles winning, 3–2, in 13 innings. The significance, it turned out, was that it was Florida State coach Mike Martin's 1,976th career victory, moving him into first place on the Division I college baseball career win list.[3]

Most lineup cards in the Baseball Hall of Fame's collection are given to the museum. There are games for which the Hall of Fame will request the lineup card from a team, manager or umpire. The Hall of Fame does not purchase lineup cards or other artifacts.

That does not necessarily mean that all cards sent to the Hall of Fame will be kept. In fact, some are not. The Hall of Fame weighs a variety of factors in making such decisions, including:

- Was the game itself, or something that occurred during the game (e.g., a player reaching a milestone), of historic significance?

Items, including a lineup card now in the Hall of Fame's collection, from Florida State coach Mike Martin's 1,976th career victory (courtesy Florida State University).

- If nothing of historical significance took place during the game, was there a player or manager involved with the game that might warrant the lineup card being kept at the Hall of Fame?
- Is the card's authenticity certain or near certain?
- Is the card in good enough condition?

John Hirschbeck: Former MLB umpire finds worthy cause for his collection

Former MLB umpire John Hirschbeck diligently kept his lineup cards throughout his lengthy career.

Whether it was a spring training, regular season, All-Star, playoff or World Series game, if Hirschbeck was behind the plate—the home plate umpire gets an official batting order card from each team before the game—he kept almost all of them over the course of his more than 30 years of umpiring.

Why did Hirschbeck hang on to all his cards?

"I would say someone said something to me, an old timer said something to me when I first came up," said Hirschbeck, who retired after the 2016 season.

So if a fan asked him for the cards after a game, which did not happen often according to Hirschbeck, he would politely say no. "I would say, 'I'm saving them for my kids, but here's a ball for you, or here's a ball for your son,'" said Hirschbeck.

He even declined the National Baseball Hall of Fame's request for a lineup card.

"I had the plate when [Barry] Bonds broke the [all-time home run] record, so I have those lineup cards also," Hirschbeck said. "The Hall of Fame wanted something. ... But I said I'm not giving up the lineup cards. I'm keeping those."

"I'll bet in 34 years, there's only several times—maybe 25 times at the most—where I gave them away, and that was something special. If like my son brought a friend to the game.... I'd give them to [the friend] as a little present," he continued.

Another set of cards he recalls giving away was Joe Mauer's MLB debut game in 2004.

"Mauer, his first game in the big leagues, I sent the lineup cards over and said, give them to him," Hirschbeck said. "A couple things like that, where I knew they'd be special to someone, I've give them away." "But that was it," added Hirschbeck. "I [kept] all the other ones."

Hirschbeck had a routine during the season for collecting the cards.

"I would go home at the All-Star break, take the lump [of cards] out of my trunk and put them in an envelope, label it," Hirschbeck said. "Then, at the end of the season, I would put the rest of them in there so they were in order, even spring training, playoff cards, World Series."

Hirschbeck was behind the plate for many meaningful games over the course of his career, including:

- The 2013 All-Star Game
- The first game of the 2010 National League Division Series between Philadelphia and Cincinnati, when Roy Halladay threw the second-ever playoff no-hitter

Former MLB umpire John Hirschbeck was behind the plate when Hall of Famer Carl Yastrzemski hit his final career home run (courtesy Jeffrey Lazarus).

- The August 7, 2007, game between the Nationals and Giants in which Barry Bonds hit his 756th career home run, surpassing Hank Aaron for first place in career home runs
- The September 19, 2011, game between the Yankees and Twins in which Mariano Rivera notched his 602nd career save to become MLB's all-time career saves leader
- Five World Series games:
    - Game 4 of the 1995 World Series
    - Game 5 (deciding game) of the 2006 World Series
    - Game 1 of the 2010 World Series
    - Game 1 of the 2013 World Series
    - Game 3 of the 2016 World Series

The cards most important to him, he eventually pulled out for either himself or family members. For example, Hirschbeck framed his five World Series lineup cards.

Adrian Beltre hit his first of 477 home runs on June 30, 1998, with John Hirschbeck behind the plate (courtesy Jeffrey Lazarus).

The 2013 All-Star Game was the only All-Star Game for which Hirschbeck called balls and strikes.

"I had the plate in the '13 All-Star Game in New York," he recalled. "I kept every change so it was official, and I had [the cards] framed, and game them to one of my daughters."

When Hirschbeck retired after the 2016 season, he had no specific plan for his collection of roughly 3,000 MLB official batting order cards.

That changed in 2020.

Hirschbeck's sons Michael and "Little" John were both diagnosed with a rare neurological disease called Adrenoleukodystrophy (ALD) in 1992.

Eleven months after the diagnosis, "Little" John passed away at the age of eight. Michael survived a bone marrow transplant that slowed the rapid progression of the disease, but still suffered debilitating seizures throughout the rest of his life. Michael passed away in 2014 at the age of 27.

Shortly after Michael's death, Hirschbeck's family and some friends established a charitable organization named "The Magic of Michael" to honor Michael's memory by doing something to help others. One of the ways the organization raises money to help families endure "the curveballs of life" is through an annual charity golf tournament.

But the 2020 event was canceled due to COVID.

Still determined to raise money that year, Hirschbeck decided to sell the many items that Michael had been given over the years, as well as the bulk of his own sports memorabilia collection.

The Brewers printed home plate umpire John Hirschbeck's name on the bottom of this batting order card, a rare occurrence.

Among the items Hirschbeck had accumulated included baseballs signed by former U.S. presidents, including Ronald Reagan, Jimmy Carter and George W. Bush; seats from Fenway Park; and a Roy Halladay autographed baseball after his playoff no-hitter.

Included in what was sold was the vast majority of Hirschbeck's lineup card collection.

"My lineup cards were one of the things I never thought I'd part with, but I did," he said.

Hirschbeck's generosity in giving up his so much of his sports memorabilia collection paid off in the form of a $134,000 contribution to "The Magic of Michael" that year.

Advice to younger umpires

Whether or not younger umpires will ultimately find as rewarding a purpose as Hirschbeck did with their lineup cards, his advice to them has always been to keep the cards after a game.

"I would say to any young umpire I would come in contact with over the years, 'what do you do with your lineup cards?' If they said, 'I save them,' I'd say 'good, save them all. Someday, you'll want them whether it's for your children or whatever.'

"To guys that didn't, I would say, 'Do yourself a favor, save them because there's

Steve Carlton earned his last MLB victory in 1987 with John Hirschbeck calling balls and strikes (courtesy Jeffrey Lazarus).

going to be reasons you might want them in years to come,'" Hirschbeck continued. "'If nothing else, it might turn out to be a memorable game.' And, I would always say, 'For your children if nothing else, family members. You can give them to them someday. There's no sense in just throwing them in the trash. It's part of the game.'"

For Hirschbeck, the only cards he kept were the ones when he was the home plate umpire. If another umpire on his crew ignored Hirschbeck's advice to keep the cards and instead left them in the locker room after a game, Hirschbeck had no interest in those cards.

"No, I never kept them because they have no meaning to me. They meant nothing to me if I didn't have the plate," he said.

The lineup card that stood out above all others

Of all the lineup cards Hirschbeck collected over his career, one stands out as the most unique and meaningful, so much so that Hirschbeck gave it to his wife, Denise. And it is not from a World Series, All-Star or player milestone game.

"I was working in Milwaukee shortly after my son Michael passed away," recalled Hirschbeck. "Jerry Narron, who was the [Milwaukee] bench coach, came out with the lineup cards. I've known Jerry since '76 in the Florida State League."

"He came out with the lineup cards, and he shook my hand and gave them to me. I looked at the lineup cards and I passed one over to the other manager. Then I looked at the other manager's [lineup card] and passed one over to Jerry. And he said, 'did you look at those close?' I said, 'yeah.' He goes, 'well, look at them again.' On the computer, he had taken a picture of my son Michael, just a little, tiny picture—because the lineup cards aren't that big—and put it on top of the lineup cards. Right at home plate, he got teary-eyed, I got teary-eyed, and I gave him a hug and said, 'it means a lot, Jerry.'"

Hample, Voda & Johnson: Some ball hawks collect lineup cards, too

Ball hawks—those trying to catch or pick up a hit or thrown baseball before, during or after a game—collect baseballs they get at games.

A small but growing number are also starting to dabble in collecting lineup cards, too.

It starts with Zack Hample, who revolutionized ball hawking and has inspired tens of thousands of kids along with a few adults to become ball hawks through his blog and videos (Hample has nearly 650,0000 YouTube subscribers as of mid–2022). It has become rare to go to a professional baseball game in recent years without seeing kids chase baseballs, and many of them learned it from Hample.

In the process, Hample has also introduced some of his followers to the art of chasing and collecting lineup cards, albeit on a much smaller scale.

Before Hample, very few people at baseball games knew that you could ask a manager, coach or umpire for a lineup card after the game, and they may very well give it to you.

Former minor league umpire Bob Serino said he was never asked for lineup cards when he umpired in the late 1970s and 1980s. "They only asked for baseballs," he said of fans. "Ninety-nine percent of people don't even know we have lineup cards."

But Hample's blogs and now videos about occasionally getting lineup cards from managers, coaches and umpires at MLB games has changed that.

In fact, it has become common to see at least one if not multiple fans asking for lineup cards after minor league and MLB games. And they are increasingly promoting their successes on social media, fostering even more interest.

Following are profiles of the lineup card collections of Hample as well as two other ball hawks, Tony Voda and Erynn Johnson, who both learned about chasing lineup cards from Hample.

Zack Hample

Hample, a self-described "baseball superfan," has a knack for snagging baseballs at MLB games with more than 12,000 baseballs to his name as of late 2022.[4]

Two of his most noteworthy snags were Mike Trout's first career home run and Alex Rodriguez's 3,000th hit, which was a home run.

A pair of batting order cards given to Zack Hample after a 2013 game (courtesy Zack Hample).

While not nearly as extensive as his baseball collection, Zack Hample's MLB lineup card collection is still impressive.[5]

For starters, Hample has never paid a dime for any of the MLB lineup cards in his collection. They all have been given to him by a manager, coach, player or grounds crew member after games.

And he has collected more than 50 cards dating back to 1999, despite lineup cards not being his primary focus.

"I decided long ago to *always* go for a ball before anything else," Hample said.

"I've attended more than 1,300 games, and I've probably tried to get lineup cards at several hundred," continued Hample in a 2015 interview. "I didn't even know about lineup cards at first, and lately I've been going to games in New York where it's basically impossible to get down to the dugouts. Sometimes, regardless of the stadium, I stay in the outfield all game because I'm more interested in catching home runs."

But when he ends up near the umpire exit, bullpens or dugouts after a game looking for a baseball toss-up or two, he has gotten his share of lineup cards.

Hample learned about the possibility of snagging a lineup card after a game by watching another fan ask for, and receive, a card at the dugout after a game in the late 1990s.

Having already been to hundreds of MLB games in his life, Hample got his first lineup cards—a pair of batting order cards—on June 26, 1999, at a Twins-Tigers game in Detroit.

Hample has a variety of types of cards in his collection, including dugout,

1999 OFFICIAL BATTING ORDER (VISITING CLUB)				1999 OFFICIAL BATTING ORDER DETROIT			
ORIGINAL	POS.	CHANGE	ALSO ELIGIBLE	ORIGINAL	POS.	CHANGE	ALSO ELIGIBLE
1 Jones				1 POLONIA	DH		CATALANOTTO / GARCIA
2			GATES	2 AUSMUS	2		HASELMAN
3 WALKER				3 KAPLER	3		MACIAS
4				4 PALMER	5		BRUNSON
5				5 CLARK	3		NITKOWSKI
6				6 ENCARNACION	1		BLAIR / FLORIE
7				7 HIGGINSON	9		LIDA / BRJCAIL
8				8 EASLEY	4		JONES / CRUZ N.
9				9 CRUZ D.	6		
P				P MLICKI	1		WEAVER / THOMPSON / MOEHLER

The first lineup cards Zack Hample was ever given were carbon copies from this Twins–Tigers game in 1999 (courtesy Zack Hample).

bullpen, batting order and pitcher usage cards. Pitcher usage cards chart the recent use of one or both teams' relief pitchers so a manager or coach knows which of their pitchers to rest or use, or which relief pitchers the opposing team is most likely to use.

One card in Hample's collection that is of historical significance is the Giants batting order card from the night Randy Wynn hit for the cycle in August 2005.

He also has gotten dugout lineup cards written by Jerry Narron, who pens some of the nicest-looking cards with his calligraphy penmanship, and Dusty Baker, known for jotting down various notes on his batting order cards during games.

Chasing lineup cards at MLB games is fraught with failure, but Hample encourages would-be collectors to give it a shot whenever possible.

"At major league stadiums, you might get rejected 19 out of 20 times, but when you finally succeed, it feels incredible," he said.

Tony Voda

Tony Voda was familiar with lineup cards before he started reading Hample's "The Baseball Collector" blog some 15 years ago, primarily to follow Hample's ball hawking exploits.

He "had bought a couple old school ones from the early '90s" that included Voda's childhood Minnesota Twins heroes Robin Ventura and Kirby Puckett. "Having Robin

Opposite page: Dusty Baker wrote a number of notes on this pair of cards he gave Zack Hample in 2005 (courtesy Zack Hample).

The Lineup Card Collectors

151

Ventura on a card makes me happy, same with having Puckett, whom I named my dog, Kirby, after," said Voda.

He did not know, however, that you could potentially get a lineup card after a game without paying for it.

"I think I first knew about gathering lineup cards after reading about it on Zack Hample's website," Voda said. "Every once in a while, he'd get one and it intrigued me."

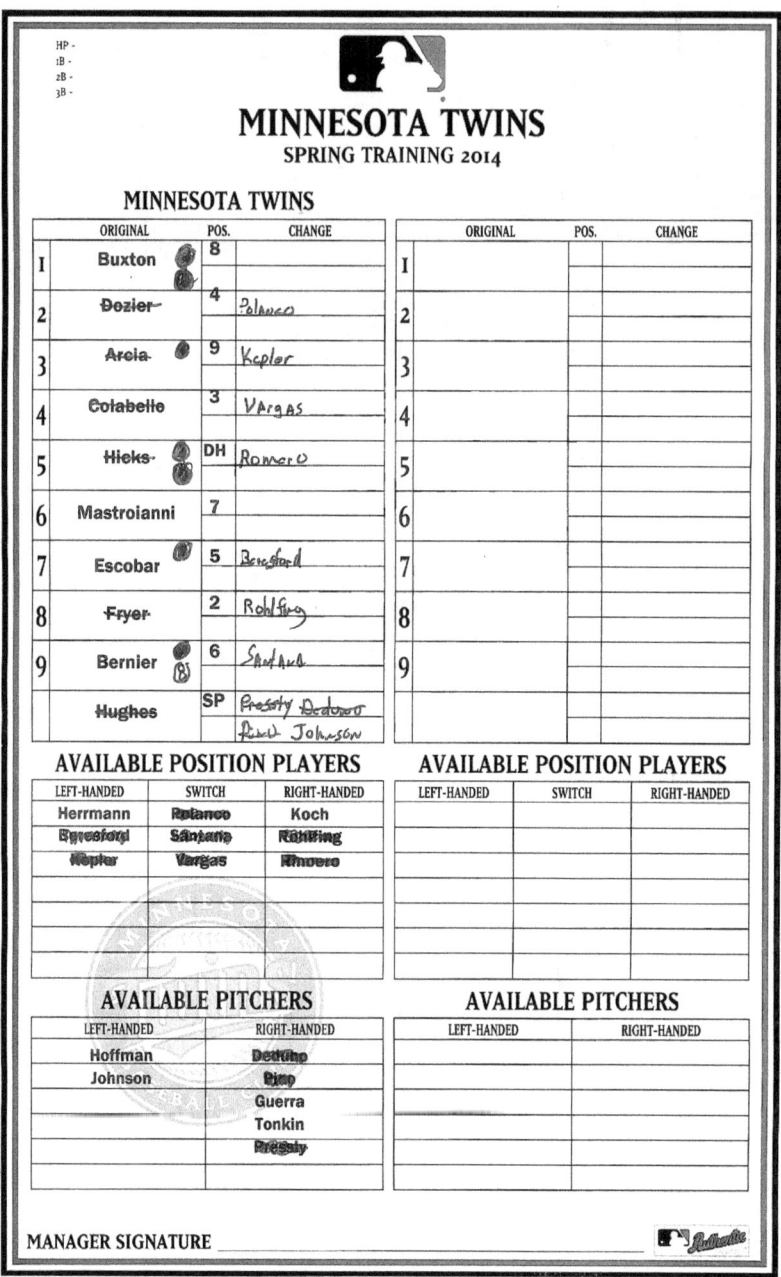

One of the first lineup cards Tony Voda was given after a game (courtesy Tony Voda).

Enough so that Voda has collected about three dozen lineup cards from managers, coaches and umpires since the first time he tried at a 2013 spring training game, through mid–2022. The vast majority are from MLB regular season and spring training games, but he also has three from a Liga Mexicana de Beisbol (LMB) trip he made in 2022. Not counted are the concert lineup cards he also collects.

BALTIMORE ORIOLES AT TORONTO BLUE JAYS
SAHLEN FIELD • BUFFALO, NY • JUNE 24, 2021

HP - Nick Lentz 1B - Edwin Moscoso 2B - Joe West 3B - Bruce Dreckman

BALTIMORE ORIOLES

#	ORIGINAL	POS.	CHANGE
1	Mullins, C	8	
2	Mancini, T	DH	
3	Mountcastle, R	3	
4	Santander, A	9	Stewart
5	Hays, A	7	
6	Galvis, F	6	
7	Franco, M	5	
8	Severino, P	2	
9	Valaika, P	4	
P	Kremer, D	1	Plutko Lakins

TORONTO BLUE JAYS

#	ORIGINAL	POS.	CHANGE
1	Semien, M	4	
2	Bichette, B	6	Espinal
3	Guerrero Jr., V	DH	
4	Hernández, T	9	
5	Grichuk, R	8	
6	Biggio, C	5	
7	Gurriel Jr., L	7	
8	Panik, J	3	
9	McGuire, R	2	
P	Kay, A	1	Castro Murphy / Barnes Saucedo

AVAILABLE POSITION PLAYERS (Baltimore)

LEFT-HANDED	SWITCH	RIGHT-HANDED
Stewart, D	Wilkerson, S	Wynns, A

AVAILABLE POSITION PLAYERS (Toronto)

LEFT-HANDED	SWITCH	RIGHT-HANDED
		Adams, R
		Espinal, S
		Springer, G

AVAILABLE PITCHERS (Baltimore)

LEFT-HANDED	RIGHT-HANDED
Akin, K	Eshelman, T / Harvey, H
Fry, P	Harvey, M / Jannis, M
Scott, Tan	Lakins Sr., T / López, J
	Plutko, A / Sulser, C
	Tate, D / Wells, T

AVAILABLE PITCHERS (Toronto)

LEFT-HANDED	RIGHT-HANDED
Mayza, T	Barnes, J / Castro, A
Ray, R	Chatwood, T / Manoah, A
Ryu, H	Murphy, P / Payamps, J
Saucedo, T	Romano, J / Stripling, R
	Thornton, T

MANAGER SIGNATURE _____

The Orioles gave Tony Voda their authenticated dugout lineup card after a 2021 game at Sahlen Field in Buffalo (courtesy Tony Voda).

154   The Lineup Card

"I have a collection of concert setlists," said Voda. "I love getting these from the musician or roadie after the concert. It allows me to remember the set and even replay the concert via my own mix later on."

Back to baseball. Voda has managed to collect some notable lineup cards.

"The one I got from Sahlen Field might be my favorite, since it is so rare and will

A dugout lineup card from the Tecolotes Dos Laredos of the Liga Mexicana de Beisbol (courtesy Tony Voda).

tell a story of the weird 2020 and 2021 seasons," said Voda of the authenticated dugout lineup card he was given by an Orioles coach after a game against the Blue Jays in Buffalo in summer 2021 when the Blue Jays used Buffalo's Sahlen Field as their home stadium for a few weeks due to Canadian COVID restrictions.

Aside from the uniqueness of an MLB game played in Buffalo, it is almost unheard of these days for an MLB team to give away its authenticated dugout card, as those are almost always sold or given to players.

A batting order card from a 2013 White Sox at Twins game, signed by Ventura, then Chicago's manager, is also high on Voda's list, followed by a batting order card from Kennys Vargas's first career home run game in 2014.

Then there are the LMB cards he got on a 2022 road trip.

The first two were from a game played north of the border. The Owls of the Two Laredos (in Spanish, the Tecolotes de los Dos Laredos) play games in both Mexico and the U.S.

"I really did want to get one from my trip, since it would be a dated and specific example of memorabilia from that league, team and trip," said Voda. "Night one ends, I am allowed on the field for the team celebration, allowed into the dugout, and as time goes on the dugouts get cleaned up and no one took the lineup cards off the wall. So as the fireworks went off for the Fourth of July celebration in Laredo, I peeled them off the wall and held on to them, and soon after got team permission to keep them."

The next night, he went to a game in Nueva Laredo, Mexico, and was able to get the dugout cards from both teams.

Priorities: Ball hawking first, lineup cards second

Like Hample, Voda's first passion is chasing baseballs.

"I am a ball hawk first and foremost, so I often forget about chasing a lineup card, or lower it on my list of priorities," Voda said.

But lineup cards have worked their way into a close second.

"I have received a ton of memorabilia over the years," said Voda. "Outside of baseballs, my favorite being Kennys Vargas's first career home run and my first home run caught on the fly, I've received many bats, hats, batting gloves, cleats, a rosin bag, and even a fielding glove."

"Lineup cards, to me, are like a step below baseballs," he continued. "They are the second most common collection I have from MLB games, but the great thing about them is they are lighter, less cumbersome, and I know that if I got one on the road, I can bring it back with me. Getting a bat when you flew somewhere presents a problem. But lineup cards? They travel nicely and are also much more specific to the game than just about any other piece of memorabilia."

Voda estimates that he's gotten a lineup card about half the times he has asked over the years. His success rate goes up to about 80 percent when he gets to have a dialogue with whoever he is asking.

"Asking a coach and having a conversation with them is much more successful than a quick shout as an umpire heads to the tunnel," Voda said.

Home sweet home

The majority of cards Voda has gotten have been at Target Field, his local stadium.

156   The Lineup Card

"I am not sure if Target Field is easy for lineup cards or just more familiar to me," Voda said. "I think certain coaches and teams are better than others, as well as certain locations. Target Field has great access to the umpires [as they exit] after the game, so that really helps with getting those lineup cards. It also just helps being a genuine fan of a team or coach."

However, Target Field has not always been friendly to Voda, lineup card–wise.

"I went through a dry spell between 2015 and 2019 for two reasons," Voda said. "First, the Twins weren't handing out their lineup cards anymore, for some reason due

 **OFFICIAL BATTING ORDER**
Minnesota Twins
Tuesday, September 28, 2021

#	ORIGINAL	POS.	CHANGE	ALSO ELIGIBLE
				POSITION PLAYERS
1	Buxton, B	8 B / C		Arraez, L
2	Polanco, J	4 B / C		Cave, J
				Gordon, N (D)
3	Garver, M	2 B / C		Jeffers, R
				PITCHERS
4	Donaldson, J	5 B / C		1. Coulombe, D
				2. Moran, J
5	Sanó, M	DH B / C	(3) / (1)	3. Thielbar, C (C)
				4. Alcala, J (A)
6	~~Rooker, B~~ (D)	7 B / C	(5)	5. Barraclough, K
				6. Colomé, A (F)
7	Astudillo, W	3 B / C	(2)	7. Duffey, T (B)
				8. Farrell, L
8	Kepler, M	9 B / C		9. Gant, J
			(4)	10. Garza Jr., R (E)
9	Simmons, A	6 B / C		11. Jax, G
				12. Minaya, J
P	(A)(B)(C)(E)	SP B / C (F)		13. Pineda, M
				14. Vincent, N
		D		~~15. Barnes, C (SP)~~
		E		

Version 1 - 9/28/2021 at 5:36 PM

The Minnesota Twins included their logo as a watermark on this 2021 batting order card (courtesy Tony Voda).

to Paul Molitor being manager, and I was always on their side for the end of games. And second, after I got denied a few times and was told they wouldn't hand them out, I just focused on ball hawking and trying for other pieces of memorabilia. Bats, hats, and batting gloves all still seemed to find their way to me, so I wasn't complaining."

Voda is appreciative of the generosity of so many managers, coaches, players, umpires and stadium workers who give away lineup cards, especially as baseball ephemera is starting to disappear in the digital age.

"Now that hard tickets are becoming a thing of the past, this is the one piece of memorabilia that is game specific and can be pinpointed without detective work to the game you attended," said Voda. "For us tactile folks who have that collector's itch, these mean the world to us."

Erynn Johnson

Erynn Johnson, a ball hawk, Detroit-area native and Tigers fan, also took note of Hample's lineup card success.

"I learned by seeing other people like Zack asking umpires, coaches, and bullpen catchers. By watching Zack, I began to think about giving it a try, and I did," she said.

Her first lineup card at a game was given to her by a friend who got a pair of batting order cards from home plate umpire Nestor Ceja after an Astros at Tigers game in June of 2021.

"He was generous enough to give me the Astros card, and this is what jump-started my collection," Johnson said of her friend. "An excellent part of this piece is that manager Dusty Baker signs it."

Johnson got her first lineup card on her own a few days later.

"On July 4th, 2021, after the game I got the Tigers' lineup card from home plate umpire Mark Ripperger," said Johnson. "This was a cool piece because my dad and I showed up late to this game and I wasn't expecting to get anything, but I went home with my second lineup card."

The thrill grew when Johnson got home. "I was excited ... because I realized this was possible and I [had] started a new collection," she said. But she quickly found out that asking for cards after MLB games does not always work out. "I have asked several umps at the end of games [since] and gotten turned down," Johnson said.

Enter Juan Nieves, Detroit's assistant pitching coach in 2021 and 2022. Nieves, who threw a no-hitter as a pitcher for the Milwaukee Brewers in 1987, works out of the bullpen during Tigers games, where he keeps a lineup card.

"Juan has hooked me up twice," said Johnson of a pair of cards she got from July 2022 games.

The first card she got from Nieves was from the game Kansas City rookie Vinnie Pasquantino hit his first MLB home run. It also was a game in which future Hall of Famer Miguel Cabrera and Detroit rookie Riley Greene each collected a hit.

"I think it is very cool," said Johnson. "I hope to get Vinnie to sign it one day when the Royals are in town."

Johnson appreciates the authenticity of the batting order and bullpen cards she has been able to get.

"It is a piece of the game, and there are only a couple each game, so they are quite unique," she said. "They represent America's greatest pastime."

158 The Lineup Card

OFFICIAL BATTING ORDER
Houston Astros — A

Thursday, June 24, 2021

ORIGINAL	POS.	CHANGE	ALSO ELIGIBLE
			POSITION PLAYERS
1 Straw, M	8 B		Castro, J
	C		
2 ~~Brantley, M~~	7 B 3		Altuve, J
	C		Jones, T
3 Gurriel, Y	3 B	3	~~McCormick, C~~
	C		**PITCHERS**
4 Alvarez, Y	DH B		1. Raley, B
	C		①2. ~~Taylor, B~~ 591
5 Correa, C	6 B		3. Valdez, F
	C		4. Bielak, B
6 Tucker, K	9 B		④~~5. Garza Jr., R~~ 625
	C		6. Greinke, Z
7 Toro, A	5 B		7. Javier, C
	C		8. McCullers Jr., L
8 Garcia, R	4 B		9. Odorizzi, J
	C		10. Pressly, R
9 Maldonado, M	2 B		②11. ~~Stanek, R~~ 3½
	C		12. Urquidy, J
P ~~Garcia, L~~	SP ~~P~~		13. Garcia, L (SP)
	C		
	D		
	E		

Version 1 - 6/24/2021 at 3:57 PM

MANAGER'S SIGNATURE _Johnnie B Baker Jr_

Erynn Johnson's first-ever MLB batting order card. Dusty Baker signed it with his full name, Johnnie B. Baker Jr., which he rarely does (courtesy Erynn Johnson).

Her advice to other would-be lineup card collectors?

"It never hurts to ask even if you get turned down," she said. "Even though it's just a piece of paper, it is so cool and represents some of the greatest players to ever touch the field."

Todd Osborne: Manners matter

The hobby of collecting lineup cards started by accident for Ohioan Todd Osborne.

Osborne was at a Dayton Dragons game in 2001. The Dragons were the Cincinnati Reds Class A Midwest League entry at the time.

"I found myself by the dugout after the game and the manager just handed it to me," said Osborne of getting his first lineup card. "The funny thing is I didn't even ask for it."

BLUE JAYS LINEUP CARD

March 15, 2018

	1	2	3	4	5	6	7	8	9	10	11	12	13	R	H	E
VISITOR	0	0	0	1	0	2	0									
HOME	0	0	0	0	0	4										

#	NEW HAMPSHIRE	POS	#	vs. PHILLIES	POS
1	PALACIOS	DH	1	●	
2	JONES · / BARRETO	4	2	●	
3	GUERERRO · / KNIGHT	5	3	●	
4	JANSEN · / SMITH	2	4		
5	WILLIAMS	3	5	● ⑨	
6	~~ADAMS~~ / MINEO	DH	6	●	
7	THOMAS · / POLIZZI	7	7		
8	LUNDQUIST	9	8	●	
9	CARDENAS	6	9	●	
10	OBESO	8			

LHH EXTRA MEN RHH
JACOB
~~BARRETO~~
~~POLIZZI~~
~~SMITH~~
PENTECOST
MINEO
~~KNIGHT~~

LHP PITCHERS RHP
SP - PEARSON
SAUCEDO
BERGEN
WEATHERLY
HALL

BU - ELLER

This 2018 Blue Jays minor league spring training card includes future big league star Vladimir Guerrero Jr (courtesy Todd Osborne).

The Lineup Card

"Well, after that game, I started asking for them now and then," continued Osborne. "There was a group of about six of us who collected and we'd take turns asking for the lineup cards. Some managers were willing to give them out and others not so much as they write game notes, etcetera, on them."

Osborne has been fortunate to come across managers willing to give him their cards more often than not in the 20 years since, growing his collection to about 500 lineup cards as of fall 2021.

"Most of my lineup cards are from games that I personally have attended. I have bought some because they have a favorite player on it," he said.

Osborne's collection spans the gamut of baseball levels, including cards from college games, collegiate summer wood bat leagues, independent leagues, affiliated minor leagues, minor league spring training and MLB.

Two cards are particularly meaningful to Osborne, both cards he got in person.

"One was in minor league spring training where I saw Ronald Acuña with the Mississippi Braves [Atlanta's AA team] versus the Blue Jays AA [team] during spring training in 2017, and the other was during spring training 2018 while I was watching Vladimir Guerrero Jr. and the Blue Jays AA [team] take on the Phillies AA squad,"

Todd Osborne watched Florence's Preston Vancil spin a no-hitter, then got both of the dugout lineup cards (courtesy Todd Osborne).

Osborne said. "I could tell Acuña and Guerrero Jr. were the real deal and destined for stardom. Guerrero Jr. was very nice and signed a couple of baseball cards that day, so if I could only keep one [lineup card] it would be that one."

Guerrero Jr. and Acuña are just two of many big-name players in Osborne's collection. Others include Ken Griffey Jr., Eddie Murray, Mike Schmidt, Johnny Bench, Mike Piazza, Steve Carlton, Frank Thomas, Tim Raines, Carlton Fisk, Alex Rodriguez, Barry Bonds and Tony Gwynn.

His favorite experience getting a card was snagging both dugout cards after a no-hitter thrown by Preston Vancil of the Florence Freedom in the Frontier League on July 26, 2009.

Like any collector chasing lineup cards, there is always that one card that got away.

"It is pretty tough to get dugout lineup cards at MLB games, and I was at a Yankees game one time where the manager just crumpled up the lineup card and tossed it in the trash," Osborne recalled. "I should have taken the chance and asked."

Osborne does not necessarily have a preference between dugout cards and batting order cards. It is more about who is on the card than what type of card it is.

"If the team lineup card is signed by a manager that is in the Hall of Fame or was a huge star, I'd take that," he said. "If the dugout lineup card has future stars on both sides, then I'd pick that one."

On a final note, Osborne offered this advice for other lineup card chasers.

"I have found that using manners with managers goes a long way," he said. "Always call them mister and then their name. Manners can pay dividends!"

Seth Swirsky: Lineup cards are a piece of the game

Former baseball memorabilia collector Seth Swirsky loved lineup cards.

"The lineup card, the manager participated with that," said Swirsky, an author and songwriter among other things, with the 1980s Thomas's English Muffins jingle and Grammy-nominated "Tell It to My Heart" sung by pop artist Taylor Dane to his credit. "I think they are fabulous pieces of history."

Calling Swirsky a former collector is not entirely accurate. He did sell most of his collection, ranging from "the Buckner ball" to a Beatles signed baseball from a Shea Stadium concert (Swirsky is a Mets fan) in 2012 for nearly $1.5 million. The Buckner ball alone, which Swirsky purchased from actor Charlie Sheen, sold for $418,250.[6]

Included in that sale were about 10 lineup cards, including a signed dugout card from Tom Browning's 1988 perfect game, and the batting order cards from the 1974 game in which Hank Aaron tied Babe Ruth's career home run record.

But Swirsky has hung on to a few items, and while he is not actively in the market, if the right item popped up for sale, he might be interested.

What lineup card would get Swirsky's attention?

Game 4 of the 1969 World Series between Swirsky's Mets and the Baltimore Orioles. Swirsky, then age nine, was at the game.

"A lineup card from that game? Oh my God, I would've paid anything," said Swirsky hypothetically. "It's also that much more cool when you have been to the game."

LOS ANGELES DODGERS   LINEUP CARD   DATE 9/16/88

#	L.A. Dodgers	#	Opponents
1	GRIFFIN	1	Larkin
2	HATCHER	2	Sabo
3	~~GIBSON~~ / Gonzalez	3	Daniels
4	MARSHALL	4	Davis
5	SHELBY	5	O'Neill
6	HAMILTON	6	Esasky
7	Dempsey	7	Reed
8	SAX	8	Oester
9	BELCHER	9	Browning

LH	EXTRA	RH	LH	EXTRA	RH
HEEP	Anderson		Griffey		Concepcion
STUBBS	Sharperson		Snider		McClendon
DAVIS	Woodson		Harris		McGriff
GWYNN	~~Gonzalez~~		Winningham		M. Brown
SCIOSCIA	Devereaux				Quinones
	Reyes				Collins

PITCHERS *(signed)* Tom Browning   **LHP**   PITCHERS   **RHP**

	Murphy	Williams
	Birtsas	Dibble
	Franco	St. Claire
		K. Brown

Dodgers dugout lineup card from Tom Browning's 1988 perfect game, signed by Browning (imaged by Heritage Auctions, HA.com).

    Swirsky has always seen lineup cards as far more than light cardboard with writing.

    "I consider them very historic," Swirsky said. "I mean the manager, he was the general in the war. Imagine seeing Eisenhower's list of who he wanted to go into battle, and he had to sign it. Imagine what that would be worth? That's what it is. It's the general of the team, the manager, who has a choice of 25 players, and says these are the ones I'm going to put out there on the field for today's game, and it turns out to be a historic game. I always saw that when I saw lineup cards. I saw them as very undervalued, and they are real pieces of the actual event that occurred."[7]

The Lineup Card Collectors

"I think the first one I got was Hank Aaron's [714th] home run [game]. I thought, 'wow, this is amazing. How is it available?'"

When possible, Swirsky liked to get multiple items from the same event.

"I also like to get cards that were not only historic but also went with historic pieces that I already had," he said. "I had the last home run hit in the twentieth century. Jim Leyritz hit the home run. So nobody thought about it at the time, but somebody collected it. And then I got it because I thought, wow, there's been 100 years of baseball, think about all the people who have hit home runs."

(Author's Note: Technically, the 20th century ended on December 31, 2000, so the Leyritz home run hit in the eighth inning of the fourth and final game of the 1999 World Series was the last MLB home run hit in the 1900s.)

Batting order card from Hank Aaron's 714th home run game (imaged by Heritage Auctions, HA.com).

"I then ran into the lineup card from that Leyritz game. I thought, how perfect would that go with that baseball?"

"I always had my collection in my head," Swirsky continued. "I know what I've got. It's not 10,000 things. It was 200, 300 really serious things, really good things, historic things."

While the larger (11" × 17") and more colorful dugout lineup cards MLB switched to around the year 2000 are more appealing to the eye than the dugout cards in use for the previous 40 or so years, Swirsky is not a fan.

"They're bigger and to me, they're less eye appeal," he said. "They don't have quite the oomph that old ones have, because the old ones, from the 50's and 60's, they were smaller, they didn't take themself so seriously as a piece just looking at it. It was just the manager's handwriting in there. It was kind of simple, and I liked that. There was a visual appeal.

"When they had the lineup cards way back in the old days, it wasn't about collecting them," he continued. "Nobody was thinking of that. And that's why they're so great."

Swirsky raises a good point. As soon as something like a dugout lineup card is made for the purpose of selling it after its use, it loses some of its charm.

"It's like playing a guitar through an amplifier in the 60's," Swirsky said. "Nobody was thinking, is this going to be a collectable amp, or a collectable guitar? They just made them. They were creative and they were good, and they sound so great today. But today, there are a million knockoffs of those kind of guitars."

"It's the same with lineup cards," he continued. "I'm not saying don't collect one if they come up and they're of value, from a valuable game. I still believe in that, of course. But they're less appealing because, I don't know, they speak louder to me when they're simpler and you have the understanding that no one was thinking of it as a piece of art. No one was thinking of it as memorabilia that should be collected."

Regardless of what the card looks like or the time frame it is from, "it's part of that game. It's not a minor, little nothing thing," said Swirksy. "It was part of that game. The game doesn't happen without that. Those are the troops. There's a war that goes on for two-and-a-half hours in those nine innings. It's a war. And this is the general and these are the troops. His hand filled it in."

Swirsky considers lineup cards unappreciated by baseball memorabilia collectors.

"To me ... it's got so much more value than I think people recognize," summed up Swirsky. "I find lineup cards to be very exciting. The fact that it was in the manager's hands. He held that card. He thought about it."

"I just loved collecting lineup cards," Swirsky continued. "I thought it was just such a thing of beauty."[8]

The hunt for hidden gems drives Jeff Garfinkel's collection

Jeff Garfinkel loves searching for buried treasure.

In Garfinkel's case, the "buried treasure" is historically significant sports items found within bulk ephemera collections that he purchases.

He has done a lot of digging in 30-plus years, with a collection of more than 30,000 yearbooks, programs, photographs, letters and, yes, lineup cards. A lot of Garfinkel's collection revolves around his favorite sports teams, which include the New York Mets, Brooklyn Dodgers, Army football and the New York Giants football team.

Garfinkel's collecting focus has evolved over the years. He started as a baseball card collector but quickly transitioned into ephemera, primarily publications. Even that has now changed. "I was really into the publications, but I've sort of moved away. I don't buy them as much," he said.

One of the challenges with publications is the large amount of space they take up. For that reason, Garfinkel has since emphasized collecting single-page items, including photos, tickets, Christmas cards, schedules and other items.

Lineup cards are another single-page item that was not on Garfinkel's radar screen in his early collecting days. That changed when he realized (1) they are easy to store, particularly batting order cards, and (2) given his interest in one-off type items, lineup cards essentially fit the bill given there are only a few from each game.

"I really like things like letterheads and letters, things that are one-offs," Garfinkel said. "Even lineup cards, which aren't necessarily one-offs, but there's [only] three or four copies."

Over the last 10 to 15 years, they have grown on him, to the point where his collection of lineup cards has grown to nearly 1,700 cards as of early 2022 and become his sports memorabilia item of choice.

"If I was going to pick a type of collectible that I would only want to focus on.... I would pick the lineup cards probably, because they are historic," he said.

Almost all the items in Garfinkel's collection come by way of bulk purchases at local card shows, auctions or online.

"I almost never buy a single lineup card," said. "That's not my M.O. My M.O. is to buy in bulk."

And he has never bought or asked for a lineup card after a game he attended in person. "I never even thought about that as a way to get them," Garfinkel said of asking the manager or umpire for their lineup card after a game.

He stays in his lane when it comes to sports memorabilia, and it has worked out well for him, both in the items in his collection and the financial aspect.

"I don't pursue anything in particular, and I can't think of any one item that I must have, which has probably saved me a lot of money, because I'm not a collector that way," said Garfinkel. "But if there was something let's say Mets-wise that I really like, I'd buy the whole collection."

Garfinkel keeps the items he likes from the collections he purchases and sells as much of the rest as he can. Most of his sales are through eBay, where he sells lineup cards and other printed sports memorabilia under the seller ID "sportmags."

"I've turned it so that I probably own all this stuff for free by selling enough to get out of the collection," he said.

Garfinkel has also established a good relationship with fellow sports memorabilia/lineup card collector Jeffrey Lazarus. They have, on a couple of occasions, teamed up to purchase a collection and split the items between them based on their preferences.

Getting his hands on a new collection and figuring out what is in it is where the fun begins for Garfinkel.

He uses a free website called Retrosheet to help with that task. Retrosheet (*www.retrosheet.org*) is a baseball encyclopedia of sorts, including features such as box scores and lists of noteworthy events (e.g., triple plays), to name just a couple.

Garfinkel especially looks for baseball games played in April as well as late September and early October to try and find player debut and last game played lineup cards.

"Retrosheet makes a lot of that very easy to figure out," he said.

"I enjoy that part of it, doing the detective work," continued Garfinkel. "Most of the time, it doesn't work out. But the couple of times it does work out, you're like, wow, that's awesome!"

And it has worked out enough times for Garfinkel to have put together an impressive list of milestone and other notable lineup cards that includes

- The game of Chipper Jones's first home run
- Dugout and batting order cards from the first-ever Colorado Rockies game against the New York Mets at Shea Stadium in 1993
- Tommy Lasorda's batting order cards from Kent Mercker's 1994 no-hitter against the Dodgers, including notes written on the cards by Lasorda

Undated Rockies card with a Mets lineup that included Dwight Gooden on the mound for the Amazins (courtesy Jeff Garfinkel).

- Mike Scioscia's last game as an MLB player
- Eric Karros's MLB debut game and his first home run game
- The Dodgers batting order card from their April 29, 1992, game against the Phillies in Los Angeles, the same night the "Rodney King Riots" began in LA
- Lee Smith's National League saves record game
- Lenny Dykstra's last career MLB game
- A minor league card from when Bryce Harper played with the Double-A Harrisburg Senators

The Lineup Card Collectors 167

Batting order cards from Kent Mercker's no-hitter, as noted by Los Angeles manager Tommy Lasorda (courtesy Jeff Garfinkel).

Garfinkel's lineup card collection spans more than 60 years. His oldest are minor league cards from the Minneapolis Millers (signed by then-manager Gene Mauch), Fort Worth Colts and Dallas Rangers, dating back to 1959.

Ask Garfinkel which is his favorite lineup card, and you'll get a surprising response.

"I get that question all the time, and people are disappointed," he said. "I'm not a true collector in that respect. So no, there's not really one [card]. After a while when you have so much stuff, it's all blurred," Garfinkel added. "It's not less significant, it's just moving on to the new things."

Jeff Garfinkel bought an ephemera lot that included a Colorado batting order card from the franchise's first-ever game (courtesy Jeff Garfinkel).

A pair of Minneapolis Millers batting order cards from 1959 (courtesy Jeff Garfinkel).

It is the process of digging into a new collection of cards that gets Garfinkel's juices flowing, more than any single card itself.

"All of it, researching it, touching it, inventorying it," he said. "That's the exciting part, that's the fun part."

As for which type of lineup card is his favorite, he will take "the first top copy, signed by the manager, with the date on it. Those are, to me, the gems."

Bill Haelig: Ripken bet pays off

Bill Haelig took a calculated gamble 40 years ago.

Fresh out of college in 1983 and wanting to collect items from a player from his favorite team, the Baltimore Orioles, he had two primary choices: Brooks Robinson, his boyhood idol and about to be enshrined in the Hall of Fame, or Cal Ripken Jr., just 23, but a promising Oriole newcomer.

"I decided I could go and get one Brooks [trading] card, or I could get like six Cal Ripken cards," said Haelig of the price premium commanded by Robinson items at the time. "I had read that Brooks was Cal's favorite player as a child, so I kind of felt like a kinship with him. So I thought, I'm just going to collect everything related to Cal."

Keep in mind that while Ripken showed promise, he was far from certain stardom in 1983. Ripken was the 47th pick in the 1978 MLB draft, and no one had any idea that the consecutive games streak that started in June 1982 would amount to anything.

You know the rest of the story. Ripken went on to not only a Hall of Fame career, but also set the standard for durability by playing in 2,632 straight MLB games, a record considered to be among the least likely to ever be broken in all professional sports.

"Back in those days, everyone was concerned about Strawberry and Gooden ... outside of Baltimore, [Cal] was kind of like not a big deal," said Haelig. "And I guarantee that benefitted me."

Haelig, meanwhile, has gone on to collect more than 15,000 items, the vast majority related to Cal Jr., but also his father, Cal Sr.; brother, Billy; or just generally the Orioles.

There is no shortage of Ripken pieces to collect given his success and fame, and the time period he played in. The Ripken items in Haelig's collection speak to that fact, including trading cards, ticket stubs, advertisements, even a commemorative pocketknife, to name just a few.

Oh, and he has lineup cards, too.

Haelig estimates he has nearly 100. He does not have a preference between batting order cards and dugout cards, estimating he has about an equal number of each.

Most but not all are Cal specific. For example, he has a neat pre–Cal dugout card from Game 3 of the 1970 World Series, the only time a pitcher (Dave McNally) ever hit a grand slam in a World Series. Haelig's Orioles would go on to win the title that year in five games over the Reds.

Haelig bought the card and ticket stub from someone who asked a policeman to pull the lineup card off the dugout wall for him after the game, and the policeman obliged. It still has marks from being taped to the dugout wall.

Haelig, who has developed a personal relationship with Ripken over the years, has had Ripken sign and even inscribe some of his lineup cards. He is more likely to get a dugout lineup card signed than a batting order card due to the extra space to sign.

For example, he had Ripken sign and inscribe the Orioles 2001 opening day dugout lineup card. It was the last opening day of Ripken's playing career.

Baltimore's dugout lineup card from Game 3 of the 1970 World Series. Starting pitcher Dave McNally hit a grand slam for the Orioles, the only World Series grand slam hit by a pitcher (courtesy Bill Haelig).

From trading cards to lineup cards

"At one point in my collecting days, [trading] cards started to bore me, particularly when they came out with 17 parallels of this card, things like that," Haelig said. "I started to look for the things that are more unique, things not necessarily replaceable."

Enter lineup cards.

Of course, back in the 1980s, the availability of lineup cards was a virtual unknown to 99.9 percent of baseball fans, even hardcore fans like Haelig. Few were kept.

"For the longest time, they were generally considered trash, given away or just discarded," he said. Even today, "They're not everyone's cup of tea."

"When I first saw them, I remember thinking, 'wow, these are pretty cool,'" Haelig continued. "They were either in the umpire's pocket, or they were hanging up on a dugout wall. I always thought of these things as being one of a kind, used as part of a game."

Haelig began to include lineup cards in his collection before MLB and teams started to market them. That helped him cultivate an impressive set of cards from many of Ripken's milestone games, including

- Ripken's first MLB game as a starting player, including his first at-bat
- The first MLB game that a father (Cal Sr.) managed two sons (Cal Jr. and Billy)
- The first game of the 2,632-game streak
- Ripken's 1,000th consecutive game played
- A July 12, 1989, Seattle Mariners game dugout card that not only had Billy and Cal Jr. on it, but also had Ken Griffey

1988 OFFICIAL BATTING ORDER

(VISITING CLUB)

DATE 6/25/88

	ORIGINAL	POS.	CHANGE
1	STANICEK	7	B
			C
2	B. RIPKEN	4	B
			C
3	C. RIPKEN	6	B
			C
4	MURRAY	DH	B
			C
5	TETTLETON	2	B
			C
6	TRABER	3	B
			C
7	GERHART	8	B
			C
8	SHEETS	9	B
			C
9	SCHU	5	B
			C
P	BODDICKER	1	B
			C
			D
			E

Manager's Signature *Frank Robinson*

Baltimore's batting order card from Cal Ripken Jr.'s 1,000th consecutive game. The card is signed by manager and fellow Hall of Famer Frank Robinson (courtesy Bill Haelig).

Jr. playing in his rookie season and Hall of Famer Randy Johnson (Johnson took the loss)
- Ripken's 2,131st game, in which he broke Lou Gehrig's record
- His 2,500th consecutive game played
- Opening Day 2001, Ripken's last
- Rays at Orioles, September 1, 2015; the Orioles celebrated the 20th anniversary of Ripken breaking Gehrig's record by having him throw the ceremonial first pitch

Reputation and knowledge

That Haelig's collection includes so many historic lineup cards related to Ripken is impressive enough. But how he got them, and for some of the ridiculously low prices, is just as compelling.

Yes, getting into the game early helped, but other factors have also contributed to his success.

For the first decade-plus of Haelig's collecting days, there was no eBay. The Internet itself didn't start to take off until about 1995. The framework of Haelig's collection was built by attending card and memorabilia shows, as well as advertising in *Sports Collectors Digest*, and responding to the ads of others. He earned a reputation as "the Ripken guy."

"I was fortunate to be in positions where I had these opportunities," said Haelig. "I think a lot of these opportunities arose because I had been collecting so long, people were aware of my collection, and I always had my ear to the ground of anything going on."

It was not just the fact that Haelig was a Ripken collector, though. People appreciated the way he went about collecting, too.

"After a while, things started finding me," Haelig said. "People knew what my intent was. I never obtained anything to flip it. To me these things don't have monetary value other than just [because I'm] a collecting guy. It just feels good to own these things."

The reputation has paid off over the years. In fact, a cornerstone of Haelig's entire

Cal Ripken Jr. got his first major league at-bat in this August 12, 1981, game (courtesy Bill Haelig).

172   The Lineup Card

A pair of carbon copy batting order cards from Cal Ripken Jr.'s record-setting 2,131st consecutive game (courtesy Bill Haelig).

Ripken collection—not just his lineup card subset—is a pair of official batting order cards from the 2,131 game that were given to him.

Yes, "given" as in Haelig did not pay anything for a pair of arguably the most famous batting order cards.

"I got that from someone who gave it to me on the condition of anonymity," said Haelig. "[The person] knew it was something that my collection had to include, and I was very happy to accept it."

Another such person Haelig connected with was a former Towson University professor and part-time umpire who had befriended some Orioles staffers in the late 1970s and would do errands for them in return for some game-used items.

Being an umpire himself, the professor had particular interest in umpire items, including the batting order cards they used during games. "After games, he would get umpire's lineup cards. He had a collection … it had to be 200," said Haelig.

The professor, knowing Haelig's reputation, gave him first crack at making him an offer on any of the 1970s and 1980s Orioles lineup cards he had collected.

One date immediately jumped out at Haelig: May 30, 1982. "The first game of the streak," said Haelig, who of course bought the card. "I know that date better than I know my wedding anniversary."

And that is the other thing that has helped Haelig's collection immensely, his knowledge, particularly dates of relevance related to the Orioles and Ripken specifically.

"It's just using context clues, being a fan," Haelig said. "I couldn't do it for George

No one could have guessed that this May 30, 1982, game would be the start of 2,632 straight games for Cal Ripken Jr (courtesy Bill Haelig).

Brett or Tony Gwynn because I don't know any of those dates of significance. But when it comes to the Orioles, and Cal specifically…. I lived through that time period and followed the team day by day.

"I had almost committed to memory the significant dates in his career, and I'm talking pre–2131," he continued. "It always helped me [to have an] encyclopedic memory of significant games in Cal's career."

Case in point, Haelig saw a small classified ad in *Sports Collectors Digest* advertising 10 to 12 items, including an Orioles lineup card billed as being signed by then-manager Frank Robinson.

The card was dated June 25, 1988, and the cost was $50.

"I don't think I could have jumped to the phone fast enough," recalled Haelig. "I called the guy to see if it was still available. I didn't want to sound too excited about it, but fortunately it was."

Why all the excitement about an Orioles card dated June 25, 1988? "That was Cal's 1,000th consecutive game," said Haelig. "I knew that date … because I remember listening to [the game] on the radio."

In another example, Haelig was perusing eBay one day and saw an Orioles lineup card dated April 25, 1998. The Orioles beat the A's, 8–2. Ripken had a good day, 2-for-5 with three RBI, and Rickey Henderson had a couple of hits for the A's.

But Haelig immediately knew it had far more significance based on the date: it was Ripken's 2,500th-straight game.

"In the back of my mind I'm thinking, I wonder if anybody else really knows, so I had to cross my fingers and put a pretty healthy snipe bid on it," he said. "But my recollection is I got it for under $20."

Another eBay hidden gem was an Orioles card where Hall of Famer Jim Palmer was listed as the third relief pitcher used in an early season 1984 game. In this case, the date was only part of the clue that led Haelig to find another hidden gem.

"I just thought that was odd because a pitcher like Jim Palmer, he probably started 99 percent of the games he was in," said Haelig. "I looked at the date, and it was May something '84. I looked it up, and it was his last career game because I remember his last career game he got hit hard."

Bill Haelig found a hidden gem with this card, Jim Palmer's last MLB appearance. Palmer signed and inscribed the card (courtesy Bill Haelig).

The price was pretty good. "For $10, I was able to pick up the lineup card from Jim Palmer's last career game," Haelig said.

Still on the lookout

It has gotten more difficult in recent years to find the hidden gems like a sub–$20 Ripken 2,500th-game lineup card or a $10 Palmer final-game lineup card.

Haelig's penchant for dates and clues does not carry the same weight it did before the Internet took off.

"Back in the day, you may have a lineup card, but you really didn't know what happened that date," he said. "Yeah, you could go to the library and pull-out microfilm, but no one was going to go to that trouble. I really think the turning point with tickets, lineup cards was that you could go on BaseballReference.com and within 30 seconds, you knew what the results of the game were, if anyone had hit a home run, and if there was any significance to it or not."

While it is tougher to find gems, it does not mean Haelig is not still having some success.

Like in late 2015 or early 2016 at Orioles Fan-Fest. Said Haelig, "I'm just flipping through and all of a sudden—" Haelig spotted the Baltimore lineup card from the 20th anniversary celebration of Ripken's 2,131st game. "The game was on September 1 because they weren't home on the 6th—again, knowing dates helped. It was just in there mixed in with everything else. I had Cal sign and note it."

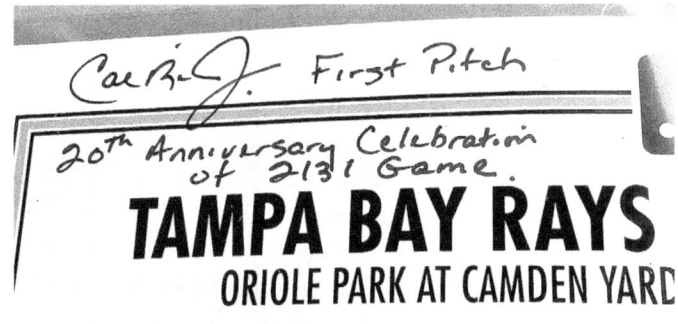

Cal Ripken Jr. signed and inscribed the Baltimore lineup card from the 20th anniversary celebration of his 2,131st game (courtesy Bill Haelig).

You can be sure that if there is an Orioles lineup card of relevance for sale, particularly if it has anything to do with Ripken, Haelig will not be far away.

Look out, eBay: Scott Meza has a lot of lineup cards to sell

If you have bought or looked at lineup cards on eBay recently, or plan to do so in the future, there is a good chance you come across one or more cards being sold by Scott Meza (eBay profile "baseball-usa").

As of early August 2022, Meza had about 175 cards for sale on eBay, including the following:

- An April 18, 1971, Atlanta Braves batting order card for $300. Hank Aaron went 1-for-3 and Orlando Cepeda went 5-for-5 in a Braves victory.
- The Boston Red Sox batting order card from the 1990 ALCS Game 1 for $280. Roger Clemens started and threw six scoreless innings, but the A's eventually won, 4–1.
- A September 24, 2015, Yankees batting order card from a game in which the Yankees held a memorial ceremony for the passing of Yogi Berra for $250. The card has a full-size watermark image of Berra from his playing days.
- A September 30, 1980, Cincinnati Reds batting order card for $100. Starters

for the Reds included Johnny Bench, Ken Griffey Jr. (1 hit) and Dave Concepcion (2 hits).

- A September 2, 2005, Oakland dugout lineup card from an A's-Yankees game for $80. Players included Derek Jeter (1 hit) and Alex Rodriguez.
- A May 27, 1989, Detroit Tigers batting order card for $50. Fred Lynn, Lou Whitaker (1 hit) and Alan Trammell started for the Tigers.

And there will be more to come from Meza. Many more.

Meza plans to divest most of his collection of approximately 4,300 lineup cards, which includes nearly 4,000 MLB and about 300 minor league cards.

"I retired at the end of [2021], so now I have time to start going through things," said Meza. "At this point, I'm reorganizing the collection."

Three of Houston's "Killer B's"—Craig Biggio, Derek Bell and Jeff Bagwell—led off on this 1997 Astros batting order card (courtesy Jeff Garfinkel).

The focus going forward will be on his favorite team, the Houston Astros and their predecessor, the Colt 45s.

"I've decided to keep the Astros and Colt 45s and basically let everything else go," Meza said.

Building a collection of nearly 4,300 lineup cards

How does one build a collection of nearly 4,300 lineup cards without being an umpire, manager or coach?

It does not happen overnight, according to Meza.

"I get a lot from umpires," Meza said. "I [also] get them from other collectors, dealers. I pick some up off of eBay."

Buying lineup cards from umpires is a long-term project, according to Meza, who spends a fair amount of time introducing himself and following up with both current and former MLB umpires.

"Get to know the umpires and let them know what you're collecting," said Meza of his approach. "The majority of them, or the current ones, keep their own cards and have no interest in getting rid of them. It's usually once they retire or get older, when they are looking to move on, or they don't have any family that's interested in them."

"There are other people that contact them," Meza continued. "There are businesses that try to buy the collections. That's why I try to establish a relationship with them and they might not be interested in selling this year, next year or in some cases even decades go by, literally. But as long as you have a relationship with them, when it does get to that point, that helps."

Meza has been collecting lineup cards for 30-plus years. He got his first lineup card in 1989, also the year he became aware they were available.

Lineup cards fall third on Meza's list of favorite collectibles, behind jerseys and bats. He considers himself a jersey guy first—he has 600—but others consider him a bat guy given that he has 1,500, including 500 on display. All but 25 of the bats and 20 of the jerseys are tied to the Astros.

Longtime MLB manager Dusty Baker likes to keep notes on his batting order cards (courtesy Jeffrey Lazarus).

Meza generally likes cards with game-use markings or notes on them. He likes umpire cards the best for that reason, but he does "like some of the manager ones, like from Dusty Baker, especially when he was with the Giants because he keeps notes on the back of his card so you can actually follow what he's thinking is important in the game," Meza said.

"Not too many managers put notes on the cards, nowhere near like [Dusty] does," he continued. "Dusty's really the only one I've come across who keeps extensive notes. Every now and then you'll see something from the umpires about something that happened in the game, usually involving an ejection."

Baker's notes cover a variety of topics.

"There's one where he mentions he's going to fine Barry Bonds $100 for not hustling down to first base," Meza said.

Another one of his favorite lineup cards was one he was not supposed to get.

"I had bought a lineup card from a gentleman, and after I bought it, he contacted me and said that he couldn't find it but he had another one, and asked if I wanted that one instead," said Meza. "I didn't even know what [the card] was. I just said, 'sure, go ahead and send it, that'll be fine.'"

The replacement card turned out to be from Houston's October 7, 1980, game, not just any playoff game, but the first in Astros history.

Meza also has a pair of batting order cards from Houston's June 3, 1989, game. "That was the first lineup card I got from a game I attended," said Meza. That game was a 22-inning affair against the Dodgers, which was the longest night game in National League history. Houston eventually won the 7-hour, 14-minute contest, 5–4, at 2:52 a.m. local time.

"I actually got both [cards], Astros and Dodgers. 'Those are probably the most beat-up cards I've ever seen,'" said Meza.

And Meza has eight Colt 45s cards, including two from 1962, the team's inaugural season. He keeps about 40 lineup cards on display in his home, and the rest are in binders.

Lineup cards for sale

As mentioned earlier, Meza is now in the process of selling most of his lineup card collection. "I've pretty much decided that anything that's not Astros or Colt 45s, I'll go ahead and sell," he said. "There's been a few that are kind of hard [to let go of]"—cards with names like Willie Mays, Hank Aaron, Bob Gibson that "really don't fit into the collection."

Meza does not have a specific time frame in mind for getting the cards sold. "If I sold it all tomorrow or 10 years from now, it'd still be fine either way with me," he said.

Unless someone comes along and purchases the entire collection, eBay will be Meza's primary vehicle for selling the cards. He has already sold some on eBay and continues to post more on the e-commerce site.

Meza has found selling lineup cards on eBay to generally be a good experience. "eBay brings you a larger market than you would have otherwise," said Meza, who noted that he has even sold cards to international customers in Canada and Japan. Not surprisingly, lineup cards with Japanese players like Shohei Ohtani, Ichiro Suzuki and Hideo Nomo are popular with Japanese baseball fans.

HOUSTON ASTROS		VISITING CLUB	
1	~~BIGGIO~~ BOGAR	STOVALL (6)	
2	~~BELL~~ (5) EVERETT	~~GRUDZIELANEK~~ MORDECAI	
3	~~BAGWELL~~ (7) HOWELL	~~GUERRERO~~ (4) McGUIRE	
4	BERRY	FULLMER	
5	ALOU (2)	~~WHITE~~ (2) MAY	
6	HIDALGO	VIDRO	
7	GUTIERREZ	~~ANDREWS~~ DEMMY	
8	AUSMUS (4)	HUBBARD	
9	~~BERGMAN~~ (3)(6) MILLER (8)	~~MOORE~~ (3) ~~VALDES~~ LIVINGSTON	
HOWELL	EUSEBIO	~~	
SPIERS	BOGAR	~~LIVINGSTONE~~	WIDGER
		~~McGUIRE~~	~~MORDECAI~~
		~~MAY~~	
	EVERETT		SANTANGELO
~~MILLER~~	SCANLAN	KLINE	~~VALDES~~
MAGNANTE	HENRY	~~ABBOTT~~	BENNETT
NITKOWSKY			TELFORD
WAGNER			URBINA

An undated Astros dugout card (courtesy Jeff Garfinkel).

eBay has also helped Meza connect with other lineup card collectors, such as Jeffrey Lazarus.

Of the cards Meza sold in the first half of 2022, he had only one return, a Mike Trout card from his minor league days.

"The guy gets it and returns it because even though it was listed as Arkansas Travelers and there were pictures of it, he thought it was when Trout was with the Angels," said Meza.

"The only downside on eBay, really, is you get a whole lot of questions and then you never hear back," said Meza. "The one big question where you never hear back from them is, does it have a COA [certificate of authorization]? You really don't get COA's with [lineup cards], and it doesn't pay to send it to a grading service."

Selling, but still collecting, too

Just because Meza is selling many of his lineup cards does not mean he is not still buying cards, too. In the first seven months of 2022 alone, he communicated with 132 former or current MLB umpires, and bought 293 cards.

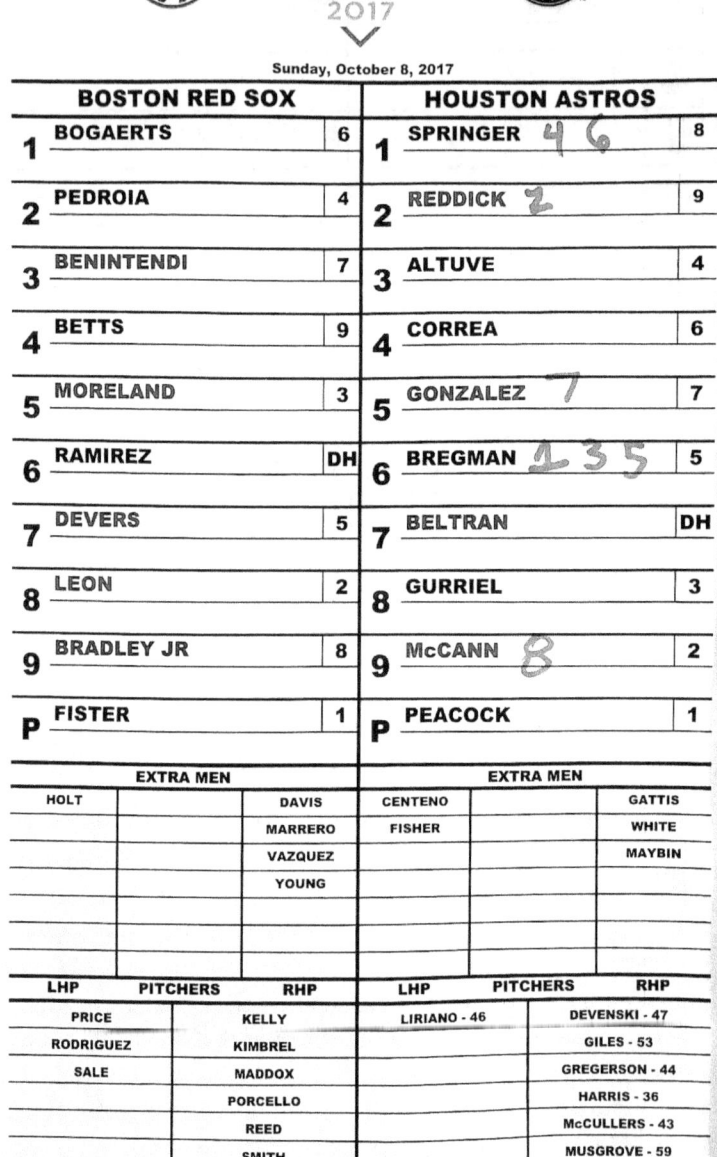

Boston's bullpen lineup card from Game 3 of the 2017 ALDS against Houston. The Astros lost this game, but went on to win the World Series a few weeks later.

"The collector in me just can't let that go," he laughed.

There is one type of lineup card that has not yet found its way into Meza's collection: an Astros World Series card.

He is on the lookout, particularly for something reasonable, but adds, "maybe even if it was unreasonable. When you collect, sometimes you don't always do everything rationally. It's more what the heart wants."

Rick Levy: Always on the lookout for vintage Dodgers lineup cards

Rick Levy has 11 lineup cards from seven MLB games in his collection. He would like to increase the number.

"I'd love to find more of them; they're just hard to find," said Levy.

Levy is not looking for your run-of-the-mill lineup cards. He is a sports memorabilia collector with a penchant for the Dodgers, particularly Sandy Koufax and Jackie Robinson.

"I collect a broad spectrum of things that are vintage," Levy explained. "The lineup cards are kind of a neat fit. I have picked them up where I can."

The cards Levy does have are historic, both in terms of age and the event. All but one is from the 1960s. The lone 21st-century card is from Cody Bellinger's cycle game in 2017.

He has batting order cards from four World Series games, a dugout card from Koufax's perfect game and the Dodgers batting order card from the game of Maury Wills's only career grand slam.

Rick Levy's Lineup Card Collection

Event	Type of Card	Team(s)
1963 World Series, Game 1	Both batting orders	Dodgers, Yankees
1963 World Series, Game 3	Both batting orders	Dodgers, Yankees
1963 World Series, Game 4*	Both batting orders	Dodgers, Yankees
9/9/65 Koufax Perfect Game	Cubs dugout	Cubs, Dodgers
1965 World Series, Game 7*	Both batting orders	Dodgers, Twins
8/16/69 Maury Wills Grand Slam**	Dodgers batting order	Dodgers, Expos
7/15/17 Cody Bellinger Cycle	Miami dugout	Dodgers, Marlins

*deciding game
**only career grand slam

Levy uses the lineup cards in baseball event displays. "So I don't just have a lineup card, I have a lineup card with other items that relate to the event," he said.

"They are incredibly hard to find, especially anything related to Koufax," said Levy of vintage Dodgers' lineup cards. "These days, with all the information available, you still won't find much because people didn't save this stuff."

Rick Levy created this display commemorating Brooklyn's sweep of the Yankees in the 1963 World Series, including a pair of batting order cards from the final game (courtesy Rick Levy).

Levy's first lineup cards: A surprise find

Levy scored his first lineup cards in the 1990s.

At that time, he said, "everything that was for auction was advertised in *Sports*

Collectors Digest, and people would have to either mail in their bid or call up to put in a bid," he said.

A full-page auction announcement from a business in Long Island advertised, among many lots, a "Sandy Koufax package ... an autographed 16" × 20" photo of Koufax pitching and it included World Series lineup cards, and they weren't even pictured," said Levy.

Levy was living in southern Connecticut at the time and was close enough to drive to the auction house and look at the lot in person.

"They show me the lot and I look at it, and I'm like, these are pretty impressive because this is like Game 7 of the Yom Kippur [1965 World] Series, the series where Koufax came back and pitched on two days' rest and threw a three-hit shutout and the Dodgers won the World Series," he said.

The provenance on the batting order cards was solid. The cards came from legendary sports memorabilia collector Al Rosen, who obtained them from a Minnesota bat boy.

He liked not only what he saw, but also what he felt in handling the cards.

"I felt pretty good about having these in my hands because I could tell they were

Sandy Koufax and the Dodgers bested the Twins in Game 7 of the 1965 World Series (courtesy Rick Levy).

old, I could tell the stock and where it was from," Levy said. "The fact that it had come from Al Rosen…. I felt pretty good from where they were coming from."

Interestingly, the autographed Koufax picture used to advertise the lot was from a different World Series, 1963. But Levy was more interested in the lineup cards at this point.

Rick Levy used the Game 7 batting order cards in this 1965 World Series display, which also includes the score sheets, a ticket and picture of Game 7 winning pitcher Sandy Koufax (courtesy Rick Levy).

Levy put in the opening bid of $1,500 with a callback request, meaning that the auction house would contact him if someone outbid him. The night of the auction, he was surprised not to receive a callback, assuming someone else would outbid him. He twice called the auction house that night to check and was assured both times that his bid was still the highest.

"The next morning, I called them up and they said, 'you were the only one to bid.' So I paid them and picked them up," Levy recalled.

Levy created a 1965 World Series Game 7 display that includes the pair of batting order cards, a ticket and the scorebook pages from the game. The 1963 Koufax picture in the lot went into a 1963 World Series display.

Maury Wills hits only career Grand Slam – Aug. 16, 1969

Wills's grand slam

Another good find was an undated Dodgers batting order card posted on eBay.

The seller listed about 15 batting order cards.

"I researched them because a lot of them were undated," said Levy. His research found that the Dodger starting lineup shown on one undated card only occurred one time.

"I was able to identify the game, and it turned out to be the game where Maury Wills, who was not known as a slugger, hit his only grand slam," said Levy. "And I was a big Maury Wills fan growing up. I didn't have anything related to Maury Wills and his career, so I thought that was pretty cool."

Levy bought the card for about $75.

"Some of these, when they appear like that, it takes a little legwork to figure it out," he continued.

Maury Wills hit just one grand slam in his 14-year MLB career, on August 16, 1969 (courtesy Rick Levy).

The one that got away

Every collector has an item or two that they really wanted, but it somehow managed to escape them.

For Levy, a case of bad timing

and poor Internet connection got in the way of a set of batting order cards he really would have liked to buy.

"I was at a [2018] World Series game with my daughter at Dodger Stadium, and closing that night was an auction for the 1988 World Series lineup cards from Game 1 where Kirk Gibson hits the home run," said Levy of a Goldin Auctions lot.

"I'm at Dodger Stadium and I figured I'd be able to bid," he continued. "Well, I couldn't get reception. There were 55,000 people all on cell phones, so the auction closed, and I was never able to get in my final bid, so I wasn't able to get the lineup cards to that game."

Instead, the cards, from Tommy Lasorda's personal collection, went to another bidder for $7,200.[9]

Of course, the combination of Gibson's walk-off home run and Scully's call is one of the most iconic moments in World Series history. The Dodgers would go on to beat the A's in five games.

That the auction for such an important piece of Dodgers history would close while the Dodgers were literally playing in another World Series game was highly disappointing to Levy.

"I was so frustrated by it," he said. "I actually talked to Ken Goldin about it afterward, and I said, 'Ken, never have an auction during the World Series.'"

"That was the one that got away," summed up Levy.

Keeping an eye out

Levy likes lineup cards as a collectible because "it's really a picture of the game. I have a lot of fun looking and seeing in the '63 World Series some great names that Koufax faced.... Mantle, Maris, Boyer," he said.

"I like having both sides," he continued. "I like having the Dodgers side, but I like seeing the other side as well, to see the lineup you had to play against to win the World Series."

He keeps an eye on various auctions for more such cards, but lineup cards from the mid–20th century are few and far between.

"I basically just wait for them to pop up somewhere," Levy said. "I keep hoping they're going to show up in auctions, but they don't."

On the positive side, the scarcity of such cards helps him appreciate the ones he has.

"I am very thankful I was able to grab the stuff I did when I did," Levy said.

Jeffrey Lazarus: A collection unlike any other

There are lineup card collections, and then there are lineup card *collections*.
Jeffrey Lazarus has the latter.

It is not just the quantity, which is remarkable in its own right with more than 3,000 lineup cards. But it is the cards themselves that truly distinguish Lazarus's collection, offering a unique insight into some of the many historical moments and figures that have shaped professional baseball's history over the last 90 years.

The Lineup Card Collectors

A small sampling of the cards owned by Lazarus. Keep in mind that all the players noted are Hall of Famers:

- A 1933 card from an A's and Indians game in which Philadelphia's Jimmie Foxx and Mickey Cochrane each had a pair of hits, and Cleveland's Earl Averill hit for the cycle, the 104th time the feat was performed by a major leaguer

Dugout lineup card from Derek Jeter's 2,000th hit game, signed and inscribed by Jeter (imaged by Heritage Auctions, HA.com).

- The unused Orioles Dugout card from 9/11/01 described in an earlier chapter
- Cards from the games in which George Brett and Cal Ripken Jr., respectively, recorded their 3,000th hits
- A dugout card from Derek Jeter's 2,000th-hit game, signed and inscribed by Jeter
- Cards from the games in which Tom Glavine, Jack Morris and Pedro Martinez each earned their first MLB victory
- Cards from games in which Foxx, Yogi Berra, Willie Mays and Hank Aaron hit home runs
- Cards from the games of Ken Griffey Jr.'s 400th career home run and Barry Bonds' 400th and 700th career home runs
- The card from the game in which Carl Yastrzemski hit his final MLB home run
- The card from the game in which Gaylord Perry recorded his 3,000th strikeout, which also happened to be the game in which Ozzie Smith introduced his signature backflip[10]
- The Atlanta Braves' four dugout lineup cards from the 1999 World Series, in which they were swept by the Yankees, 4–0

Like most lineup card collectors, lineup cards were not Lazarus's item of choice in his early sports memorabilia collecting days. In fact, he was not even aware of them.

"I had not been familiar with lineup cards, when I stumbled across a vintage

Batting order cards from George Brett's 3,000th hit game (courtesy Jeffrey Lazarus).

Ken Griffey Jr. hit his 400th career home run on April 10, 2000 (courtesy Jeffrey Lazarus).

Cleveland Indians lineup card signed by Walter Johnson on eBay a number of years back," recalled Lazarus. "I recognized the distinctive last name and handwriting. I did some research and learned about them and was able to acquire the card."

"The seller also had a 1935 Washington Senators lineup card signed by Hall of Famer Bucky Harris, which I bought," continued Lazarus. "This led to my first project, trying to find a lineup card signed by each manager who is in the Hall of Fame, whether they are there for their performance as a player or manager."

Not only did Gaylord Perry notch his 300th career victory on October 1, 1978, Ozzie Smith debuted what would become his trademark back flip that day against the Padres (courtesy Jeffrey Lazarus).

Lazarus has collected about 25 lineup cards signed by Hall of Famers, including all of what he refers to as "the easier ones," such as Tommy Lasorda, Joe Torre, Tony La Russa, Sparky Anderson and Casey Stengel.

"Casey Stengel lineup cards are likely the most abundant from that era, as he managed for an extended period of time, and the Yankees were highly popular," Lazarus said.

"I have almost all of the ones from the last ... call it 20 or 30 years," Lazarus said. "Collecting every manager who has made the Hall is an impossibility as it includes players who were active in the 1800s, and some of the toughest autographs in the hobby. But it's a fun chase."

What are some of the tougher ones that Lazarus has gotten? Yogi Berra and Ryne Sandberg were particularly difficult, despite both managing fairly recently, according to Lazarus. Another tough one was Tony Perez, whose entire managerial career (split between two teams over two seasons) was less than 160 games. And "when you get to managers from ... call it before 1980, finding anything from anyone particular is just hard. It is even harder with managers who did not always sign for themselves. I had a ghost-signed Leo Durocher long before I was able to acquire a lineup card that he had signed. Another interesting one is Mel Ott. He was a player-manager for six years. While I have not been able to find a lineup card where he signed his name in the manager spot, I do have one where he penned the lineup card, including penciling himself into the lineup."

And then there's Bill Terry, who managed the New York Giants from 1932 through 1941, to go along with a Hall of Fame playing career. Terry lived until the age of 90, so his autograph is

Tony Perez is in the Hall of Fame as a player, but also managed parts of two seasons (courtesy Jeffrey Lazarus).

Casey Stengel played 14 years of pro baseball, but is best known as a manager (courtesy Jeffrey Lazarus).

not necessarily hard to find. But on a lineup card?

"I would be a little bit surprised if there's another Bill Terry lineup card that's still in existence," said Lazarus. His Terry card is a 1937 World Series lineup card. The opposing lineup card featured a slew of Hall of Famers and Yankee legends, including Lou Gehrig, Joe DiMaggio, Bill Dickey, Tony Lazzeri and Red Ruffing, and was signed by Hall of Fame manager Joe McCarthy. It is also the earliest World Series lineup card in existence, as best Lazarus can tell.

A Hall of Famer as a player, Ryne Sandberg managed the Phillies, 2013–2015 (courtesy Jeffrey Lazarus).

Hall of Famer Bill Terry was a player/manager for the 1937 New York Giants (courtesy Jeffrey Lazarus).

Iván "Pudge" Rodriguez made his MLB debut for the Texas Rangers in 1991 (courtesy Jeffrey Lazarus).

Other projects

As for what he is looking for lineup card–wise these days, Lazarus says, "I've expanded the collection in a number of different directions as I just find them

OFFICIAL BATTING ORDER
LOS ANGELES

DATE: 9/3/2011

	ORIGINAL	POS	CHANGE	
1	BOURJOS	8	B	WILSON
			C	ROMINE
2	CALLASPO	5	B	BRANYAN
			C	CONGER
3	KENDRICK	4	B	ABREU
			C	MOORE
4	HUNTER	DH	B	NAVARRO
			C	IZTURIS
5	TRUMBO	3	B	
			C	
6	WELLS	7	B	RAMIREZ
			C	DOWNS
7	TROUT	9	B	TAKAHASHI
			C	WALDEN
8	AYBAR	6	B	CASSEVAH
			C	THOMPSON
9	MATHIS	2	B	RODNEY
			C	PINEIRO
	WEAVER	1	B	HAREN
			C	SANTANA
			D	WILLIAMS
			E	CHATWOOD

Manager's Signature

Batting order card from Mike Trout's 25th MLB game, and his first game to collect three hits (courtesy Jeffrey Lazarus).

incredibly fascinating. I'm always looking for milestones, World Series games, as well as vintage lineup cards. My favorite to find are MLB debuts," Lazarus said.

He has not just limited himself to debut game cards, though. "I've built up a collection of lineup cards from players' rookie seasons," Lazarus said, referencing baseball trading cards. "It's my take on a player's 'rookie card.' It's often far cheaper and far rarer than an actual rookie baseball card. That works well for me. The search is a lot of fun and the price tag can still be fairly reasonable."

"Take Frank Thomas for example," Lazarus continued. "Thomas's most famous rookie card is the 1990 Topps NNOF [No Name on Front] error which leaves out his name from the front of the card. One hundred-twenty copies have been graded by PSA in grades of 8 (officially 'Near-Mint/Mint') or better. At the time this is being typed in early 2022, a PSA 8 is worth $10,000 according to the PSA online database, with the most recent sale at $9,600. Meanwhile, the umpire lineup card from one of the 60 games that Thomas played during his 1990 rookie season just sold on eBay for $295, a small fraction of the price."

Carbon copy Baltimore batting order card, signed by Earl Weaver, from one of Cal Ripken Jr.'s first MLB games. Since Ripken didn't start and lineup changes weren't kept on the cards, his name doesn't appear (courtesy Jeffrey Lazarus).

Lineup cards from World Series games are another project, and he has had the good fortune to add cards from 18 World Series to his collection, including lineup cards from the opening games of the 1979, 1991, 1999 and 2009 World Series, and the clinching game of the 1976, 1981, 1999, 2003, 2007 and 2018 World Series.

Given that Lazarus is a Yankees fan, getting all four of Atlanta's dugout lineup cards from the 1999 World Series in which the Yankees swept the Braves is a highlight. "For me, the '90's dynasty, that was the Yankees I was introduced to growing up," Lazarus said. "My first season as a fan was '95. Next year, they started a

Hall of Famer Frank Thomas went 0-for-4 with one RBI in his MLB debut (courtesy Jeffrey Lazarus).

Batting order cards from Game 1 of the 1979 World Series (courtesy Jeffrey Lazarus).

The Yankees beat the Braves 7–2 in Game 2 of the 1999 World Series en route to a sweep (courtesy Jeffrey Lazarus).

dynasty, so '99 was smack in the middle of that. To have the whole run of those is pretty cool."

He also cites another World Series lineup card—the 2007 World Series Game 4 card—as one of his favorites.

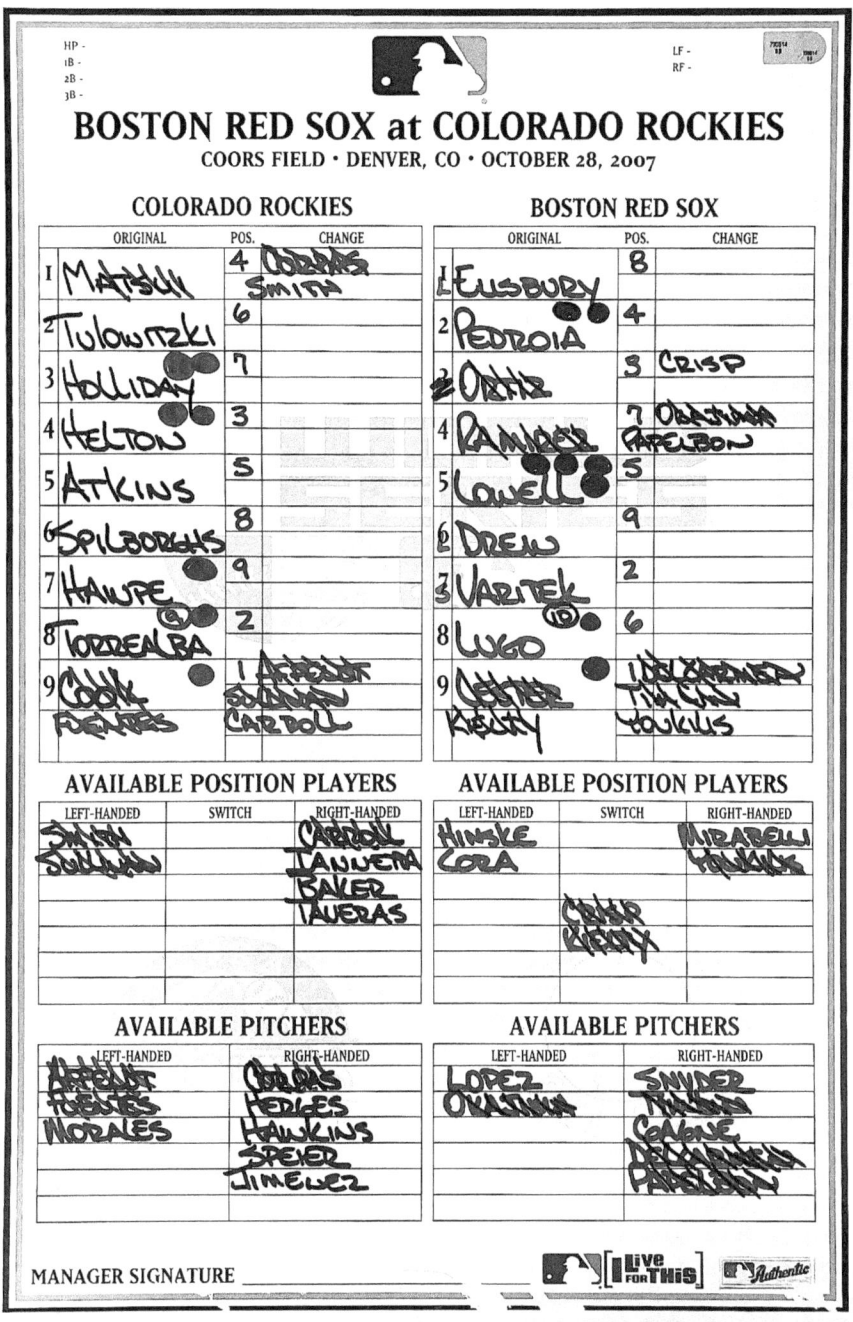

Less than two years after being diagnosed with cancer, Jon Lester started and won Game 4 of the 2007 World Series to cap a Boston sweep of Colorado (courtesy Jeffrey Lazarus).

That one is a surprise, given that it was New York's hated rivals, the Red Sox, who clinched the 2007 World Series against the Colorado Rockies in Game 4. But Lazarus has a very personal reason for liking that card.

Jon Lester was the winning Game 4 pitcher for Boston, throwing 5 2/3rd shutout innings. Lester had returned to the Red Sox in late July of that season after undergoing treatment for a rare form of cancer known as anaplastic large cell lymphoma, a form of non–Hodgkin's lymphoma.

For Lazarus, Lester's overcoming cancer to pitch in the deciding game of the 2007 World Series transcended the Yankee-Red Sox rivalry.

"The 2007 one for me is one of the most significant from a personal perspective. I'm a Yankees fan, not a Red Sox fan, but as a young child, I lost an uncle to cancer, who I was close to," said Lazarus. "During 2006–2007, I was following Lester's story closely, accumulating a large collection of rookie cards, et cetera. When the 2007 World Series reached Game 4, and Jon Lester was on the mound, it was a big deal. Him winning the game was enormous, given his personal medical journey. When the lineup card went up for sale on MLB.com, I was thrilled to be able to acquire it. And thankfully, the price tag was far less than what the [card for the] 2004 clinching game sold for, or I would not have been anywhere close to being able to afford it.

"That personal element, whether we're on the same side or other side of the field, when you see people overcoming challenges, stepping up … that's very powerful to me," continued Lazarus.

A piece of the game, yet economical

While Lazarus continues to also collect non-lineup cards—including items related to integration, World War II and the Negro Leagues—lineup cards have become his primary collectible.

"I love the fact that they play an actual role in the game, in establishing the official lineup," he said.

"The lineup card is like a game-used program," continued Lazarus. "It tells the story of the game in a way that a jersey or bat can't, with the names written on it, particularly if the manager or umpire tracked the changes throughout the game."

Another reason Lazarus likes lineup cards is the value proposition.

"Compared to other game-used items, they are simply much cheaper," said Lazarus. "It has enabled me to acquire items from significant games and players, games for which I am far priced out on jerseys, bats, etc."

Lazarus gives the example of Cal Ripken Jr.'s 3,000th-hit game. The bat Ripken used for his 3,000th hit, signed and inscribed, sold at auction for more than $247,000.[11]

However, the lineup card from the Orioles dugout from that game sold for just over one percent of that price, $3,075, according to Lazarus. Lazarus believes that the price was somewhat suppressed in an auction with hundreds of other significant Ripken items (Ripken sold his personal collection via Goldin Auctions with the bulk of the collection hitting the market in early 2021).

Lazarus is open about the fact that he recognizes that the ability to spend as much money on a sports collectible as he does is an enormous luxury. But as it relates to other items from the game, the price of lineup cards is far less.

Barry Bonds hit his 400th career home run on August 23, 1998, as noted by Dusty Baker on the batting order cards (courtesy Jeffrey Lazarus).

Sharing the hobby

One of Lazarus's favorite parts of the hobby is the community and connections it has created for him.

"It's amazing to be able to get a lineup card to the person who will value it most," he says. An example was working out a deal to get Juan Gonzalez's major league debut card into the hands of one of the biggest Gonzalez super-collectors.

But Lazarus has stories even better than that.

"Recently, I was cataloguing some old lineup cards, when I came across one with a player whose name I didn't recognize. When I searched Steve Macko online, I discovered that he played just 25 games for the Cubs between 1979 and 1980, before passing away from testicular cancer in 1981. Eerily, I discovered the lineup card shortly before midnight on Nov 14, 2021. Looking at the date Macko passed I realized that the next day, November 15, would be 40 years to the day that he had passed away," said Lazarus.

"I posted information about the lineup card on Facebook to see if anyone had any connection to the Macko family, and someone pointed me to a scholarship fund created in his memory. I reached out to them and they were gracious and friendly in responding. I offered to send them the lineup card, and within a week or so, the lineup card from one of just 25 games that Steve played in the major leagues was now in the hands of family members. It's an honor to be able to make that happen, and I imagine being able to see his name written into the lineup was very meaningful to them."

1985 OFFICIAL BATTING ORDER (VISITING CLUB) DATE 10/6/85			
	ORIGINAL	POS.	CHANGE
1	HENDERSON	CF	
2	MATTINGLY	1B	
3	WINFIELD	RF	
4	BAYLOR	DH	
5	ROBERTSON	3B	
6	RANDOLPH	2B	
7	COTTO	LF	
8	WYNEGAR	C	
9	MEACHAM	SS	
P	P. NIEKRO	P	

Home Manager's Copy — Billy Martin

1985 OFFICIAL BATTING ORDER TORONTO DATE 10/6/85			
	ORIGINAL	POS.	CHANGE
1	GARCIA	4	
2	LEACH	7	
3	THORNTON	9	
4	FIELDER	3	
5	BURROUGHS	DH	
6	GRUBER	5	
7	SHEPHERD	8	
8	HEARRON	2	
9	LEE	6	
P	CERUTTI	1	

Home Manager's Copy — Bob Cox

A Billy Martin–signed batting order card from Phil Niekro's 300th victory (courtesy Jeffrey Lazarus).

Lazarus also connected with former MLB umpire John Hirschbeck in early 2022 after purchasing much of Hirschbeck's personal lineup card collection a couple of years earlier.

"We spoke about his time in the game, the charity he established after losing sons to a rare genetic disorder; the charity was the impetus for his selling his personal collection, as he was raising money to help support the charitable efforts. During the conversation he reminisced about an experience early in his career where legendary manager Billy Martin confronted him. He mentioned that he wished he had kept that lineup card. I immediately told him that while I was not sure I had the exact game he mentioned—based on the description I was pretty sure I did not—I would be happy to send him a Yankees' lineup card signed by Martin from a collection I had purchased. He graciously offered to compensate me for it, but I was happy for him to rather apply that money towards the charity," recalled Lazarus.

"As expected, I couldn't find the particular game in my collection—he may have misplaced it over the years, since I do not believe it was part of the collection

I bought—but at least he will have a lineup card from a game that he umpired with Billy Martin in the dugout to recall the memories," he said.

The last word

What has Lazarus learned from his days of collecting lineup cards?

"Ultimately lineup cards are unlike many other collectibles. If you miss a Jeter

Dugout lineup card from the 2000 Subway World Series between the Yankees and Mets (courtesy Jeffrey Lazarus).

signed baseball online, you'll get 10 other ones, 20 other ones. If you miss Frank Thomas's major league debut or George Brett's 3,000th hit [lineup card], there isn't another one to go get," he said. "Even if the lineup card you are pursuing is simply from a game you attended, finding the exact game is near impossible. The scarcity and particularity is appealing to me, both from a collectible standpoint and what I have been able to do with them."

Signatures/Autographs on Lineup Cards

Autographs and baseball have long gone hand in hand. And while baseballs are the primary vehicle for baseball autograph collecting, lineup cards have and continue to play a role in the autograph space.

There are two types of signatures on lineup cards: managers' signatures on batting order and dugout lineup cards and more traditional autographs on both batting order and dugout lineup cards.

Autographs, whether from a manager, player, or both, almost always make a lineup card worth more than if there were no signature. "Anything signed, that's going to add to the value," said Phil Weiss of Weiss Auctions in Lynbrook, New York.

Managers' signatures

Managers were long been required to sign their batting order cards, until 2020, when COVID restrictions implemented by MLB prevented them from doing so. As noted, beginning in 2022, managers have the option of either hand-signing or digitally printing their signature on their

A unique Reds batting order card signed by both manager Dusty Baker and bench coach Chris Speier; Baker left the stadium a few hours before the game to have chest x-rays performed, and Speier managed the team in his place (courtesy Jeffrey Lazarus).

PAKISTAN vs. BRASIL
MCU PARK • BROOKLYN, NY • SEPTEMBER 22 2016

BRASIL

#	ORIGINAL	POS.	CHANGE
1	MACIEL	8	
2	CHIRINOS	7	
3	REGINATTO	5	
4	BICHETTE D.	3	
5	SATO	DH	
6	MUNIZ	9	
7	BICHETTE B.	6	
8	CAMARGO	2	
9	ROJO	4	
P	TOME	1	

AVAILABLE POSITION PLAYERS

LEFT-HANDED	SWITCH	RIGHT-HANDED
ITO		LUCIANO
PAZ		GARMENDIA
		COBAS

AVAILABLE PITCHERS

LEFT-HANDED	RIGHT-HANDED
BATISTA (L)	FERNANDEZ (R)
KANABUSHI (L)	FUKUDA (R)
	GOUVÊA (R)
PARPINHO (R)	MATSUMOTO (R)
RIENZO (R)	NORIS (R)
SALES (R)	OLIVEIRA (R)
TAKAHASHI (R)	VIEIRA (R)

PAKISTAN

#	ORIGINAL	POS.	CHANGE
1	ZAWAR	8	
2	JAMSHAID	6	
3	ALI	3	
4	NAWAZ	5	
5	KHAN		
6	JOHAR	DH	
7	UBAID ULLAH	9	
8	BHATTI	2	
9	FAQIR HUSSAIN	4	
P	INAYAT KHAN	1	

MANAGER SIGNATURE

Hall of Fame player Barry Larkin has never managed in MLB, but has managed Brazil's national baseball team.

batting order cards, although there is evidence of digitally signed cards going back to 2004.

All those years of hand-signed cards has been a boon to both lineup card and autograph collectors, given how many Hall of Famers have managed over the years.

As of the writing of this book, there are 23 individuals that have been inducted into baseball's Hall of Fame specifically as managers, and another 63 players elected into the Hall of Fame who also managed in MLB.[1]

Another 18 Negro league players/executives who also managed are in the Hall of Fame, too.[2]

Further, there are other Hall of Fame players who have managed at other levels of baseball. For example, Barry Larkin is currently the manager of Brazil's national baseball team.

But not all Hall of Fame manager–signed batting order cards are equal in terms of value. How many games they managed and when they managed them play big roles.

Tony La Russa, for example, managed more than 5,400 games in his career. Multiply that by at least three batting order cards per game and the fact that lineup cards have become more popular and are more likely to still be in existence, and there is no scarcity of batting order cards signed by La Russa.

Fellow Hall of Famer Yogi Berra was only born about 20 years before La Russa and is a Hall of Famer based on his playing career. While he managed 930 games in the majors, all but 178 of those games were prior to 1976, so a lineup card signed by Berra is far rarer than a La Russa–signed card.

Ghost-signing, digital signatures and unsigned cards

Umpires have not thoroughly policed the manager signature requirement to any great length over the years. There are examples through the years of cards that either were not signed at all, or were ghost-signed.

"The idea of people ghost-signing for the manager also goes back a long way. In 1937, Tigers manager Mickey Cochrane sustained an injury

One of many Tony La Russa–signed batting order cards (courtesy Jeffrey Lazarus).

and was unable to manage the team for a period of time. A lineup card from that era has been found which has a ghost-signed 'Mickey Cochrane' with the initials 'C.P.' underneath, presumably from one of the 15 games where [Cy] Perkins had stepped in to manage for Cochrane," lineup card collector Jeffrey Lazarus shared, adding that other Tigers games that season were managed by Del Baker.

In more recent years, a bigger issue is whether the manager's signature was actually handwritten or digitally printed. It is not always easily determined. For example, this 2021 Mets batting order card signed by then-manager Luis Rojas needs to

OFFICIAL BATTING ORDER
New York Mets
Game 1
Tuesday, September 28, 2021

	ORIGINAL	POS.	CHANGE		ALSO ELIGIBLE
1	Nimmo, B	8	B		POSITION PLAYER
			C		Guillorme, L
2	Lindor, F	6	B		McNeil, J
			C		Smith, Do
3	Conforto, M	9	B		McCann, J
			C		Peraza, J
4	Alonso, P	3	B		PITCHERS
			C		1. Hand, B
5	Báez, J	4	B		2. Hill, R
			C		3. Loup, A
6	Villar, J	5	B		4. Carrasco, C
			C		5. Castro, M
7	Pillar, K / McNeil	7	B		6. Díaz, E
			C		7. Familia, J
8	Nido, T	2	B		8. Hembree, H
			C		9. Lugo, S
9	Stroman, M / PH	1	B (9)(6)		10. May, T
			C		11. Megill, T
			B		12. Reid-Foley, S
			C		13. Syndergaard, N
			D		14. Walker, T
			E		15. Williams, T

Version 1   9/28/2021 at 2.46 PM

MANAGER'S SIGNATURE

Even with the card in hand, it is hard to tell if Luis Rojas signed it in pen, or the signature was digitally printed.

be looked at a few times to determine if the signature is handwritten or not, and even then, it is not crystal clear.

In some rare cases, there are batting order cards that were never signed, according to Lazarus.

One such example is from Hall of Fame manager Casey Stengel.

Lazarus acquired an unsigned Yankees lineup card from 1950, as well as the 1951 AL All-Star Game lineup card, a team managed by Stengel which is signed "Stengel" in print, which PSA/DNA has verified is in Stengel's hand.

Casey Stengel printed his name onto this batting order card (courtesy Jeffrey Lazarus).

Ozzie Guillen's headshot, but not his signature, adorns this 2007 White Sox batting order card (courtesy Jeffrey Lazarus).

Hall of Fame manager Bobby Cox signed this card "B Cox" (courtesy Jeff Garfinkel).

... but simply "Cox" on this card (courtesy Jeffrey Lazarus).

Of the handful of Walter Alston 1950s Dodgers batting order cards that have been found, some are signed and some are not. "So it's clear the inconsistencies go back a long way," said Lazarus.

Lazarus also has an unsigned White Sox batting order card from 2007 when Ozzie Guillen managed the team. There is a head shot of Guillen on the card, though.

Full name versus partial name

While a manager is technically required to sign his batting order cards, there is

A Connie Mack–signed batting order card (courtesy Jeffrey Lazarus).

KANSAS CITY ROYALS AT CLEVELAND GUARDIANS
PROGRESSIVE FIELD • CLEVELAND, OH • OCTOBER 5, 2022

HP - Dan Merzel   1B -   2B -   3B -

CLEVELAND GUARDIANS

#	ORIGINAL	POS.	CHANGE
1	Kwan, S	DH	
2	Rosario, A	6	
3	Ramirez, J	5	
4	Gimenez, A	4	
5	Naylor, J	3	
6	Gonzalez, O	9	
7	Brennan, W	7	
8	Maile, L	2	
9	Straw, M	8	
P	Civale, A	1	

KANSAS CITY ROYALS

#	ORIGINAL	POS.	CHANGE
1	Melendez, M	DH	
2	Witt Jr, B	6	
3	Pasquantino, V	3	
4	Olivares, E	9	
5	Massey, M	4	
6	Waters, D	8	
7	Isbel, K	7	
8	Eaton, N	5	
9	Rivero, S	2	
P	Heasley, J	1	

AVAILABLE POSITION PLAYERS (Cleveland)

LEFT-HANDED	SWITCH	RIGHT-HANDED
Benson, W		Arias, G
Naylor, B		Hedges, A
		Miller, O

AVAILABLE POSITION PLAYERS (Kansas City)

LEFT-HANDED	SWITCH	RIGHT-HANDED
Lopez, N		Dozier, H
O'Hearn, R		Perez, S
		Taylor, M

AVAILABLE PITCHERS (Cleveland)

LEFT-HANDED	RIGHT-HANDED
Hentges, S	Bieber, S / Clase, E
McCarty, K	De Los Santos, E / Karinchak, J
	McKenzie, T / Morgan, E
	Morris, C / Plesac, Z
	Quantrill, C / Sandlin, N
	Stephan, T

AVAILABLE PITCHERS (Kansas City)

LEFT-HANDED	RIGHT-HANDED
Bubic, K	Barlow, S / Castillo, M
Garrett, A	Coleman, D / Greinke, Z
Lynch, D	Hernandez, C / Keller, B
Misiewicz, A	Singer, B / Snider, C
	Weaver, L

MANAGER SIGNATURE _____

The "Manager Signature" line is sometimes left blank on MLB dugout cards as the card does not have to be signed.

no specific rule about how he has to sign it. He may either sign his full name or an abbreviated version. In some cases, managers have changed what they signed over time.

Take Hall of Fame manager Bobby Cox. There are batting order cards that he signed "Bobby Cox," "Bob Cox," "B Cox" and others that he simply signed "Cox." A couple of examples appear above.

Cox was not the only one to vary his signature, and full name versus abbreviated name is not just a recent phenomenon.

"I have two Connie Mack [cards]," said Lazarus. "One of them he signed 'C. Mack.' One of them he signed his full name, 'Connie Mack.' And I've also seen one that I don't own that he just signed 'Mack.' Walter Johnson sometimes signed his whole name, and at other times just his last name."

Dugout cards

Dugout lineup cards from about 2000 and on typically have a line for the manager to sign the card, but because there is no rule that dugout cards need to be signed, many are not.

Dugout cards from before 2000, given that they typically were not seen as a collectible, usually did not have a place for the manager to sign.

In some cases, however, managers did still sign them, like this 1995 card signed by Milwaukee manager Phil Garner.

Players' signatures

Some fans have players sign lineup cards. Due to both the size difference and increased accessibility, dugout lineup cards are more likely to be signed by a player than batting order cards, especially in recent years as they have become far more available to the public.

Milwaukee manager Phil Garner signed this 1995 dugout card. Cal Ripken Jr. went on to break Lou Gehrig's consecutive games played streak later that season.

CLEARWATER THRESHERS

VS Stone Crabs

PLATE: Branson BASES: Nick

July 25, 2010

#	Threshers	Pos	#	Stone Crabs	Pos
1	GOSE	8	1	FRONK	9
2	HERNANDEZ	4	2	BECKHAM	6
3	SUSDORF	7	3	VOGT	2
4	RUF	3	4	SEXTON	5
5	KENNELLY	9	5	SHERIDAN	3
6	MURPHY	DH	6	BALDELLI	DH
7	PERDOMO	5	7	KANG	7
8	STUMPO	2	8	VELASQUEZ	8
9	HANZAWA	6	9	HALL	4
P	CORREA	1	P	CRUZ	1

LHH	EXTRA MEN	RHH	LHH	EXTRA MEN	RHH
MINTKEN	LANGLEY			MURRILL	
	MITCHELL			SCELFO	
	MYERS			JEFFERIES	

LHP	PITCHERS	RHP	LHP	PITCHERS	RHP
DIEKMAN	SANDOVAL		SCHOUSE		QUATE
LOOP	VELASQUEZ		JARMAN		OLIVEROS
	CLOYD		SCHENK		FLEMING
	KISSOCK				ANDUJAR
	ELLIS				

A team-signed 2010 MiLB lineup card.

An autograph from a popular player or Hall of Famer can greatly increase the worth of a lineup card.

Compare, for example, a Boston Red Sox dugout lineup card from their August 17, 2019, game against the Baltimore Orioles, listed on MLB Auctions in June 2020 for a "buy now" price of $100, and the Red Sox–Orioles card from their September 21, 2016, game that is signed by David Ortiz, also listed on MLB Auction in June 2020, but for $350. Both games were Red Sox wins, and there is no clear difference between the two cards beyond Ortiz's autograph, which apparently added $250-worth of value to that card in the mind of the Red Sox.

For star players, a signed pre–MLB lineup card can also be worth significant money. For example, in the spring of 2021, a Cedar Rapids (High-A Midwest League) lineup card for a game in which Mike Trout started and played center field, and was one of 32 players to sign, sold for $1,558.80.³

Pedro Martinez signed and inscribed this batting order card from his first career victory (courtesy Jeffrey Lazarus).

According to Nik Key, owner/operator of Game 7 Authentics, the card might have sold for more money if it was only signed by Trout.

"For investment and value, it would be best to just have the important people [or person] sign it," Key said. "There's no need to chase the guy who pinch hit and struck out in the 6th inning."

Inscriptions, yes or no?

Key gives a thumbs-up to inscriptions: "Getting lineup cards signed is good because it adds historical significance to it, especially if the signer inscribes the event that took place in that specific game," said Key. "I have seen one collector who collected Angels' lineup cards and would have [Mike] Trout sign and inscribe them with whatever he did that day, such as, 'career home run #56.'"

Authenticity: Caveat emptor ("Let the buyer beware")

Fake items—mostly forged autographs, but also items themselves—are a significant thorn in the side of the sports collectibles business.

There is no industry standard number as to what portion of sports collectible items are counterfeit but estimates generally start at 50 percent and go up from there.[1]

Those in or close to the lineup card piece of the market agree that while caution still needs to be taken, the category's small size and relatively lower prices have generally shielded it from significant forgery issues.

"Lineup cards have not reached any kind of stratosphere level at all, price-wise," said sports memorabilia collector Seth Swirsky. "People aren't taking their time forging things for something that's not going to make them a lot of money."

"It's incredibly difficult to forge a full lineup card's worth of handwriting," added collector Jeffrey Lazarus. "In almost all cases, both based on the difficulty and based on the value of the item, forgers have recognized that it is easier to forge a baseball, which is one of the reasons I think that, thankfully, forgeries haven't really penetrated the lineup card market deeply. It also helps that many people are not aware of lineup cards. I can't say that [lineup card forgeries] don't exist at all, but [they are] incredibly, incredibly rare."

"Since it's not a huge collectible area, there aren't going to be a lot of people forging them or faking them," offered Phil Weiss of Weiss Auctions.

Due diligence should still be done when purchasing lineup cards, the experts agree, especially higher-end cards.

"If it's a very big game that you're getting this from, you have to have an extra red flag," said Swirsky. "There's always a red flag for something like a seventh game of a World Series. You have to look out for that."

Far more likely than a forged lineup card, collectors need to look out for lineup cards that are misidentified—either mistakenly or purposefully—or are not actually owned by the person trying to sell it.

A few high-profile examples:

- An item billed as Babe Ruth's MLB debut "lineup card" was auctioned off in 2020, selling for $100,000.[2] While it is a noteworthy piece, given that it is not game used—it was penned after the game, perhaps years later—the $100,000 price raised questions within the industry as to whether or not the purchaser

knew that the piece was not a game-used lineup card. A more detailed account of the item follows later in this chapter.
- Similarly, a thread on baseball collectible forum Net54.com in early 2020 about the authenticity of a batting order card from Hank Aaron's 714th home run game led the auction house to update its item description to "acknowledge the possibility that this card was created subsequent to the event."[3]
- Sky Lucas paid more than $165,000 in late 2004 to purchase the Red Sox 2004 World Series Game 4 lineup card, which clinched Boston's first World Series title in 86 years. However, a would-be scam artist took a high-resolution copy of the card that Lucas had made and tried to sell it on eBay. Fortunately, Lucas and his friend and lawyer David Campbell found out and were able to get the listing pulled off eBay before anyone was conned.[4]
- According to newspaper reports at the time, Maryland businessman James Ancel thought he was paying $35,000 for the handwritten batting order card from Cal Ripken Jr.'s record-breaking 2,131st consecutive game along with the original card from the 2,130st consecutive game and pen used to fill both cards out.[5] In fact, he was buying one of the carbon copies. Ancel got bailed out of the planned purchase because the Baltimore Orioles sued the sellers, Baltimore manager Phil Regan and his daughter.[6] Ancel ended up buying a different carbon copy card from the game for $20,000, and Regan and his daughter found a different purchaser after the lawsuit was settled.[7]

Do your homework

While the above examples are extreme cases, it is important for collectors to know exactly what they are buying, particularly if it is a high-end item. That includes not assuming the description is accurate.

Being well-versed in baseball history in general, as well as lineup cards specifically, is vital.

"You have to do all the authentication you possibly can," said Swirsky. "It's so, so important for people to understand."

But given that it is impossible for one person to be familiar with all aspects of lineup cards, it is also necessary to connect and communicate with other collectors to get their input on the authenticity and value of lineup cards.

"You have to build relationships," Swirsky said. "The way to make money in business is relationships. Like anything else, it's relationships. That's true of collecting. Find the expert in what they do and make those calls. You have to go with your two or three people that you trust, not that they're always going to be exactly right. You have to use your own common sense. If you're going to go buy a stock, you ask two or three advisors or friends that you trust that do that, but it still comes down to you."

MLB authentication helps, to an extent

MLB began its own authentication program in 2001. Since then, MLB and its teams collect whatever a fan or collector might be willing to buy after a game.

Authenticity: Caveat emptor ("Let the buyer beware")   215

A 2017 Jackie Robinson Day lineup card written by Don Wakamatsu, including an authentication sticker on the top, right-hand corner of the card (courtesy Don Wakamatsu).

"I would say it was the last 10 or 15 years that everything that wasn't tied down was sold, whether it's the foul balls, the broken bats," said Don Wakamatsu, who coached and managed in MLB from 2003 through 2021.

And yes, that includes lineup cards.

Dugout lineup cards are almost always authenticated by MLB, while official batting order cards and bullpen lineup cards are sometimes collected and authenticated.

But MLB's authentication program is far from perfect from a collector perspective. MLB and its teams are trying to make money, and just because MLB deems a lineup card "authentic" doesn't necessarily mean it is game used. In fact, some are not. Therefore, it is important to read the authentication certificate closely, regardless of what a seller—MLB, a team or third party—claims the card is.

For example, MLB authenticates not only dugout lineup cards and some official batting order cards, but also clubhouse cards and even replica cards. Club house cards are not used during a game, and replica lineup cards are mass-produced after a game, and do not meet the definition given early in this book of what a lineup card is.

Clubhouse and replica cards are fine for what they are as long as the purchaser understands what they are buying and that they are paying a price that reflects that the cards are not game used.

But that is not always the case.

First, here is an example of a title/description of a card for sale on eBay that is accurate, but the lack of details in the title and description could be confusing to a prospective buyer:

The June 2022 eBay listing was titled:

Juan Soto 2018 Game Used HR #16 Lineup Card Rookie August 29 Nationals GU RC.

An MLB authentication sticker on a lineup card.

The item description added:

> Tied Griffey Jr for HR's [sic] by a teenager. Mammoth 2 Run HR! Would be great signed!

The listing's main picture shows what appears to be a game-used Nationals dugout lineup card. It sounds, at least on the surface, like a neat dugout lineup card, and is perhaps worth close to, if not the $200 asked for it.

What is not mentioned, save for the last picture of the MLB authentication certificate in relatively small print, is that the card was not in Washington's dugout.[8] It was in the bullpen. In fairness to the seller, the person never claimed it was in the dugout, it just looks like it may have been, to those unfamiliar with lineup cards. Why does it matter? Dugout cards are considered more important than bullpen cards, so the buyer might be disappointed if they eventually find out it was in the bullpen rather than the dugout.

The good news is that no one purchased the card for the $200 the seller was originally asking for, so the seller eventually changed the item to an auction-style format. The card sold in September 2022 for $42, much closer to what it is likely worth.

Next is an example of a card for which the eBay title/description is either untrue or the MLB authentication certificate is incorrect:

The June 2022 eBay listing was titled:

> Game Used Mets Vs Nationals 8/24/18 Dugout Lineup Card Juan Soto Bryce Harper.

The item description for the $125 lineup card reads:

> Up for sale is a great game used Mets Vs Nationals Dugout Lineup Card. This lineup card is from the game played August 24, 2018. In this game Jason Vargas started for the Mets and the Nationals countered with Gio Gonzalez. The card was from the Nationals dugout and is signed by manager Dave Martinez. It's MLB Authenticated with a hologram # of JD357908.

One of the pictures with the listing is of the MLB authentication hologram, #JD357908. The MLB authentication certificate for that code states that the item is a "Replica Line-up Card" for the Nationals-Mets August 24, 2018, game.[9]

One would assume that MLB has it right and the seller is wrong that the card was in the dugout and game used. It is a little surprising, however, that the Nationals would create replica lineup cards for a seemingly ordinary regular season game that they lost, 3–0.

Regardless of who is wrong, the seller or MLB, it is a prime example of "buyer beware."

Managers' signatures: Handwritten vs. electronic

An area of importance when it comes to lineup card authenticity is managers' signatures on batting order cards, as some collectors purchase lineup cards either partially or fully for managers' signatures.

Over the years, it has been well proven that it is not uncommon for managers to have a coach fill out and sign the lineup card for them. Hall of Famers Leo Durocher and Eddie Mathews are two examples of managers who were known to have coaches fill out and sign their batting order cards, according to Lazarus.

In the 21st century, as batting order cards have more typically been computer printed, it has become more common that managers' signatures are electronically produced as opposed to handwritten, significantly decreasing the value of the "autograph." Particularly, since 2020, umpires no longer care if the signature is digitally produced instead of handwritten, according to former MLB umpire Jim Reynolds.

OFFICIAL BATTING ORDER
Seattle Mariners

Wednesday, June 30, 2021

	ORIGINAL	POS.	CHANGE		ALSO ELIGIBLE
					POSITION PLAYERS
1	Crawford, J	6	B		
			C		Fraley, J
2	Haniger, M	9	B		Long Jr., S
			C		**PITCHERS**
3	France, T	3	B		1. Gonzales, M
			C		2. Kikuchi, Y
4	Seager, K	5	B		3. Misiewicz, A
			C		4. Santiago, H
5	Torrens, L	2	B		5. Chargois, J
			C		6. Flexen, C
6	Bauers, J	7	B		7. Gilbert, L
			C		8. Graveman, K
7	Murphy, T	DH	B		9. Middleton, K
			C		10. Montero, R
8	Moore, D	4	B		11. Ramirez, Y
			C		12. Sewald, P
9	Trammell, T	8	B		13. Steckenrider, D
			C		14. Vest, W
P	Sheffield, J	SP	B		15. Sheffield, J (SP)
			C		
			D		
			E		

Version 1 - 6/30/2021 at 3:36 PM

MANAGER'S SIGNATURE

Seattle manager Scott Servais's signature was pasted digitally onto this batting order card.

OFFICIAL BATTING ORDER

| CLUB | PHILADELPHIA PHILLIES | | DATE | 3/8/2020 |

#	ORIGINAL		CHANGE	ALSO ELIGIBLE	
1	HASELEY	8	B	C	LARTIGUE
			C	1B	HALL
2	FORSYTHE	DH	B	2B	RIVERA
			C	SS	MATON
3	BRUCE	3	B	3B	BOHM
			C	LF	LISTI
4	WALKER	4	B	CF	MAHTOOK
			C	RF	GOSSELIN
5	HARRISON	5	B	DH	GAMBOA
			C		BETHANCOURT
6	WILLIAMS, N.	7	B		O'HOPPE
			C		MONIAK
7	GARLICK	9	B		
			C		DOMINGUEZ
8	GRULLON	2	B		NORRIS
			C		PARKER
9	TORREYES	6	B		GUERRA
			C		RUSS
	VELASQUEZ	1	D		HENNIGAN
			E		ROSS
				/	KILLGORE

MANAGER'S SIGNATURE _[signature]_

Joe Girardi hand-signed this 2020 spring training batting order card.

And it is not always easy at quick glance to tell if a lineup card signature has been added digitally or written.

In the example above, the 2021 Mariners card signed by manager Scott Servais appears to be an electronically produced signature when looked at closely.

Meanwhile, Joe Girardi's signature on the Phillies 2020 spring training batting order card above is clearly handwritten.

More transparency needed?

It begs the question of whether there should be formal rules and regulations as to how sports memorabilia items are marketed, given the billions of dollars spent on such items each year.

"A lot of industries have regulations as to what you can say and what you can't say," said Richard Roth, founding partner of New York City–based The Roth Law Firm, which represents athletes, teams and companies in sports memorabilia cases.

The stock market, real estate market and medical field are three of many regulated industries. "I don't know of any in this industry," said Roth of the sports memorabilia business. "In this industry, there's no real stringent guidelines for doing anything other than what you would expect reasonable certification companies and auctioneers to do."

Until such regulation is brought to the sports memorabilia business, if it ever is, let the buyer beware.

Babe Ruth's MLB debut "lineup card"

The headline on a Christie's auction item in December 2020 read: "Significant July 11, 1914, Babe Ruth First Major League Game "Lineup Card" (Tommy Connolly Collection) (PSA/DNA)."[10]

A lineup card from Babe Ruth's MLB debut would be the holy grail of lineup cards for two reasons:

1. Ruth is arguably the most iconic and well-known baseball player ever; and
2. it would also be the oldest known lineup card still in existence by more than 15 years.

"The face of Babe Ruth is known today," said baseball memorabilia collector and Grammy-nominated songwriter Seth Swirsky. "He's the Beatles. Everything that he touched, or had anything to do with, is valuable. But if it's from the day he played that first game, that's another story. That's a major, major piece."

The Babe Ruth "lineup card" sold for $100,000 at auction, which would make it one of the most expensive lineup cards ever sold. But is it just a lineup card?

The item's description read as follows:

On July 11, 1914 Tommy Connolly along with umpire O'Loughlin, presided over a game played between the Boston Red Sox and the Cleveland Naps at Fenway Park in Boston. The game was, for the most part, fairly insignificant save for the debut of a young pitcher by the name of George "Babe" Ruth. Ruth played his first Major League game on this date departing with a no decision after six innings. Ruth surrendered only five hits and one run to the mighty Cleveland team, whose lineup included Nap Lajoie and Joe Jackson. Ironically, on the offensive side of the ball, Ruth struck out in his first at bat. The lineup card itself is neatly penned in Connolly's hand, including positions, date, site, umpires (including a last name autograph of Connolly), and even the substitution of left fielder Duffy Lewis for Olaf Henriksen (misspelled "Hendrickson" by Connolly). The Babe is simply listed as "Ruth-P." just above the name of the substitute Duffy. The size of the paper stock card is 4¼" × 4½" with a single horizontal fold line.

This particular item originated from the personal collection of Hall of Fame umpire Tommy Connolly. Connolly was documented to have preserved additional noteworthy items of memorabilia within his collection including the first pitch baseball in the history of Fenway Park (See Hunt Auctions, April 2012, lot 335) and the Eddie Collins single signed baseball within this auction. Given the impeccable provenance of the offered card and the mundane nature of Ruth's debut, the card is certainly unique and possibly one of the more significant lineup cards of its type extant.

The lot also includes an original photograph of Connolly posed in full umpire gear on the field by Louis Van Oeyen, c. 1910. Image measures 5"x8" signed by Van Oeyen with surface abrasion at bottom margin. Includes full LOA from JSA and encapsulated by PSA/DNA: EX

4¼ × 4½ in., the lineup card

In addition, the description references the card's PSA/DNA Certification, which can be found by going to PSA's authentication web page and entering certification #84262381.[11] The certification includes the following information:

Item: "Lineup Card"
Primary Subject: "TOM CONNOLLY"
Result: "Authentic"

It is worth noting:

1. The Ruth MLB debut "lineup card" was previously auctioned off by Hunt Auctions in 2005, and sold for $20,000.[12] The Hunt item description in 2005 is similar to Christie's, although it does not place "lineup card" in quotation marks like the Christie's listing; and
2. Both the Hunt and the Christie's item description state: "Ruth played in his first Major League game on this date departing with a no decision after six innings. Ruth surrendered only five hits and one run."

In fact, according to the game box scores found at MLB.com, Retrosheet and *Baseball Almanac*, Ruth pitched seven innings, allowed eight hits and three runs (two earned), and earned the victory.[13] Assuming the box scores are correct—and one should be able to assume that MLB.com has it right—it is a significant error in the write-up because it undervalues what the item is purported to be. Not only does the card represent Ruth's MLB debut game; it is also his first career pitching victory, making it even more valuable.

As noted in both descriptions, Ruth also batted for the first time in his career in the game, going 0-for-2.

"It makes for a very interesting story," said Richard Roth. "Either it's the first lineup card ever, or, and my guess more likely, logically, it's not."

The verdict

Roth opines above that the Ruth debut "lineup card" is not the oldest lineup card still in existence, and the facts support his take. The card is not a lineup card, at least not the way baseball memorabilia collectors would define a lineup card and the way it is defined at the beginning of this book: "a physical document, either hand-written or computer printed before a game, that includes at least one team's lineup. It contains information including the starting lineup, batting order and positions, and reserve players. Lineup cards are used by managers, coaches, players and umpires for reference before and during a game."

The point of distinction in the definition is that the card is written *before* the game and used *before* and *during* the game. Tommy Connolly's card was written *after* the game. How can we be certain?

On the right-hand column of the lineup card penned by Connolly, under

"Boston," the second name is "Leonard," short for Dutch Leonard. Leonard replaced Ruth as pitcher and took Olaf Henriksen's spot in the lineup.

Had Connolly written the card before the game, he would not have known to leave a space for Leonard. Further, he did not leave any other spaces for substitutions because writing this after the game, he knew the only additional space he needed was for Duffy Lewis coming on as a pinch-hitter for Ruth in the bottom of the seventh inning.

Whether Connolly penned this "lineup card" 40 minutes, four months, or 40 years after the game (Connolly died in 1961) is not clear, but what is certain is that it was written *after* the game.

As for the PSA/DNA Certification, the company was likely authenticating the item as having been penned by Connolly. The fact that PSA/DNA identifies the item simply as a "lineup card" is almost certainly in the generic sense that it is a card with the lineups on it.

In fairness to Christie's, Hunt and PSA/DNA, none of them claimed that the card was game used.

The question is, did the buyer who paid $100,000 for this item think they were buying a game-used lineup card, or did they realize they were buying a piece that Connolly penned after the game?

"The piece is wonderful, but..."

The fact that Connolly's card is not a game-used lineup card does not mean that it is insignificant, Swirsky points out. Connolly was a Hall of Fame umpire who wrote the lineups down from a very historical game for which he was behind the plate.

"This piece is wonderful, but it could have been done 10, 20, 30 years later for all I know," Swirsky said. "That's not good enough for me to bid in the [$100,000] range."

Lineup Cards:
What Are They Worth,
and Where to Buy/Sell

Because lineup cards are a tiny speck in the vast universe of baseball memorabilia, trying to calculate annual lineup card sales would hardly be worth the effort, Chris Ivy, director of Sports Auctions at Heritage Auctions, said in a 2020 *Sports Collectors Digest* article.

"It would be a tiny fraction of one percent," said Ivy. "Probably signed baseballs alone outnumber lineup cards by tens of thousands to one."[1]

But while their annual sales may be little more than a rounding error in the overall baseball memorabilia market, we have seen how lineup cards have become an important niche in telling the story of baseball's history, and there is a market for them.

Recall collector Seth Swirsky's military metaphor, quoted earlier: "I consider them very historic. I mean the manager, he was the general in the war. Imagine seeing Eisenhower's list of who he wanted to go into battle, and he had to sign it? Imagine what that would be worth?"[2]

As noted, fellow collector Jeff Garfinkel likes the fact that there are a very limited number of lineup cards from a game; they "aren't necessarily one-offs, but there's three or four copies."

"They are, effectively, the official documents of a particular game, in the same way a player's contract is the official document of his particular season, so they are absolutely historically relevant," added Ivy.[3]

Vintage sports memorabilia collector Rick Levy echoes the comments of fellow collectors.

"I think they are really underappreciated," said Levy of lineup cards. "A lot of the paper stuff isn't as appreciated as baseball cards, which doesn't make a lot of sense to me because these are really part of the game, and the baseball cards really aren't."

But there are reasons why lineup cards make up such a microscopic piece of the market.

Ivy mentions the "meager supply of available examples from anything other than the 21st century, when MLB started marketing them directly."[4]

"For most of baseball history, the person who used the card during the game—each manager and the home plate umpire—was effectively the owner," Ivy continued. "Virtually all of them were tossed in the trash after the game, and that's why they are so rare today. When you consider that that well over a thousand MLB games

Batting order cards from Game 1 of the 1963 World Series (courtesy Rick Levy).

happened each year for decades, with six cards for each game, you can see that the surviving population is a microscopic sliver of the original population."[5]

While Ivy might be slightly exaggerating in claiming that virtually all cards from the 20th century ended up in the garbage, he is right that lineup cards were seen to be of little value at the time, and the vast majority did get thrown away. Thankfully, some survived and are now appreciated.

How much are lineup cards worth?

In a broad stroke, the value of any lineup card will fall between $0 and $165,000.

The high-end number is based on the most expensive lineup card ever sold publicly, the Boston dugout card for 2004 World Series Game 4. It sold for $165,010 in 2004.[6]

Of course, almost every other lineup card's value is far closer to $0.

Narrowing the lens is not always easy. Compared with other segments of baseball memorabilia, for example, baseball cards and autographed baseballs, which have pricing guides, there are few resources available to determine what lineup cards are worth.

Additionally, almost all lineup cards are unique.

"Lineup cards, there's so many of them," said Phil Weiss of Weiss Actions in Lynbrook, New York. "[The value] is going to be determined by what happened in the game, what teams were playing, what manager handled the card, assuming it was the manager that did all the writing on it and not one of the coaches."

Factors Likely to Increase a Lineup Card's Value

Some of the factors that are likely to increase a lineup card's value include:

- A significant game (e.g., All-Star game, playoffs, World Series)
- A milestone is achieved (e.g., 3,000th hit, no-hitter)
- One or more Hall of Famers, or likely Hall of Famers; the more the player(s) did of note during the game, the better
- A lineup card signed by a popular or Hall of Fame manager
- Cards from a World Series championship team's season
- Player debut or last game or even the player's rookie season, particularly Hall of Famers
- The age of the card
- A team with a large fan base (e.g., Yankees, Red Sox)
- Personal interest (e.g., a game attended, a favorite player or team)

Take the most expensive card sold to date, as an example, the Boston dugout card for 2004 World Series Game 4, which sold for $165,010 a couple of months after the game. The Red Sox had not won the World Series in 86 years, so not only was it a World Series clinching victory, but demand from a large Boston fan base was high because of how long it was between titles. All those factors played into the exorbitant price.

Another example is the pair of official batting order cards from the first-ever MLB All-Star Game at Comiskey Park in 1933 that sold for $138,000 in 2007.[7]

It was the first-ever MLB All-Star Game, included legendary baseball names like "Ruth" and "Gehrig," and pitted two of the greatest managers of all time, Connie

Alex Rodriguez batted ninth and played shortstop for the Mariners in this game during his rookie season (courtesy Jeffrey Lazarus).

Mack and John McGraw. Additionally, the American League card was signed by Mack.

"Think about the players that were in that game," said Swirsky. "A piece like a lineup card brings you to the event when you are looking at it and holding it.... These names are in folklore, every one of them on those cards. This is a fantastic piece. I think it went for what it should have gone for [price-wise]."

"My personal favorite that we've sold … is Casey Stengel's card from Game 7 of the 1960 World Series," said Ivy of the card Heritage Auctions auctioned off in 2005 for $5,377.50. "You can almost feel the anxiety coursing through him as he struggled to find an answer before Mazeroski's walk-off. This is a line-up card that is more than just a documentation. It borders on a psychological study."[8]

Of course, all of the above are famous lineup cards.

Most lineup cards from MLB games are worth $200 or less.

In 2022, MLB teams were typically selling current dugout lineup cards for between $75 and $300.

"The price varies depending on many factors including the outcome of the game, the date and players involved," said Dan Hanrahan, director, Authentics for the Texas Rangers.

"If it's just a regular old lineup card, not much happened from that day, I don't think people are going out of their way to say, 'Oh, I really have to have this,'" said collector and seller Jeff Garfinkel.

Weiss added: "If you had a lineup card from the '27 Yankees that Joe McCarthy handled, yeah, that's cool. If you have a 1970s Milwaukee Brewers lineup card in a year where they did nothing, I don't know if there'll be a lot of interest in that."

Valuation resources: Past auction house and eBay sales; colleagues

As stated earlier, while not many, there are some resources to help determine a lineup card's value, or at least a ballpark figure.

Auction houses such as Heritage Auctions and Robert Edwards Auctions, which typically sell higher-end memorabilia, often include historical listings and final selling prices on their websites.

eBay is also a resource but must be used carefully as often the "buy now" prices are high, sometimes ridiculously so.

"On eBay, it's not what someone's asking," said Garfinkel, adding that "sold" prices are a far better gauge for determining a similar card's value.

As an example, in mid–2022, someone was trying to sell a signed lineup card from Clayton Kershaw's first MLB victory for $25,000 on eBay. It is a nice card with historic merit from an almost certain Hall of Famer. But $25,000 is almost certainly overpriced.

As a point of reference, Goldin Auctions sold the MLB authenticated dugout lineup card and ticket stub for Kershaw's 100th win in 2015 for $508.[9] Granted, it is not as historic as Kershaw's first victory nor is it signed, but it might help a would-be bidder realize just how steep the $25,000 price tag is.

Then there is the Boston bullpen lineup card from Derek Jeter's last MLB game,

Heritage Auctions sold these batting order cards from Derek Jeter's MLB debut game for $23,400 in 2021 (imaged by Heritage Auctions, HA.com)

offered on eBay for $12,500. That would be a high price even if it was an authenticated dugout or batting order card from the game, but it is neither.

For comparison, Heritage Auctions sold a signed and inscribed, MLB authenticated dugout card from Jeter's 2,000th-hit game for $2,520 in 2020.[10]

This is why Garfinkel suggested searching "sold" listings on eBay as they will typically yield a more accurate perspective as to what something similar is truly worth.

Trusted lineup card collector friends can also serve as a valuable sounding board for a piece's value.

Do lineup cards offer more value than comparable items?

Some within the lineup card community believe the price of lineup cards to often be a bargain when compared to the price of other items from the same game.

As an example, the bat used by Cal Ripken for his historic 3,000th career hit, signed and inscribed by Ripken Jr., sold at auction for nearly $250,000[11]

The Milwaukee Brewers dugout lineup card from that game, also signed and inscribed by Ripken, sold for just under $2,500.[12]

Both are game-used items from one of baseball's historic moments. Surely the bat played a more significant role in the achievement, and few would argue that it is more important than the lineup card—but 100 times more?

Weiss is "a strong believer in 'the market determines what it's worth.'" In that line of thinking, the prices are what they are.

And perhaps terms like "worth," "value" or "bargain" need to be looked at from more than just a monetary sense.

If the person who bought the lineup card for $2,500 could not afford the $250,000 bat, then, yes, it was a good deal to buy a lineup card from such a historic event for $2,500.

"Collect what you love"

And that beings us to a broader definition of worth, one that transcends monetary value.

"If people have an interest in it, it's a great way to get more people into the hobby who can afford things," Weiss said. "It doesn't have to necessarily have to be something super expensive to have interest."

Ivy takes it a step further.

"The best collecting advice that exists is the most basic advice: collect what you love," he said. "So if you are intrigued by lineup cards, that's the biggest 'pro' there is."

The lineup card marketplace

There are a few primary places to acquire lineup cards, some of which also offer the opportunity to sell cards, too. The most common outlets include being given cards for free by managers, coaches or umpires after games; the MLB Auctions website; brick-and-mortar or online team stores; eBay; and auction houses. These are covered below.

Other channels include:

- E-commerce sites such as Facebook Marketplace and Mercari. While generally similar in nature to eBay, these other e-commerce sites have a very limited selection of lineup cards. For example, a September 2022 search of "lineup card" on Mercari yielded just two lineup cards, both from minor league games.
- Online baseball message boards and forums (e.g., Net54.com)
- Person-to-person sales
- Sports memorabilia dealers, card shows, etc.
- Antique stores, flea markets, garage sales: Lineup card finds at antique stores and flea markets are "extremely rare," but they do happen, said sports memorabilia collector Michael Calvello, who regularly visits flea markets in search of sports collectibles. For example, Calvello's last lineup card score at a flea market was some two years ago, but it was a good one: 75 minor league cards—including future major leaguers such as Nomar Garciaparra, Michael Cuddyer and Joe Mauer, to name just a few—plus a few minor league ticket stubs (including a Derek Jeter rehab game) all for $25. But Calvello reiterates that hits like this are few and far between.

Asking a manager, coach or umpire for their lineup cards after a game

If you stay at a game until the end and are in the right place in the stadium, you can ask the manager, a coach or an umpire and they might give you their batting order cards, whether it be at an MLB, minor league or college game.

In the case of MLB, you can also ask for the bullpen lineup card which is exclusively used at that level. And because dugout cards are almost never sold by minor league or college teams, a manager or coach will sometimes give those away.

While it is not new—for as long as lineup cards have been used, a fan could ask for a lineup card after a game—it has only become common for fans to ask for a card in recent years, largely because more and more fans are seeing the success of others doing so in blogs, social media and YouTube videos.

"'Hey, I can ask for that and maybe I'll get it,'" said Garfinkel of those chasing lineup cards after games. "I think it's an accepted part of the collectible market now. I think it will continue to expand."

Assuming you are going to the game anyway—and therefore paying for a ticket, parking and travel, anyway—then the cards are free, and a nice souvenir, much like a baseball you might catch during a game. And you can sometimes get very lucky and get a truly historic card.

MLB and team sites

The teams themselves, through the MLB Auctions website, team specific stores—both online and in-stadium—and team marketing partners (e.g., Fanatics for the Yankees and Giants) are the best source for current or recent MLB dugout lineup cards.

There are few bargains when purchasing from a team or MLB, whether it be at a stadium or online, although sometimes, when a card has gone unsold over a period of time, it will be discounted. For example, in 2022 the Minnesota Twins were selling leftover cards from games between 2013 and 2018 for $35 each on the MLB Auctions site.

Otherwise, dugout lineup card prices largely depend on the teams and players in the game, and what happened during the game.

For example, the Yankees' dugout lineup card pricing starts at $250, which the Yankees can charge because of their enormous fan base and on-field success. Pricing for Cubs dugout lineup cards from the first two months of the 2022 season ranged from $85 to as high as $250 for the May 29, 2022, game against the crosstown rival White Sox. The base price for a Rangers 2022 dugout lineup card was $75, per Dan Hanrahan, director, Authentics for the Texas Rangers.

Some teams—the Cubs and Rangers were confirmed—have begun selling batting order cards. The Cubs were selling them for $30 in 2022, when they were available.

"Available" is the key word, according to Hanrahan. It is one of the reasons he does not like to presell cards, even though teams often promote it.

"On occasion, [the lineup cards] are not made available to me, or a milestone

CAPE LEAGUE ALL-STAR Game 2014

WEST VS. EAST

JULY 25TH 2015
SPILLANE FIELD, WARHAM

#	WEST	Pos	#	EAST	Pos
1	Nick Solac	2B	1	Colin Lyman (Knapp)	LF
2	Andrew Calica	CF	2	Tommy Edman	2B
3	Blake Tiberi	3B	3	Nick Senzel (Zammarelli)	3B
4	Jacob Noll	DH	4	Kyle Lewis (Pate)	RF
5	JJ Matijevic	1B	5	Donnie Walton (Adams)	SS
6	Heath Quinn	RF	6	Gio Brusa	DH
7	Nick Cieri	C	7	Ronnie Dawson	1B
8	Michael Paez	SS	8	Cassiddy Brown (Murphy)	C
9	Jacob Robson	LF	9	Cole Billingsley	CF
P	Blake Fox	P	P	Mitchell Jordan	P

RESERVES

WEST	EAST
Errol Robinson	Cavin Biggio 4
David MacKinnon	Johnny Adams 6
Charlie Warren	Nick Zammarelli 5
Jackson Klein	Aaron Knapp 7
Ryan Boldt	Adam Pate 8
Jake Rogers	Sean Murphy 2

PITCHERS

WEST	EAST
Evan Hill	Ricky Thomas
Ian Hamilton	Eric Lauer
Jon Woodcock	Parker Dunshee
Aaron Civale	Brandon Miller
Devin Smeltzer	Thomas Hackimer
Austin Tibby	Aaron McGarity
Andrew Frankenreider	Spencer Trayner
Austin Conway	Luke Scherzer
Gavin Pittore	Nick Highberger

HOME RUN DERBY

Peter Alonso   Logan Sowers   Will Craig   Nick Senzel
Will Haynie   Willie Abreu

This Cape Cod League All-Star game lineup card was given away after the game. Several players have gone on to play in the majors, including Kyle Lewis, Cavan Biggio, Pete Alonso and Sean Murphy.

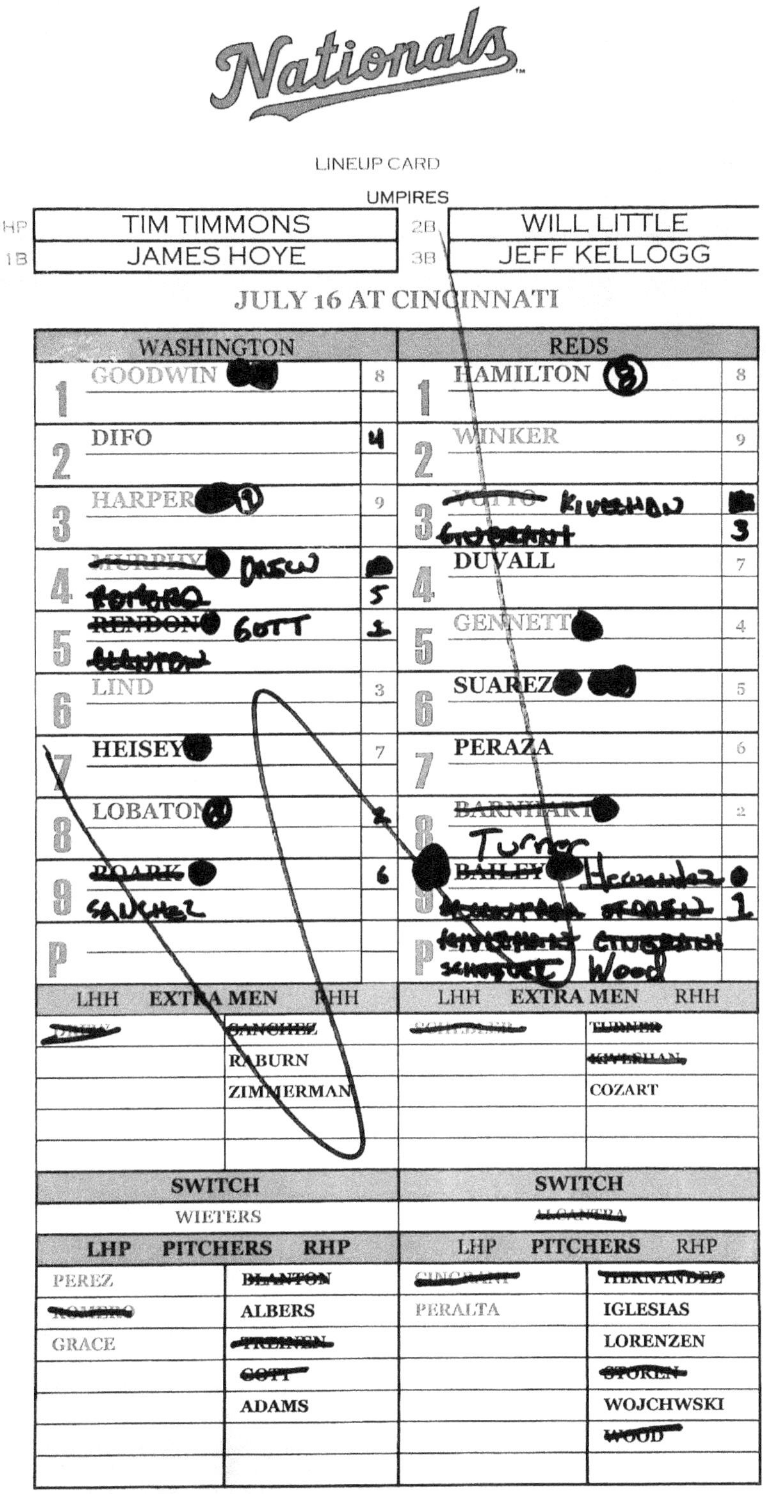

This Nationals bullpen lineup card was given away after the game.

OFFICIAL BATTING ORDER TORONTO

TORONTO   SEPTEMBER 17, 2019

#	ORIGINAL	POS.		CHANGE	ALSO ELIGIBLE
1	BICHETTE	6	A		FISHER
			B		TELLEZ / MCGUIRE
2	BIGGIO	4	A		DAVIS
			B		ALFORD / MAILE
3	GURRIEL JR	DH	A		DRURY
			B		URENA
4	GUERRERO JR	5	A		
			B		BOSHERS / PANNONE
5	GRICHUK	9	A		ROMANO / LUCIANO
			B		GAVIGLIO
6	SMOAK	3	A		GILES
			B		LAW
7	HERNANDEZ	8	A		FONT
			B		ADAM
8	MCKINNEY	7	A		ZEUCH
			B		STEWART / SHAFER
9	JANSEN	2	A		THORNTON
			B		BUCHHOLZ
10	TEPERA	SP	A		KAY
			B		WAGUESPACK

MANAGER'S SIGNATURE

Then–Toronto manager Charlie Montoyo gave his batting order card to a fan after Cavan Biggio hit for the cycle in a 2019 game.

may occur that would create more demand and value," said Hanrahan. "Unfortunately for me, many don't understand the concept."

And the prices will go up significantly if something significant took place in the game.

"If something happened that's historic or monumental, they know about it," said Garfinkel of the teams. "That was always the fun ... that you on your own can do the research and perhaps hit a home run, find a gem. When they come from the team, there's nothing that happened that's not coming cheap."

Case in point: The Rangers hosted Cleveland in the final regular season game of

Opposite page: Michael Klett pre-purchased the Yankees Aaron Judge 62nd home run of the season card (right) for $250 from the MLB Auctions web site mid-way through the season. He also bought the Rangers card (left) from MLB Auctions for $12,530 10 days after the game (courtesy Michael Klett).

Lineup Cards: What Are They Worth, and Where to Buy/Sell

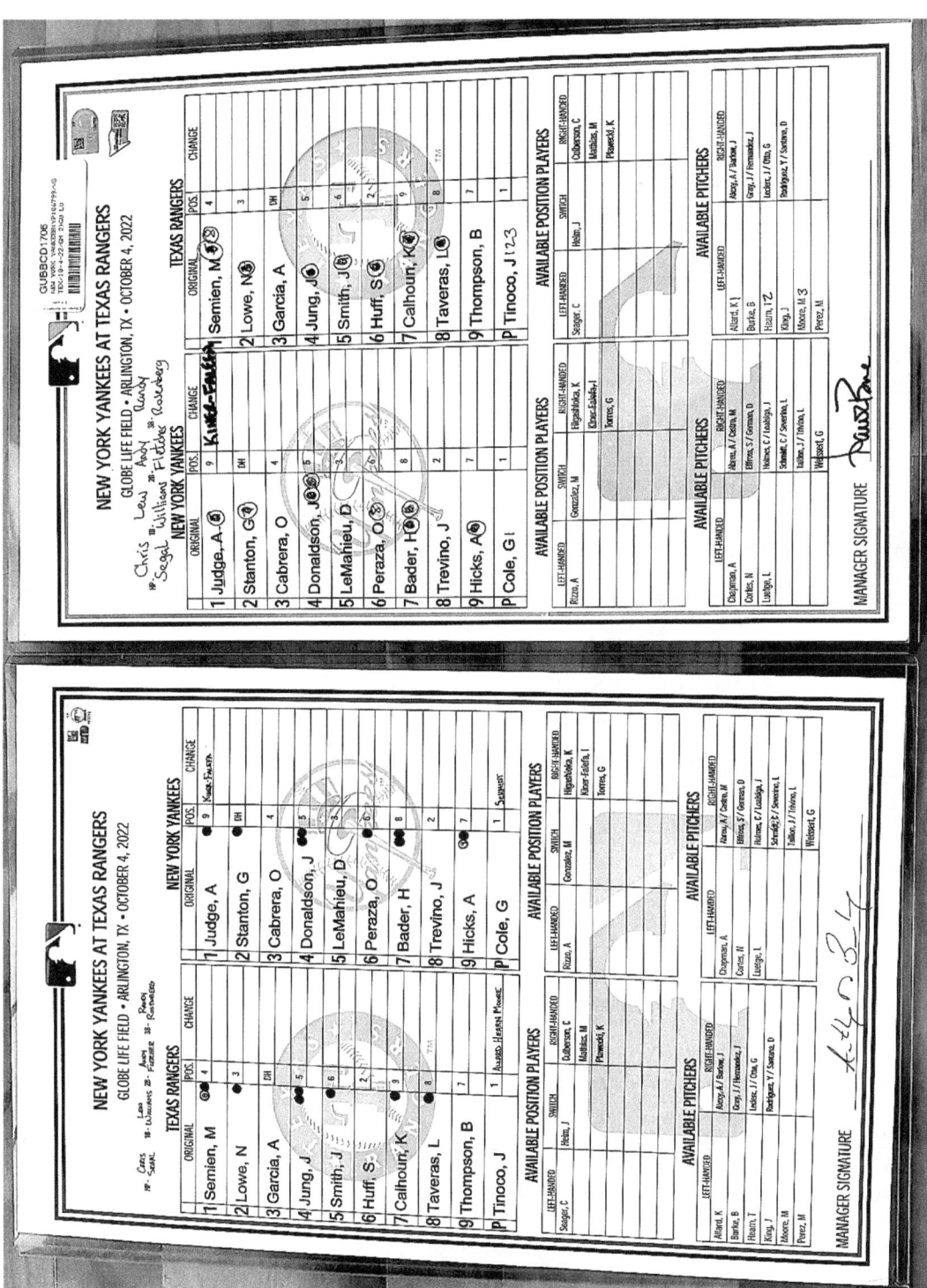

the 2021 season. It was the last game in which Cleveland was playing as the Indians as they had previously announced a nickname change to the Guardians starting in 2022.

The Texas dugout card from Cleveland's last game as the Indians would have been a fantastic pickup for $75. But the Rangers knew what they had.

Sure enough, a few weeks later, Texas's dugout lineup card from the game was put up for auction on the MLB Auctions site. The dugout lineup card was combined with a Yu Chang home run ball from the game.

The winning bid was $5,000.

No disrespect to Chang, a career .213 hitter through 2022, but it was almost certainly the last Cleveland Indians' dugout lineup card that drove the price that high.

A Sample of Cards Sold on the MLB Auctions Site		
Item	Price	Year Sold
Indians @ Rangers, 10/3/21 Cleveland's last games as Indians	$5,000	2021
Angels @ Rangers, 4/26/21 Ohtani: Pitching Win and 2 hits, 2 RBI Pujols: Last HR as an Angel	$2,750	2021
Yankees @ Cubs, 5/20/14 Jeter: last season, 2 hits	$280	2014
Blue Jays @ Orioles, 9/5/22 Bichette: 3 HRs	$495	2022
2002 WS G1, Giants @ Angels Glaus 2 HRs, Bonds HR, Snow HR Autographed by Glaus	$3,221	2014
*Yankees @ Rangers, 10/4/22 Judge 62nd HR of season	$12,530	2022
**Yankees @ Rangers, 10/4/22 Judge 62nd HR of season	$250	2022
Dodgers @ Brewers, 5/1/21 Betts HR, Shaw HR, Feliciano debut	$150	2021
Yankees @ Red Sox, 5/1/15 Rodriguez career HR #660	$355	2015
Angels @ A's, 5/14/22 Ohtani 100th career HR	$1,940	2022
*Texas dugout card **New York dugout card Source: www.auctions.mlb.com		

Why eBay is a shot in the arm for both lineup card sellers and buyers

The online auction trading company eBay has played a role in the growth of the sports collectibles market, in terms of how such items are both bought and sold. Albeit on a small scale, it has helped promote the collecting of lineup cards, too.

Lineup Cards: What Are They Worth, and Where to Buy/Sell

When told that there were 560+ lineup cards available for purchase on eBay in September 2022, Garfinkel was surprised. "That's a huge amount compared to what it used to be," he said.

With its fairly simple process for both selling and buying items, eBay has boosted the number of lineup cards for sale. "Teams, umpires, the people that had these things and saved them—there's always that collector mentality—figured out they could monetize it," said Garfinkel.

For sellers, eBay offers dozens if not hundreds or even thousands of potential customers, depending on the item, and the fees are well-detailed.

For buyers, eBay has provided a way to find a unique selection of cards, many of which never would have been available previously.

Here is a sample of the variety of lineup cards available for purchase on eBay, per an informal September 2022 survey:

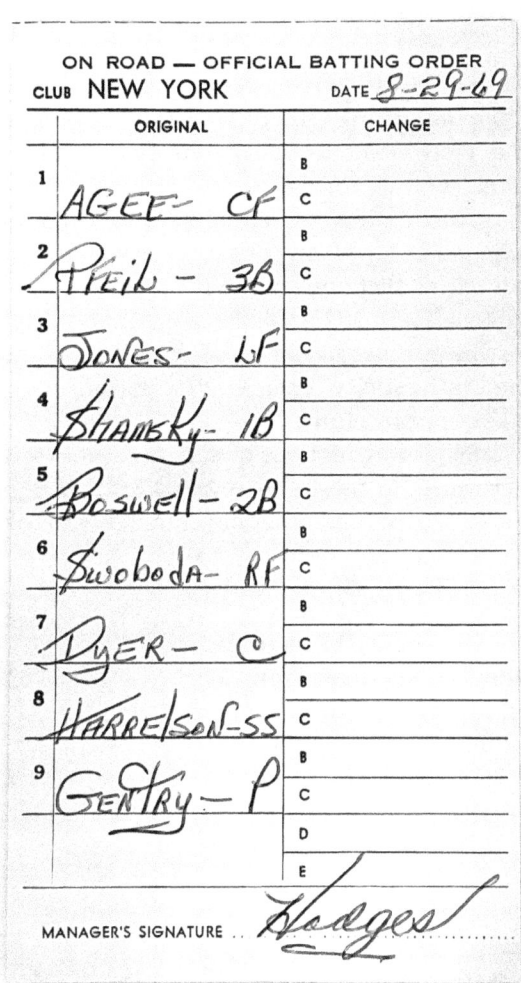

Jeffrey Lazarus bought this 1969 "Miracle Mets" batting order card off eBay (courtesy Jeffrey Lazarus).

- 2009 World Baseball Classic dugout card, USA-Venezuela
- 1988 Yankees batting order card, carbon copy
- 2008 Diamondbacks-Cubs 2008 Mother's Day dugout card, blank
- 1967 Cincinnati Reds batting order card, carbon copy
- 2020 Somerset Patriots (Atlantic League) dugout card
- 2020 Miami Marlins spring training batting order card
- 2007 Peoria Chiefs (Midwest League) batting order card
- 1986 Memphis Chicks (Southern League) dugout card
- 2000 Montreal Expos dugout card
- 2017 Detroit Tigers spring training batting order card
- 2016 Nashville Sounds (International League) batting order card
- 2007 Rhodes College batting order card

On the high end, of the 560-plus cards available at the time, the highest-priced card was a $12,500 Julio Urias debut dugout lineup card, signed by Urias.

On the low end was a 2014 dugout card from the Wilmington Blue Rocks for $12.

But as with any sports collectible purchase, buyers need to tread carefully when shopping on eBay. There are cards that are reasonably priced, especially given that you likely would not be able to find them anywhere else, but there are overpriced cards, too.

For example, in September 2022 eBay had 45 lineup cards listed at $1,000 or higher. But how many of them are worth those prices? While it is impossible to say, it is telling that none of the 161 lineup cards sold on eBay between July 23, 2022, and September 21, 2022, sold for more than $500.

Buyers also need to read descriptions and look at pictures carefully. As noted in the "Authenticity" chapter, descriptions may not always be accurate, either by mistake or purposefully.

Sellers are on their own to take pictures, write descriptions and package items. According to those interviewed for this book, if a seller does a good job with the above, returns and other buyer issues tend to be minimal.

Auction houses

Historically, auction houses have generally catered to those selling and buying higher priced sports memorabilia items.

That has changed to an extent in recent years with more auction houses entering the market, some targeting less expensive items. eBay, for example, has stepped into the space as it allows for auction-style items, including low-priced items.

Advantages of selling through a traditional auction house include:

- Most traditional auction houses, especially the good ones, will do much of the work for you, including writing descriptions, taking pictures,

This Tim Raines father/son batting order card was purchased via an auction house (courtesy Jeffrey Lazarus).

and promoting an item to their targeted customer lists and other marketing vehicles.
- The more unique or historic a lineup card is, the less likely it will get overlooked and fail to sell for what it is worth.
- If multiple bidders are interested in an item, it can drive the sale price up dramatically.

From a buyer's perspective, if you are interested in higher-end lineup cards, you almost have to keep an eye on auction houses.

On the negative side, buyers will likely pay more in additional fees—including buyer's premiums, shipping and handling, and insurance—than purchasing a lineup card through other outlets.

For sellers, read contracts carefully! There are all sorts of additional fees (e.g., authentication costs) and language (e.g., the auction house may include a clause covering their right to eventually sell the item at a lower price, which can impact how much profit you will end up with).

Sample of Lineup Cards Sold Through Auction Houses		
Item(s)	*Price*	*Year Sold*
1st All-Star Game (1933), American/National Lg cards	$120,000	2007
1995 Jeter MLB debut batting order cards	$23,400	2021
Cleveland dugout card for 2016 World Series Game 7	$14,650	2016
1974 Hank Aaron 715th HR batting order card	$11,700	2020
1985 World Series Game 7 batting order cards	$7,500	2020
Yankee batting order card from 1960 World Series Game 7	$5,377	2005
Braves batting order card from Hank Aaron 714th HR game	$4,056	2007
Jeter 2,000th-hit dugout card (signed/inscribed)	$2,520	2020
Bryce Harper MLB debut batting order card (signed)	$2,270	2012
1955 Brooklyn Dodgers batting order card	$720	2018
1991 Wilson Alvarez No-hitter batting order cards	$305	2020
Sources: various auction houses		

So, where is the best place to buy or sell a lineup card?

There is no one-size-fits-all answer as to the best place to buy or sell a lineup card. Take eBay versus auction houses, for example.

"They're very different animals," said Garfinkel.

If you are looking to sell something and cash out quickly, eBay, person-to-person or through a dealer are likely your best options. If you have time and are looking for top dollar for a high-end item, an auction house is probably the best fit.

For almost all buyers and sellers, the best approach is likely to use multiple outlets depending on the lineup card you are selling or the type of lineup card you are looking to buy at the time.

The Future of Lineup Cards

Lineup cards have become a part of baseball's fabric over the years. "The game does not start until the lineup cards are exchanged," said sports memorabilia collector Rick Levy.

But will that always be the case, or will the game reach a point where lineup cards are no longer necessary, at least not physical ones?

Unlike the NBA and NHL, MLB's lineup cards survived COVID-19

While physical lineup cards are dependent on baseball, baseball could survive without physical lineup cards.

This was proven during COVID-19 when lineups were electronically submitted to MLB headquarters. The lineups were then sent back to the stadium for batting order cards to be printed out and given to the managers and umpires before the traditional lineup card exchange at home plate.

If it were not for the home plate umpires needing to track changes on the cards, the batting order cards would not have been necessary.

While MLB went back to its normal routine, with batting order cards being exchanged at home plate before the game in 2022, the NBA and NHL did not. Both have chosen to forgo physical cards in favor of electronic lineup submission.

Baseball's official batting order cards have a few things in their favor for their continued use. First, even if not necessary, the pregame lineup card exchange has long been one of the game's foremost traditions, and traditions generally do not die easily.

Second, unlike the NBA and NHL, MLB's on-field officials keep track of lineup changes and other rules, and batting order cards are used for that purpose. But that might not always be the case.

"Baseball is slowly changing, but the one department that's been changing rapidly is the umpiring, what our responsibilities are, all that stuff," said former MLB umpire Jim Reynolds.

"I could see [the responsibilities] all changing, depending on what our job looks like five, 10 years from now," Reynolds continued. "You might have the home plate umpire communicating directly with someone in the press box. Or the managers [communicating with a fifth umpire]."

In this scenario, batting order cards may not be necessary as a fifth umpire in the press box would have other ways to track changes.

OFFICIAL BATTING ORDER
Baltimore Orioles   A

Monday, May 30, 2022

	ORIGINAL	POS.	CHANGE		ALSO ELIGIBLE
1	Hays, A	9	B		**POSITION PLAYERS**
			C		Mullins II, C
2	Mancini, T	DH	B		Odor, R
			C		Chirinos, R
3	Mountcastle, R	3	B		**PITCHERS**
			C		1. Akin, K
4	Santander, A	7	B		2. Perez, C
			C		3. Zimmermann, B
5	Urias, R	5	B		4. Baker, B
			C		5. Bautista, F
6	Rutschman, A	2	B		6. Bradish, K
			C		7. Diplan, M
7	Mateo, J	6	B	C	8. Gillaspie, L ②
			C	B	9. Krehbiel, J ①
8	McKenna, R	8	B		10. Lopez, J
			C		11. Lyles, J
9	Owings, C	4	B		12. Sedlock, C
			C		13. Tate, D ④
P	Wells, T	SP	B ABC		14. Wells, T (SP)
			C		
			D		
			E		

Version 1 - 5/30/2022 at 6:01 PM

MANAGER'S SIGNATURE

MLB went back to its traditional pre-game exchange of batting order cards in 2022. Of note, Adley Rutschman recorded his first career double in this May 30, 2022, game.

Dugout cards

Dugout lineup cards serve a different purpose than batting order cards, giving teams a quick snapshot view of the lineups and potential matchups. We have seen that MLB teams now sell the cards, too, so they generate revenue, albeit minimal in the big picture.

The former, in particular, is important.

"I think having that visual in the dugout matters," said Reynolds. "I don't know if it will be a lineup card or a video board in the dugout."

A video display in the dugout, perhaps touch-screen, could make practical sense for MLB teams. It would likely offer more information for managers and coaches than the current physical dugout card.

Safe, for now, but change will continue to be constant

For the time being, physical lineup cards will continue to maintain their role in baseball. As they have survived COVID-19, there is no immediate reason for any change. The biggest threat is to the batting order cards, if MLB were to move the role of tracking changes and notes regarding other rules from the home plate umpire to a person in the press box.

Reynolds does not know if, or when, that might happen, but he expects the umpire's role to continue to evolve, which would open the door for such a change.

"I've only been around for a short amount of time, 24 years in the big leagues, but this job has changed drastically over these past 24 years compared to the prior 24 years. And I can continue to see our department evolving," said Reynolds. "Our job has gone way beyond just calling balls and strikes. Now we're completely in charge of managing whatever baseball wants to implement, whether it be speeding up the game and those kinds of things."

Notes

Preface

1. "The Baseball Almanac Book Shelf, Baseball Book Reviews," *Baseball Almanac*, accessed March 27, 2022, https://www.baseball-almanac.com/bookmenu.shtml#:%7E:text=Over%20seventy%2Dthousand%20books%20have,what%20books%20deserve%20your%20money.

Lineup Cards Defined

1. *Official Baseball Rules, 2021 Edition*, Major League Baseball, accessed April 18, 2021, https://img.mlbstatic.com/mlb-images/image/upload/mlb/atcjzj9j7wrgvsm8wnjq.pdf.

How to Read a Lineup Card

1. "Minnesota Twins vs Chicago White Sox Box Score: April 7, 2017," Baseball Reference, accessed February 20, 2022, https://www.baseball-reference.com/boxes/CHA/CHA201704070.shtml.
2. "MLB Authentication lookup, hologram #HZ324292," Major League Baseball, accessed May 7, 2022, retrieved from https://www.mlb.com/official-information/authentication.

The History of Lineup Cards

1. "Baseball," *The New York Clipper*, April 2, 1881, retrieved from www.fultonhistory.com.
2. "Should Have Held On," *The Saint Paul Daily Globe*, September 21, 1887, retrieved from https://chroniclingamerica.loc.gov/.
3. "Base Ball of the Future: Meeting of the Joint Committee on the Playing Rules," *Press and Daily Dakotaian*, November 15, 1887. Retrieved from https://chroniclingamerica.loc.gov/.
4. Henry Chadwick, *Spalding's Baseball Guide and Official League Book for 1889*, A. G. Spalding & Bros., accessed September 15, 2021, retrieved from https://books.google.com/.
5. Bruce Donnelly, "Cleveland player manager Nap Lajoie reviews his lineup card before handing it to an umpire during a game in 1907," Facebook "Vintage Baseball" group post, November 5, 2022, https://www.facebook.com/search/top?q=%22lineup%20card%22%20%22donnelly.
6. *Spalding's Official Baseball Guide, 1910*, A. G. Spalding & Bros., accessed September 15, 2021, retrieved from https://chroniclingamerica.loc.gov/.
7. "Cub Sydelights," *The Chicago Daily Tribune*, Wednesday, April 23, 1913, retrieved from www.fultonhistory.com.
8. "Player Bats Out of Turn Four Times in Game," *The Calumet News*, August 27, 1914, retrieved from https://chroniclingamerica.loc.gov/.
9. *The Reach official American League base ball guide, 1914–1915*, A. J. Reach Co., accessed September 22, 2021, retrieved from https://library.si.edu/digital-library/book/reachofficialame19141phil,
10. "Nats May Regain 1st Division in Bargain Show Here Today," *The Sunday Star*, July 1, 1928, retrieved from https://chroniclingamerica.loc.gov/.
11. "Rare 30's Senators Lineup Card Signed Walter Johnson, HOF, 1 Of '5 Immortal's,'" WorthPoint, accessed November 2, 2022, https://www.worthpoint.com/worthopedia/30-senators-lineup-card-signed-walter-1728452785.
12. "Lot Number 137," Hunt Auctions, accessed November 28, 2022, https://huntauctions.com/live/imageviewer_online.cfm?auction_num=31&lot_num=137&lot_qual=
13. (cavaliercards), "Connie Mack Lineup Card" thread, Net54baseball.com, September 2, 2018, https://www.net54baseball.com/showthread.php?p=1809771.
14. "1960 New York Yankees World Series Game Seven Line-up Card from the Casey Stengel Collection," Heritage Auctions, accessed June 20, 2022, https://sports.ha.com/itm/baseball/1960-new-york-yankees-world-series-game-seven-line-up-card-from-the-casey-stengel-collection-to-gaze-upon-this-amazing-his/a/703-1-9648.s?ic4=ListView-ShortDescription-071515; "1960 World Series Game 7 Line-Up Carbon Sheet from the Casey Stengel Collection," Heritage Auctions, accessed June 20, 2022, https://sports.ha.com/itm/baseball/1960-world-series-game-7-line-up-card-carbon-sheet-from-the-casey-stengel-collection-the-suffering-ended-

with-a-ninth-inni/a/45111-12256.s?ic4=-ListView-ShortDescription-071515.

15. "Will McEnaney Stats," *Baseball Almanac*, accessed November 1, 2022, https://www.baseball-almanac.com/players/player.php?p=mcenawi01.

16. "Official lineup card signed by manager Red Schoendienst for game with the St. Louis Cardinals and Los Angeles Dodgers at Dodger Stadium," Alamy, accessed October 24, 2022, https://www.alamy.com/official-lineup-card-signed-by-manager-red-schoendienst-for-game-with-the-st-louis-cardinals-and-los-angeles-dodgers-at-dodger-stadium-circa-1969-image328806312.html?imageid=0C759CAC-51AE-4E6F-9931-ED79F469D4B5&p=350861&pn=1&searchId=6a536b4e97e40d0e0e5f361a5ea1b5b2&searchtype=0.

17. "Close Win Out West: 1972 Lineup Card," Mets Virtual Vault, accessed November 10, 2022, https://www.metsheritage.com/item/a-close-win-out-west/?postId=2120.

18. (RetroReaction), "Vintage 1995 Oakland Athletics Game Used Lineup Card," Etsy, accessed November 12, 2022, https://www.etsy.com/listing/1005493180/vintage-1995-oakland-athletics-game-used.

19. "Mound Visit," Major League Baseball Glossary, Major League Baseball, accessed November 15, 2022, https://www.mlb.com/glossary/rules/mound-visit.

20. "Three-batter Minimum," Major League Baseball Glossary, accessed November 15, 2022, https://www.mlb.com/glossary/rules/three-batter-minimum.

21. "Automatic Runner," Major League Baseball Glossary, accessed November 15, 2022, https://www.mlb.com/glossary/rules/designated-runner.

22. "26-man Roster," Major League Baseball Glossary, accessed November 15, 2022, https://www.mlb.com/glossary/transactions/26-man-roster.

23. "Designated Hitter Rule," Major League Baseball Glossary, accessed December 2, 2022, https://www.mlb.com/glossary/rules/designated-hitter-rule.

The Use of Lineup Cards in Other Sports

1. "2010 NHL Winter Classic Line-up Card!!," NHL Auctions Blog, January 25, 2010, https://nhlauctions.typepad.com/nhlauctions/2010/01/2010-nhl-winter-classic-lineup-card.html.

2. "Boston Bruins Framed Original Line-Up Cards from June 9, 2019 Vs. St. Louis Blues—Stanley Cup Final Game 6," NHL Auctions, accessed July 30, 2022, https://auctions.nhl.com/iSynApp/auctionDisplay.action?sid=1100803&auctionId=2709277.

3. "Boston Bruins Framed Original Line-up Cards from January 18, 2018 Vs. New York Islanders—Patrice Bergeron 3rd NHL Hat Trick," NHL Auctions, accessed July 30, 2022, https://auctions.nhl.com/iSynApp/auctionDisplay.action?sid=1100803&auctionId=2591600&isynsharedsession=rlB5zr3shXVWGQtq_O0F8HpR912d8NugDvNuuqxLirtEdaSACl02r4aCDzYhNvUm.

4. "2021 NCAA Football Rules and Interpretations," NCAA Publications, accessed May 4, 2022, https://www.ncaapublications.com/p-4627-2021-ncaa-football-rules-and-interpretations.aspx.

5. "NCAA Basketball 2021–2022 Men's Basketball Rules Book," NCAA Publications, accessed May 4, 2022: https://www.ncaapublications.com/productdownloads/BR22.pdf.

6. "NCAA Soccer 2022 and 2023 Soccer Rules Book," NCAA Publications, accessed May 4, 2022, https://www.ncaapublications.com/productdownloads/SO23.pdf.

7. "Season 2021/2022, Team Sheet and Pre-Match Briefing," Premier League Handbook, accessed May 1, 2022, https://resources.premierleague.com/premierleague/document/2021/11/30/235538a5-3927-4489-9812-7b426b80e6e1/PL_Handbook_2021_22_DIGITAL_29.11.21.pdf.

8. "Fergie's first United team sheet for sale," ESPN, June 17, 2013, https://www.espn.com/soccer/news/story/_/id/1478214/fergie-first-ever-united-team-sheet-goes-auction.

9. Charlie Skillen, "Fergie's first United team-sheet from 1986 sells for £20k at auction... six times the asking price," *Mail Online*, June 23, 2013, https://www.dailymail.co.uk/sport/football/article-2346770/Sir-Alex-Fergusons-Manchester-United-team-sheet-fetches-20k-auction.html.

Famous Lineup Cards

1. Rich Mueller, "All Star Game Auction Includes Ruth World Series Bat," *Sports Collectors Digest*, June 14, 2007, https://www.sportscollectorsdaily.com/all-star-game-auction-includes-ruth-world-series-bat/.

2. "Lot Number 137," Hunt Auctions, accessed November 28, 2022, https://huntauctions.com/live/imageviewer_online.cfm?auction_num=31&lot_num=137&lot_qual=.

3. Rich Mueller, "Ruth Bat Brings $322K in All Star Auction," *Sports Collectors Digest*, July 10, 2007, https://www.sportscollectorsdaily.com/ruth-bat-brings-322k-in-all-star-auction/.

4. "1933 Cleveland Indians and Philadelphia A's Lineup Cards Signed by Walter Johnson and Connie Mack," Robert Edward Auctions, accessed September 4, 2022, https://robertedwardauctions.com/auction/2020/spring/1537/1933-cleveland-indians-and-philadelphia-as-lineup-cards-signed-by-walter-johnson-and-connie-mack.

5. Jon Morgan, "Regan allowed to sell Ripken

card," *The Baltimore Sun*," April 19, 2000, https://www.baltimoresun.com/news/bs-xpm-2000-04-19-0004190143-story.html.

6. "1995 Baltimore Orioles Dugout Lineup Card and Pitching Chart from Cal Ripken, Jr.'s Record-Setting 2,131st Consecutive Game," Robert Edwards Auctions, accessed June 27, 2022, https://robertedwardauctions.com/auction/2014/spring/1256/1995-baltimore-orioles-dugout-lineup-card-pitching-chart-cal-ripken-jrs-record-setting-2131st-consecutive-game.

7. "Auction Item Details, Lot 316," Hunt Auctions, accessed November 28, 2022, https://huntauctions.com/live/imageviewer.cfm?auction_num=88&lot_num=316&lot_qual=.

8. Ruth Sadler, "Ruth Museum's display has a hot number: 2,131," *The Baltimore Sun*, March 24, 1996, https://www.baltimoresun.com/news/bs-xpm-1996-03-24-1996084152-story.html.

9. Jon Morgan, "For sale: the Lineup card from Ripken's record game ex-Orioles manager sets auction items from No. 2,131," *The Baltimore Sun*, December 7, 1998, https://www.baltimoresun.com/news/bs-xpm-1998-12-07-1998341062-story.html.

10. "Ripken Lineup Card Battled Over," Associated Press, December 21, 1998, https://apnews.com/article/82264d813618e2e99df4a279d831f67d.

11. Jon Morgan, "$35,650 bid for Ripken lineup card, judge will determine if Baltimore contractor is allowed to buy item," *The Baltimore Sun*, December 10, 1998, https://www.baltimoresun.com/news/bs-xpm-1998-12-10-1998344096-story.html.

12. "Ripken Lineup Card Dispute Settled," Associated Press, April 19, 2000, https://apnews.com/article/d7e213cb01aba312e354adf1a0cff890.

13. "Obituaries, Warren Fitzgibbon," *The Connection*, April 7, 2005, http://www.connectionnewspapers.com/news/2005/apr/07/obituaries/.

14. "Auction Item Details, Lot 317," Hunt Auctions, accessed November 28, 2022, https://huntauctions.com/live/imageviewer.cfm?auction_num=88&lot_num=317&lot_qual=.

15. "Auction Item Details, Lot 316," Hunt Auctions, accessed November 28, 2022, https://huntauctions.com/live/imageviewer.cfm?auction_num=88&lot_num=316&lot_qual=.

16. "2004 World Series Boston Red Sox Vs. St. Louis Cardinals Lineup Card, Pricing & History," Worthpoint, accessed October 23, 2021, https://www.worthpoint.com/worthopedia/2004-world-series-boston-red-sox-vs-1880000280.

17. "Oct. 4, 2022—New York Yankees, Texas Rangers Game-Used Dugout Lineup Scorecard from Aaron Judge 62nd Home Run Hit—MLB Authenticated, Fanatics," Goldin Auctions, accessed December 18, 2022, https://goldin.co/item/oct-4-2022-texas-rangers-game-used-dugout-lineup-scorecard-from-aaron9a9gp

18. "New York Yankees and Fanatics partner on marketing of excusive game-used Yankees memorabilia," Major League Baseball, September 26, 2019, https://www.mlb.com/press-release/press-release-yankees-fanatics-partner.

19. Bob Keisser, "The Lederer Tree," *San Gabriel Valley Tribune*, last updated August 30, 2017, https://www.sgvtribune.com/2010/09/08/the-lederer-tree/.

20. "Ripken Lineup Card Dispute Settled," Associated Press, April 19, 2000, https://apnews.com/article/d7e213cb01aba312e354adf1a0cff890.

21. "Obituaries, Warren Fitzgibbon," *The Connection*, April 7, 2005, http://www.connectionnewspapers.com/news/2005/apr/07/obituaries/.

22. "Auction Item Details, Lot 317," Hunt Auctions, accessed November 28, 2022, https://huntauctions.com/live/imageviewer.cfm?auction_num=88&lot_num=317&lot_qual=.

23. "2004 World Series Boston Red Sox Vs. St. Louis Cardinals Lineup Card, Pricing & History," Worthpoint, accessed October 23, 2021, https://www.worthpoint.com/worthopedia/2004-world-series-boston-red-sox-vs-1880000280.

24. "Auction Item Details, Lot 316," Hunt Auctions, accessed November 28, 2022, https://huntauctions.com/live/imageviewer.cfm?auction_num=88&lot_num=316&lot_qual=.

25. "Oct. 4, 2022—New York Yankees, Texas Rangers Game-Used Dugout Lineup Scorecard from Aaron Judge 62nd Home Run Hit—MLB Authenticated, Fanatics," Goldin Auctions, accessed December 18, 2022, https://goldin.co/item/oct-4-2022-texas-rangers-game-used-dugout-lineup-scorecard-from-aaron9a9gp

26. "New York Yankees and Fanatics partner on marketing of excusive game-used Yankees memorabilia," Major League Baseball, September 26, 2019, https://www.mlb.com/press-release/press-release-yankees-fanatics-partner.

27. Bob Keisser, "The Lederer Tree," *San Gabriel Valley Tribune*, last updated August 30, 2017, https://www.sgvtribune.com/2010/09/08/the-lederer-tree/.

Minor League Lineup Cards

1. Samantha Burkett, "Artifacts Tell Story of Record-Setting 33-Inning Game From 1981," National Baseball Hall of Fame, accessed November 2, 2022, https://baseballhall.org/discover/short-stops/33-inning-game.

2. "Tom Kayser Collection on the Texas League, 1895–2019: A Guide to the Collection," Texas Archival Resources Online, accessed December 4, 2022, https://txarchives.org/smu/finding_aids/00396.xml##series1.

The Lineup Card Collectors

1. Andrew Simon, "Rays' all-lefty lineup a first in MLB history," Major League Baseball News, September 11, 2020, https://www.mlb.com/news/rays-all-left-handed-lineup-makes-history.
2. "Baseball's first openly gay player makes debut—and makes history: 'It's who I am,'" *The Guardian*, June 26, 2015, https://www.theguardian.com/sport/2015/jun/26/baseball-history-sean-conroy-sonoma-stompers.
3. "Florida State's Martin meets wins milestone with grace," NCAA News, May 6, 2018, https://www.ncaa.com/news/baseball/article/2018-05-06/college-baseball-florida-states-mike-martin-meets-record-setting.
4. Zack Hample, "About," accessed November 7, 2022, https://www.zackhample.com/about.
5. Zack Hample, "Lineup cards," accessed November 7, 2022, https://www.zackhample.com/lineupcards.
6. "The Famous 'Buckner Ball' from the 1986 World Series, Game Six," Heritage Auctions, accessed December 15, 2021, https://sports.ha.com/itm/baseball-collectibles/balls/the-famous-buckner-ball-from-the-1986-world-series-game-six/a/7051-80987.s.
7. Tom O'Reilly, "Collecting History via MLB Lineup Cards," *Sports Collectors Digest*, October 8, 2020, https://sportscollectorsdigest.com/tag/mlb-lineup-cards.
8. Tom O'Reilly, "Collecting History via MLB Lineup Cards," *Sports Collectors Digest*, October 8, 2020, https://sportscollectorsdigest.com/tag/mlb-lineup-cards.
9. "Lot #158: 1988 World Series Game 1 National League And American League Official Lineup Cards From Kirk Gibson's Historic Walk Off Home Run From Tommy Lasorda Collection," Goldin Auctions, accessed February 12, 2022, https://goldinauctions.com/1988_World_Series_Game_1_National_League_And_Ameri-LOT45821.aspx.
10. Tom Larwin, "October 1, 1978: Gaylord Perry records 3,000th career strikeout and Ozzie Smith performs his first pregame backflip," Society for American Baseball Research, accessed July 21, 2022, https://sabr.org/gamesproj/game/october-1-1978-gaylord-perry-gets-3000th-career-strikeout-and-ozzie-smith-performs-his-first-pregame-backflip/.
11. "Cal Ripken, Jr.'s 3000th Career Hit Game Used, Signed & Inscribed Louisville Slugger P72 Model Bat From 4/15/2000 vs. Minnesota," Goldin Auctions, accessed June 11, 2022, https://goldinauctions.com/Cal_Ripken_Jr__s_3000TH_Career_Hit_Game_Used__Sign-LOT72646.aspx.

Signatures/Autographs on Lineup Cards

1. "Hall of Famers Who Also Managed," National Baseball Hall of Fame, accessed October 12, 2022, https://baseballhall.org/discover-more/stories/hall-of-famer-facts/hall-of-famers-who-managed.
2. "2010 Mike Trout Pre-Rookie and Cedar Rapids Kernels vs. Peoria Chiefs Team-Signed Game Used Lineup Card (PSA) Auction: Spring Classic 2021," Lelands, accessed August 3, 2022, https://lelands.com/bids/2010-mike-trout-pre-rookie-and-cedar-rapids-kernels-vs-peoria-chiefs-team-signed-game-used-lineup-card-psa.
3. Author source missing

Authenticity: Caveat Emptor ("Let the Buyer Beware")

1. "What Not to Collect in Sports Memorabilia," Chubb Corp., accessed October 14, 2022, https://www.chubb.com/us-en/individuals-families/resources/what-not-to-collect-in-sports-memorabilia.html#:~:text=The%20FBI%20estimates%20that,signature%20and%20a%20bogus%20one.
2. "Significant July 11, 1914 Babe Ruth First Major League Game 'Lineup Card' (Tommy Connolly Collection) (PSA/DNA)," Christie's, accessed July 27, 2022, https://www.christies.com/en/lot/lot-6296497.
3. Jeff Lazarus (Topnotchsy), "Aaron 714 Lineup Card" thread, Net54baseball.com, February 11, 2020, https://www.net54baseball.com/showthread.php?t=279216.
4. Jon Birger, "A Sox Suit: For Love or Money?" *Fortune Magazine*, January 11, 2006, https://archive.fortune.com/magazines/fortune/fortune_archive/2006/01/23/8367042/index.htm.
5. Jon Morgan, "Collector disappointed that it's not the original: $35,650 bid for Ripken card is withdrawn," *The Baltimore Sun*, December 17, 1998, https://www.baltimoresun.com/news/bs-xpm-1998-12-17-1998351014-story.html.
6. "Ripken Lineup Card Dispute Settled," Associated Press, April 19, 2000, https://apnews.com/article/d7e213cb01aba312e354adf1a0cff890.
7. Jon Morgan, "Regan allowed to sell Ripken card," *The Baltimore Sun*, April 19, 2000, https://www.baltimoresun.com/news/bs-xpm-2000-04-19-0004190143-story.html.
8. "MLB Authentication lookup, hologram #JD218519," Major League Baseball, retrieved from https://www.mlb.com/official-information/authentication.
9. "MLB Authentication lookup, hologram #JD357908," Major League Baseball, accessed May 7, 2022, retrieved from https://www.mlb.com/official-information/authentication.
10. "Significant July 11, 1914 Babe Ruth First Major League Game 'Lineup Card' (Tommy Connolly Collection) (PSA/DNA)," Christie's, accessed July 27, 2022, https://www.christies.com/en/lot/lot-6296497.

11. "PSA/DNA Certification #84262381," PSA Authentication & Grading Services, accessed January 17, 2022, https://www.psacard.com/cert/84262381.

12. "Completed Live Auctions, Items for the Auction of November 12th, 2005, Lot #268," Hunt Auctions, accessed September 14, 2022, https://www.huntauctions.com/online/imageviewer.cfm?auction_num=24&lot_num=268&lot_qual=.

13. "Gameday: Cleveland Naps 3, Boston Red Sox 4, Box Score: July 11, 1914," Major League Baseball, accessed September 13, 2022, https://www.mlb.com/gameday/naps-vs-red-sox/1914/07/11/86718/final/box.

Lineup Cards: What Are They Worth, and Where to Buy/Sell

1. Tom O'Reilly, "Collecting History via MLB Lineup Cards," *Sports Collectors Digest*, October 8, 2020, https://sportscollectorsdigest.com/tag/mlb-lineup-cards.

2. Tom O'Reilly, "Collecting History via MLB Lineup Cards," *Sports Collectors Digest*, October 8, 2020, https://sportscollectorsdigest.com/tag/mlb-lineup-cards.

3. Tom O'Reilly, "Collecting History via MLB Lineup Cards," *Sports Collectors Digest*, October 8, 2020, https://sportscollectorsdigest.com/tag/mlb-lineup-cards.

4. Tom O'Reilly, "Collecting History via MLB Lineup Cards," *Sports Collectors Digest*, October 8, 2020, https://sportscollectorsdigest.com/tag/mlb-lineup-cards.

5. Tom O'Reilly, "Collecting History via MLB Lineup Cards," *Sports Collectors Digest*, October 8, 2020, https://sportscollectorsdigest.com/tag/mlb-lineup-cards.

6. Jon Birger, "A Sox Suit: For Love or Money?" *Fortune Magazine*, January 11, 2006, https://archive.fortune.com/magazines/fortune/fortune_archive/2006/01/23/8367042/index.htm.

7. Rich Mueller, "Ruth Bat Brings $322K in All Star Auction," *Sports Collectors Digest*, July 10, 2007, https://www.sportscollectorsdaily.com/ruth-bat-brings-322k-in-all-star-auction/.

8. Tom O'Reilly, "Collecting History via MLB Lineup Cards," *Sports Collectors Digest*, October 8, 2020, https://sportscollectorsdigest.com/tag/mlb-lineup-cards.

9. "Lot #604, 2015 Clayton Kershaw 100th Win Game Used Line Up Card and Ticket Stub (MLB Authenticated)," Goldin Auctions, accessed November 6, 2022, https://goldinauctions.com/-2015_clayton_kershaw_100th_win_game_used_line_up_c-lot21776.aspx.

10. "2020 July 26 Sunday Sports Collectibles Weekly Online Auction #152030, Lot #44141," Heritage Auctions, accessed August 14, 2022, https://sports.ha.com/itm/baseball/-derek-jeter-signed-game-used-lineup-card-2-000th-hit-/a/152030-44141.s?ic4=GalleryView-Thumbnail-071515.

11. "Cal Ripken, Jr.'s 3000TH Career Hit Game Used, Signed & Inscribed Louisville Slugger P72 Model Bat From 4/15/2000 vs. Minnesota (PSA/DNA GU 10 & Ripken LOA), LOT #430," Goldin Auctions, accessed March 18, 2022, https://goldinauctions.com/Cal_Ripken_Jr__s_3000TH_Career_Hit_Game_Used__Sign-LOT72646.aspx.

12. "Cal Ripken, Jr. 3000th Career Hit Game Minnesota Twins Dugout Line-Up Card from 4/15/00 (Ripken LOA), Lot #532," Goldin Auctions, accessed March 18, 2022, https://goldinauctions.com/Cal_Ripken_Jr__3000th_Career_Hit_Game_Minnesota_Tw-LOT69757.aspx.

Bibliography

"Auction Item Details, Lot 316." Hunt Auctions. Accessed November 28, 2022. https://huntauctions.com/live/imageviewer.cfm?auction_num=88&lot_num=316&lot_qual=.

"Auction Item Details, Lot 317." Hunt Auctions. Accessed November 28, 2022. https://huntauctions.com/live/imageviewer.cfm?auction_num=88&lot_num=317&lot_qual=.

"Automatic Runner." Major League Baseball Glossary. Major League Baseball. Accessed November 15, 2022. https://www.mlb.com/glossary/rules/designated-runner.

"Base Ball of the Future: Meeting of the Joint Committee on the Playing Rules." *Press and Daily Dakotaian,* November 15, 1887. Retrieved from https://chroniclingamerica.loc.gov/.

"Baseball." *The New York Clipper,* April 2, 1881. Retrieved from www.fultonhistory.com.

"The Baseball Almanac Book Shelf, Baseball Book Reviews." *Baseball Almanac.* Accessed March 27, 2022. https://www.baseball-almanac.com/bookmenu.shtml#:%7E:text=Over%20seventy%2Dthousand%20books%20have,what%20books%20deserve%20your%20money.

"Baseball, Florida State's Martin meets wins milestone with grace." *NCAA News,* May 6, 2018. https://www.ncaa.com/news/baseball/article/2018-05-06/college-baseball-florida-states-mike-martin-meets-record-setting.

"Baseball's first openly gay player makes debut—and makes history: 'It's who I am.'" *The Guardian,* June 26, 2015. https://www.theguardian.com/sport/2015/jun/26/baseball-history-sean-conroy-sonoma-stompers.

Birger, Jon. "A Sox Suit: For Love or Money?" *Fortune Magazine,* January 11, 2006. https://archive.fortune.com/magazines/fortune/fortune_archive/2006/01/23/8367042/index.htm.

"Boston Bruins Framed Original Line-Up Cards from January 18, 2018 Vs. New York Islanders—Patrice Bergeron 3rd NHL Hat Trick." NHL Auctions. Accessed July 30, 2022. https://auctions.nhl.com/iSynApp/auctionDisplay.action?sid=1100803&auctionId=2591600&isynsharedsession=rlB5zr3shXVWGQtq_O0F8HpR912d8NugDvNuuqxLirtEdaSACl02r4aCDzYhNvUm.

"Boston Bruins Framed Original Line-Up Cards from June 9, 2019 Vs. St. Louis Blues—Stanley Cup Final Game 6." NHL Auctions. Accessed July 30, 2022. https://auctions.nhl.com/iSynApp/auctionDisplay.action?sid=1100803&auctionId=2709227.

"Boston Red Sox 4, Cleveland Naps 3." Retrosheet. Accessed September 13, 2022. https://www.retrosheet.org/boxesetc/1914/B07110BOS1914.htm.

Burkett, Samantha. "Artifacts Tell Story of Record-Setting 33-Inning Game from 1981." National Baseball Hall of Fame. Accessed November 2, 2022. https://baseballhall.org/discover/short-stops/33-inning-game.

"Cal Ripken, Jr. 3000th Career Hit Game Minnesota Twins Dugout Line-Up Card from 4/15/00 (Ripken LOA), Lot #532." Goldin Auctions. Accessed March 18, 2022. https://goldinauctions.com/Cal_Ripken_Jr__3000th_Career_Hit_Game_Minnesota_Tw-LOT69757.aspx.

"Cal Ripken, Jr.'s 3000TH Career Hit Game Used, Signed & Inscribed Louisville Slugger P72 Model Bat From 4/15/2000 vs. Minnesota (PSA/DNA GU 10 & Ripken LOA), LOT #430."

Calvello, Michael. Interview. September 5, 2022.

Campbell, David. Interview. November 30, 2021.

(cavaliercards). "Connie Mack Lineup Card" thread. Net54baseball, September 2, 2018. https://www.net54baseball.com/showthread.php?p=1809771.

Chadwick, Henry. *Spalding's Baseball Guide and Official League Book for 1889.* A. G. Spalding & Bros. Accessed September 15, 2021. https://books.google.com/.

"Cleveland Naps Vs. Boston Red Sox, July 11, 1914 Box Score." *Baseball Almanac.* Accessed September 13, 2022. https://www.baseball-almanac.com/box-scores/boxscore.php?boxid=191407110BOS.

"Close Win Out West: 1972 Lineup Card." Mets Virtual Vault. Accessed November 10, 2022. https://www.metsheritage.com/item/a-close-win-out-west/?postId=2120.

"Completed Live Auctions, Items for the Auction of November 12th, 2005, Lot #268."

Bibliography

Hunt Auctions. Accessed September 14, 2022. https://www.huntauctions.com/online/imageviewer.cfm?auction_num=24&lot_num=268&lot_qual=

"Cub Sydelights." *The Chicago Daily Tribune.* Wednesday, April 23, 1913. Retrieved from www.fultonhistory.com.

Dellinger, Dusty. Interview. June 22, 2022.

"Designated Hitter Rule." Major League Baseball Glossary. Accessed December 2, 2022. https://www.mlb.com/glossary/rules/designated-hitter-rule.

Donnelly, Bruce. "Cleveland player manager Nap Lajoie reviews his lineup card before handing it to an umpire during a game in 1907." Facebook "Vintage Baseball" group post, November 5, 2022. https://www.facebook.com/search/top?q=%22lineup%20card%22%20%22donnelly.

Dwyer, Brian. Interview. June 10, 2020.

"The Famous 'Buckner Ball' from the 1986 World Series, Game Six." Heritage Auctions. Accessed December 15, 2021. https://sports.ha.com/itm/baseball-collectibles/balls/the-famous-buckner-ball-from-the-1986-world-series-game-six/a/7051-80987.s.

"Fergie's first United team sheet for sale." ESPN. June 17, 2013. https://www.espn.com/soccer/news/story/_/id/1478214/fergie-first-ever-united-team-sheet-goes-auction.

"Gameday: Cleveland Naps 3, Boston Red Sox 4, Box Score: July 11, 1914." Major League Baseball. Accessed September 13, 2022. https://www.mlb.com/gameday/naps-vs-red-sox/1914/07/11/86718/final/box.

Garfinkel, Jeff. Interviews. January 4, 2022, and September 19, 2022.

Goldin Auctions. Accessed March 18, 2022. HTTPS://GOLDINAUCTIONS.COM/CAL_RIPKEN_JR__S_3000TH_CAREER_HIT_GAME_USED__SIGN-LOT72646.ASPX.

Goldstein, Aaron. Interview. October 25, 2022.

Haelig, Bill. Interview. July 18, 2022.

"Hall of Famers Who Also Managed." National Baseball Hall of Fame. Accessed October 12, 2022. https://baseballhall.org/discover-more/stories/hall-of-famer-facts/hall-of-famers-who-managed.

Hample, Zack. Interview. December 13, 2015.

Hirschbeck, John. Interview. January 11, 2022.

Ivy, Chris. Interview. June 5, 2020.

Johnson, Erynn. Interview. July 25, 2022.

Kayser, Tom. Interview. June 11, 2022.

Keisser, Bob. "The Lederer Tree." *San Gabriel Valley Tribune.* Last updated August 30, 2017. https://www.sgvtribune.com/2010/09/08/the-lederer-tree/.

Key, Nik. Interview. October 15, 2021.

Klett, Michael. Interview. November 7, 2022.

Larwin, Tom. "October 1, 1978: Gaylord Perry records 3,000th career strikeout and Ozzie Smith performs his first pregame backflip." Society for American Baseball Research. Accessed July 21, 2022. https://sabr.org/gamesproj/game/october-1-1978-gaylord-perry-gets-3000th-career-strikeout-and-ozzie-smith-performs-his-first-pregame-backflip/.

Lazarus, Jeffrey. Interviews. May 20, 2020, and September 4, 2022.

Lazarus, Jeffrey (Topnotchsy). "Aaron 714 Lineup Card" thread. Net54baseball. February 11, 2020. https://www.net54baseball.com/showthread.php?t=279216.

Levy, Rick. Interview. November 6, 2022.

"Lot #158: 1988 World Series Game 1 National League and American League Official Lineup Cards from Kirk Gibson's Historic Walk Off Home Run from Tommy Lasorda Collection." Goldin Auctions. Accessed February 12, 2022. https://goldinauctions.com/1988_World_Series_Game_1_National_League_And_Ameri-LOT45821.aspx.

"Lot Number 137." Hunt Auctions. Accessed November 28, 2022. https://huntauctions.com/live/imageviewer_online.cfm?auction_num=31&lot_num=137&lot_qual=.

"Lot #604, 2015 Clayton Kershaw 100th Win Game Used Line Up Card and Ticket Stub (MLB Authenticated)." Goldin Auctions. Accessed November 6, 2022. https://goldinauctions.com/2015_clayton_kershaw_100th_win_game_used_line_up_c-lot21776.aspx.

Lucas, Sky. Interview. November 30, 2021.

Meza, Scott. Interview. July 30, 2022.

Miller, Kenneth. Interview. July 11, 2022.

"Minnesota Twins vs. Chicago White Sox Box Score: April 7, 2017." Baseball Reference. Accessed February 20, 2022. https://www.baseball-reference.com/boxes/CHA/CHA201704070.shtml.

"MLB Authentication lookup, hologram #HZ324292." Major League Baseball. Accessed May 7, 2022. Retrieved from https://www.mlb.com/official-information/authentication.

"MLB Authentication lookup, hologram #JD357908." Major League Baseball. Retrieved from https://www.mlb.com/official-information/authentication.

"MLB Authentication lookup, hologram #JD218519." Major League Baseball. Retrieved from https://www.mlb.com/official-information/authentication.

Morgan, Jon. "For sale: The Lineup card from Ripken's record game Ex-Orioles manager sets auction items from No. 2,131." *The Baltimore Sun*, December 7, 1998. https://www.baltimoresun.com/news/bs-xpm-1998-12-07-1998341062-story.html.

Morgan, Jon. "Regan allowed to sell Ripken card." *The Baltimore Sun*, April 19, 2000. https://www.baltimoresun.com/news/bs-xpm-2000-04-19-0004190143-story.html.

Morgan, Jon. "$35,650 bid for Ripken card is withdrawn; Collector disappointed that it's not the original." *The Baltimore Sun.* December 17, 1998. https://www.baltimoresun.com/news/bs-xpm-1998-12-17-1998351014-story.html.

"Mound Visit." Major League Baseball Glossary. Accessed November 15, 2022. https://www.mlb.com/glossary/rules/mound-visit.

Mueller, Rich. "All Star Game Auction Includes Ruth World Series Bat." *Sports Collectors Digest.* June 14, 2007. https://www.sportscollectorsdaily.com/all-star-game-auction-includes-ruth-world-series-bat/.

Mueller, Rich. "Ruth Bat Brings $322K in All Star Auction." *Sports Collectors Digest.* July 10, 2007. https://www.sportscollectorsdaily.com/ruth-bat-brings-322k-in-all-star-auction/.

Narron, Jerry. Interview. April 15, 2022.

"Nats May Regain 1st Division In Bargain Show Here Today." *The Sunday Star,* July 1, 1928. Retrieved from https://chroniclingamerica.loc.gov/.

"NCAA Basketball 2021–2022 Men's Basketball Rules Book." NCAA Publications. Accessed May 4, 2022. https://www.ncaapublications.com/productdownloads/BR22.pdf.

"NCAA Soccer 2022 and 2023 Soccer Rules Book." NCAA Publications. Accessed May 4, 2022. https://www.ncaapublications.com/productdownloads/SO23.pdf.

"New York Yankees and Fanatics partner on marketing of excusive game-used Yankees memorabilia." Major League Baseball. September 26, 2019. https://www.mlb.com/press-release/press-release-yankees-fanatics-partner.

"Obituaries, Warren Fitzgibbon." *The Connection,* April 7, 2005. http://www.connectionnewspapers.com/news/2005/apr/07/obituaries/.

"Oct. 4, 2022—New York Yankees, Texas Rangers Game-Used Dugout Lineup Scorecard from Aaron Judge 62nd Home Run Hit—MLB Authenticated, Fanatics." Goldin Auctions. Accessed December 18, 2022. https://goldin.co/item/oct-4-2022-texas-rangers-game-used-dugout-lineup-scorecard-from-aaron9a9gp.

"Official Baseball Rules, 2021 Edition." Major League Baseball. Accessed April 18, 2021. https://img.mlbstatic.com/mlb-images/image/upload/mlb/atcjzj9j7wrgvsm8wnjq.pdf.

"Official lineup card signed by manager Red Schoendienst for game with the St. Louis Cardinals and Los Angeles Dodgers at Dodger Stadium." Alamy. Accessed October 24, 2022. https://www.alamy.com/official-lineup-card-signed-by-manager-red-schoendienst-for-game-with-the-st-louis-cardinals-and-los-angeles-dodgers-at-dodger-stadium-circa-1969-image328806312.html?imageid=0C759CAC-51AE-4E6F-9931-ED79F469D4B5&p=350861&pn=1&searchId=6a536b4e97e40d0e0e5f361a5ea1b5b2&searchtype=0.

"1995 Baltimore Orioles Dugout Lineup Card and Pitching Chart from Cal Ripken, Jr.'s Record-Setting 2,131st Consecutive Game." Robert Edwards Auctions. Accessed June 27, 2022. https://robertedwardauctions.com/auction/2014/spring/1256/1995-baltimore-orioles-dugout-lineup-card-pitching-chart-cal-ripken-jrs-record-setting-2131st-consecutive-game.

"1960 New York Yankees World Series Game Seven Line-up Card from the Casey Stengel Collection." Heritage Auctions. Accessed June 20, 2022. https://sports.ha.com/itm/baseball/1960-new-york-yankees-world-series-game-seven-line-up-card-from-the-casey-stengel-collection-to-gaze-upon-this-amazing-his/a/703-19648.s?ic4=ListView-ShortDescription-071515.

"1960 World Series Game 7 Line-Up Carbon Sheet from the Casey Stengel Collection." Heritage Auctions. Accessed June 20, 2022. https://sports.ha.com/itm/baseball/1960-world-series-game-7-line-up-card-carbon-sheet-from-the-casey-stengel-collection-the-suffering-ended-with-a-ninth-inni/a/45111-12256.s?ic4=ListView-ShortDescription-071515.

"1933 Cleveland Indians and Philadelphia A's Lineup Cards Signed by Walter Johnson and Connie Mack." Robert Edward Auctions. Accessed September 4, 2022. https://robertedwardauctions.com/auction/2020/spring/1537/1933-cleveland-indians-and-philadelphia-as-lineup-cards-signed-by-walter-johnson-and-connie-mack.

O'Reilly, Tom. "Collecting history via MLB Lineup Cards." *Sports Collectors Digest,* October 8, 2020. https://sportscollectorsdigest.com/tag/mlb-lineup-cards.

Osborne, Todd. Interviews. September 27, 2021, and July 7, 2022.

"Player Bats Out of Turn Four Times in Game." *The Calumet News,* August 27, 1914. Retrieved from https://chroniclingamerica.loc.gov/.

"PSA/DNA Certification #84262381." PSA Authentication & Grading Services. Accessed January 17, 2022. https://www.psacard.com/cert/84262381.

"Rare 30's Senators Lineup Card Signed Walter Johnson, HOF, 1 of '5 Immortals.'" WorthPoint. Accessed November 2, 2022. https://www.worthpoint.com/worthopedia/30-senators-lineup-card-signed-walter-1728452785.

The Reach official American League base ball guide, 1914–1915. A. J. Reach Co. Accessed September 22, 2021. Retrieved from https://library.si.edu/digital-library/book/reachofficialame19141phil.

(RetroReaction). "Vintage 1995 Oakland Athletics Game Used Lineup Card." Etsy. Accessed November 12, 2022. https://www.etsy.com/listing/1005493180/vintage-1995-oakland-athletics-game-used.

Reynolds, Jim. Interviews. November 1, 2021, and May 20, 2022.
"Ripken Lineup Card Battled Over." Associated Press. December 21, 1998. https://apnews.com/article/82264d813618e2e99df4a279d831f67d.
"Ripken Lineup Card Dispute Settled." Associated Press, April 19, 2000. https://apnews.com/article/d7e213cb01aba312e354adf1a0cff890.
Roth, Richard. Interview. May 19, 2021.
Runnells, Tom. Interview. March 30, 2022.
Sadler, Ruth. "Ruth Museum's display has a hot number: 2,131." *The Baltimore Sun*. March 24, 1996. https://www.baltimoresun.com/news/bs-xpm-1996-03-24-1996084152-story.html.
"Season 2021/2022, Team Sheet and Pre-Match Briefing." Premier League Handbook. Accessed May 1, 2022. https://resources.premierleague.com/premierleague/document/2021/11/30/235538a5-3927-4489-9812-7b426b80e6e1/PL_Handbook_2021_22_DIGITAL_29.11.21.pdf.
Serino, Bob. Interview. June 8, 2022.
"Should Have Held On." *The Saint Paul Daily Globe*. September 21, 1887. Retrieved from https://chroniclingamerica.loc.gov/.
"Significant July 11, 1914 Babe Ruth First Major League Game 'Lineup Card' (Tommy Connolly Collection) (PSA/DNA)." Christie's. Accessed July 27, 2022. https://www.christies.com/en/lot/lot-6296497.
Simon, Andrew. "Rays' all-lefty lineup a first in MLB history." Major League Baseball News. September 11, 2020. https://www.mlb.com/news/rays-all-left-handed-lineup-makes-history.
Skillen, Charlie. "Fergie's first United team-sheet from 1986 sells for £20k at auction…six times the asking price." *Mail Online*. June 23, 2013. https://www.dailymail.co.uk/sport/football/article-2346770/Sir-Alex-Fergusons-Manchester-United-team-sheet-fetches-20k-auction.html.
Spalding's Official Baseball Guide, 1910. A. G. Spalding & Bros. Accessed September 15, 2021. Retrieved from: https://chroniclingamerica.loc.gov/.
Stocking, Tyler. Interview. July 1, 2022.
Swirsky, Seth. Interviews. June 12, 2020, and June 11, 2021.
"Three-batter Minimum." Major League Baseball Glossary. Accessed November 15, 2022. https://www.mlb.com/glossary/rules/three-batter-minimum.
"Tom Kayser collection on the Texas League, 1895–2019: A Guide to the Collection." Texas Archival Resources Online. Accessed December 4, 2022. https://txarchives.org/smu/finding_aids/00396.xml##series1.

"26-man Roster." Major League Baseball Glossary. Accessed November 15, 2022. https://www.mlb.com/glossary/transactions/26-man-roster.
"2004 World Series Boston Red Sox Vs St. Louis Cardinals Lineup Card, Pricing & History." Worthpoint. Accessed October 23, 2021. https://www.worthpoint.com/worthopedia/2004-world-series-boston-red-sox-vs-1880000280.
"2010 Mike Trout Pre-Rookie and Cedar Rapids Kernels vs. Peoria Chiefs Team-Signed Game Used Lineup Card (PSA) Auction: Spring Classic 2021." Lelands. Accessed August 3, 2022. https://lelands.com/bids/2010-mike-trout-pre-rookie-and-cedar-rapids-kernels-vs-peoria-chiefs-team-signed-game-used-lineup-card-psa.
"2010 NHL Winter Classic Line-up Card!!" NHL Auctions Blog. January 25, 2010. https://nhlauctions.typepad.com/nhlauctions/2010/01/2010-nhl-winter-classic-lineup-card.html.
"2020 July 26 Sunday Sports Collectibles Weekly Online Auction #152030, Lot #44141." Heritage Auctions. Accessed August 14, 2022. https://sports.ha.com/itm/baseball/derek-jeter-signed-game-used-lineup-card-2-000th-hit/a/152030-44141.s?ic4=-GalleryView-Thumbnail-071515.
"2021 NCAA Football Rules and Interpretations." NCAA Publications. Accessed May 4, 2022. https://www.ncaapublications.com/p-4627-2021-ncaa-football-rules-and-interpretations.aspx.
Voda, Tony. Interview. July 21, 2022.
Wakamatsu, Don. Interview. March 18, 2022.
Weiss, Phil. Interview. March 3, 2022.
"What Not to Collect in Sports Memorabilia." Chubb Corp. Accessed October 14, 2022. https://www.chubb.com/us-en/individuals-families/resources/what-not-to-collect-in-sports-memorabilia.html#:~:text=The%20FBI%20estimates%20that,signature%20and%20a%20bogus%20one.
White, Rick. Interview. June 13, 2022.
"Will McEnaney Stats." *Baseball Almanac*. Accessed November 1, 2022. https://www.baseball-almanac.com/players/player.php?p=mcenawi01.
Wojtkun, Jim. Interview. June 1, 2022.
Zackhample.com. "About." Accessed November 7, 2022, https://www.zackhample.com/about.
Zackhample.com. "Lineup cards." Accessed November 7, 2022, https://www.zackhample.com/lineupcards.

Index

Aaron, Hank 44, 140, 144, 161, 163, 175, 178, 188, 214, 237
Acuña, Ronald, Jr. 160-161
Albany A's 131-132
All-Star Game 2, 41, 115, 143, 145, 147, 225; (1933) 88-89, 99, 225, 237; (1950) 207; (1951) 207; (2013) 145; (2015) 117; (2016) 116
Alonso, Pete 230
Alou, Felipe 30
Alston, Walter 208
Alvarez, Wilson 237
Amalfitano, Sandy 106
American Association 38
American League 39-41, 48, 53, 88, 103, 116, 142, 226, 237; 2017 Division Series 180
Anaheim Ducks 70-71
Ancel, James 91, 214
Anderson, Sparky 113, 120, 190
Aoki, Nori 120-121
Arizona Diamondbacks 53-54, 235
Arkansas Travelers 179
Asche, Cody 30
Atlanta Braves 59, 95, 175, 188, 194, 196, 237
Atlantic League of Professional Baseball 130, 235
auction 1, 2, 41, 49, 71, 79, 89, 91-92, 98-99, 101-102, 140, 182-183, 185, 186, 198, 212, 214, 217, 220, 226-229, 232, 234, 236-237
Averill, Earl 89, 187

Baker, Dusty 150, 157-158, 177-178, 199, 203, 206
Baldelli, Rocco 65
Baldwin Wallace University 76
Baltimore Orioles 3-4, 9, 26, 45-46, 53, 87, 90-92, 95-98, 119, 141, 153, 155, 161, 168-175, 188, 198, 212, 214, 234
Banks, Ernie 104
Banks, Tanner 122
Barnett, Larry 91
Baseball Almanac 1, 4, 221
Baseball Guide and Official League Book for 1889 39
Baseball Reference.com 175
basketball 67, 71; *see also* National Basketball League

batting order card 5-7 9-12, 15, 26, 28, 30-31, 39-42, 44, 45, 47-50, 52-53, 56-60, 62-66, 72, 77, 80-81, 84, 87-92, 95, 97, 99, 107-108, 113, 115, 119-127, 129-130, 133, 139-141, 143, 145-146, 149-150, 155-158, 161, 163-170, 172-178, 181-186, 188, 193-194, 196, 199-200, 203-208, 210, 212, 214, 216-218, 221, 224-225, 227, 229, 232, 235-240
The Beatles 161, 220
Bell, David 31
Bellinger, Cody 181
Beltran, Carlos 21
Beltre, Adrian 20, 145
Bench, Johnny 161, 176
Berra, Yogi 175, 188, 205
Berry, Quintin 135
Betts, Mookie 234
Bichette, Bo 234
Bielecki, Mike 133
Biggio, Cavan 230, 231
Binghamton Rumble Ponies 124
Blank, Trent 17
Boggs, Wade 123, 141
Bonds, Barry 143-144, 161, 178, 188, 199, 234
Bonilla, Bobby 134-135
Boston Braves 88
Boston Celtics 75
Boston Red Sox 4, 6, 9, 20, 27-28, 42, 44-45, 57, 84, 86-87, 98-100, 123-124, 132, 137, 141, 175, 180, 197-198, 212, 214, 220, 222, 224-226, 234
Bowling Green State University 91
Boyer, Clete 186
Brach, Brad 136
Brazilian national baseball team 204-205
Brett, George 95, 173, 188, 202
Brooklyn Dodgers 43-44, 164, 182, 237
Browne, Byron 104
Browning, Tom 161-162
Bryant, Kobe 75-76
Buckner, Bill 161
bullpen lineup card 3, 16-19, 25, 84-87, 93-94, 125, 150, 157, 180, 216-217, 226, 229, 231

Bush, George W. 122, 146
Buxton, Byron 29

Cabrera, Miguel 16, 57, 119, 157
Calgary Flames 69
California Angels 91, 141, 179, 212, 234
calligraphy 84, 107, 109, 112-113, 115, 117-119, 150
The Calumet News 40
Calvello, Michael 228
Campbell, David 98-100, 214
Cangelosi, John 134-135
Cape Cod League 230
Carew, Rod 141
Carey, Max 89
Carlton, Steve 147
Carolina League 130
Carter, Jimmy 146
Cedar Rapids Kernels 212
Ceja, Nestor 157
Cepeda, Orlando 175
Chicago Bulls 75
Chicago Cubs 18-20, 32, 40-41, 87, 103-106, 181, 199, 229, 234-235
The Chicago Daily Tribune 40
Chicago White Sox 28-30, 46, 60, 84, 107, 113, 115, 122, 133, 155, 207-208, 229
Christie's 220-221
Chronicling America 1
Cincinnati Reds 19, 31-32, 40, 57, 108, 112, 143, 159, 175, 235
Citi Field 59
Clemens, Roger 132, 175
Clemente, Roberto 44
Clemson University 142
Cleveland Cavaliers 73
Cleveland Guardians 234; *see also* Cleveland Indians; Cleveland Naps
Cleveland Indians 52, 56, 64, 89, 187, 232, 234, 237; *see also* Cleveland Guardians; Cleveland Naps
Cleveland Naps 39, 220; *see also* Cleveland Guardians; Cleveland Indians
Cliburn, Stan 23
Cobb, Ty 40
Cochrane, Mickey 89, 187, 205

Index

Collins, Eddie 89, 220
Colorado Rockies 55, 108, 110, 112, 165-167, 197-198
Comerica Park 140
Comiskey Park 41, 88, 225
Concepcion, Dave 176
Connolly, Tommy 220-222
Conroy, Sean 141
Coors Field 112
Cora, Alex 84, 86
Cornell University 15
Cottier, Chuck 90, 92-93
COVID-19 7, 34, 62-63, 67, 72, 101, 141, 145, 155, 203, 238, 240
Cox, Bobby 208, 210
Cronin, Joe 41-42
Cuddyer, Michael 228
Curry, Stephen 76

Dallas Rangers 167
Dallas Stars 70-71
Dane, Taylor 161
Davidson, Matt 30
Dayton Dragons 159
Dayton Dutch Lions 80
Dayton Dynamo 79
DeGolyer Library 129
DeGrom, Jacob 34
Dellinger, Dusty 125, 130
Denorfia, Chris 125, 139
DeSclafani, Anthony 136-137
designated player (DP)/flex player (FP) 80
Detroit Tigers 16, 40, 48, 57, 140, 149-150, 157, 176, 205-206, 235
Dickey, Bill 191
DiMaggio, Joe 191
Dodger Stadium 105, 186
dugout lineup card 2-4, 12-20, 25, 29-30, 34-35, 37, 44-49, 53-54, 56, 59, 61, 81-86, 90-96, 98-110, 112-113, 115-119, 121-122, 124, 126, 140-142, 149-150, 153-155, 160-163, 165, 169-170, 176, 179, 181, 187-188, 194, 198, 201, 203, 209-210, 212, 216-217, 224-227, 229, 234-235, 237, 239
Duncan, Tim 76
Durocher, Leo 190, 217
Dwyer, Brian 83
Dykstra, Lenny 166

Eastern League 130-133
eBay 41, 68, 71, 78, 100, 139, 165, 171, 174-176, 178-179, 185, 189, 194, 214, 216-217, 226-228, 234-237
ECHL 67-68
Edmonton Oilers 69
Enroth, Johnas 71
Équipe Québec 34-35

Facebook 39, 199, 228
Facebook Marketplace 228
Fairchild, Stuart 31

Fanatics 103, 229
FC Cincinnati 77
Federal League 141
Feliciano, Mario 234
Fenway Park 146, 220
Ferguson, Sir Alex 78
Fitzgibbon, Warren 91
Flanagan, Mike 90-93
Florence, Freedom 161
Florida Fall Instructional League 134
Florida State League 148
Florida State University 142
football 71, 164
Fort Worth Colts 167
Foxx, Jimmie 89, 187-188
Franco, Maikel 34
Francona, Terry 100
Fraser, Charlie 137
Frazier, Jeff 136
Frazier, Todd 136
Friedl, TJ 31
Frisch, Frankie 41
Frisco Roughriders 14
Frontier League 11, 34, 161
Fulton Search 1

Gallego, Mike 132
Garciaparra, Nomar 228
Gardenhire, Ron 58
Garfinkel, Jeff 164-168, 223, 226-227, 229, 232, 235, 237
Garner, Phil 211
Gehrig, Lou 41, 90-91, 141, 171, 191, 210-211, 225
Giamatti Research Center 140
Gibson, Bob 178
Gibson, Kirk 186
Girardi, Joe 219
Glaus, Troy 234
Glavine, Tom 95, 188
Golden State Warriors 74-75
Goldin, Ken 186
Goldin Auctions 186, 198, 226
Goldstein, Aaron 71
Gomez, Lefty 41
Gonzalez, Gio 217
Gonzalez, Juan 199
Gosewisch, Tuffy 135
Green, Elijah Jerry "Pumpsie" 123
Greene, Riley 157
Greensboro Grasshoppers 35-36
Griffey, Ken, Jr. 161, 170-171, 176, 188-189, 217
Groome, Jay 137
Grove, Lefty 41
Guerrero Vladimir, Jr. 159-161
Guillen, Ozzie 60, 207-208
Gwynn, Tony 161, 173

Haelig, Bill 91-92, 140, 168-175
hall of fame 1, 75, 88-89, 91, 101, 113, 141-143, 161, 168, 189-191, 204-205, 207-208, 210, 220, 222, 225; *see also* National Baseball Hall of Fame
Halladay, Roy 143, 146

Hamilton, Jeff 129
Hample, Zack 140, 148-150, 155
Hanrahan, Dan 226, 229, 232
Harper, Bryce 137, 139, 166, 217, 237
Harris, Bucky 189
Harrisburg Senators 137, 166
Hartford Yard Goats 125, 139
Hefner, Jeremy 18
Henderson, Rickey 174
Hendley, Bob 104
Henriksen, Olaf 220
Heritage Auctions 223, 226-228
Hernandez, Yadiel 34
High-A East 35
Hirschbeck, Denise 147
Hirschbeck, John 122, 140, 143-148, 200
Hirschbeck, "Little" John 145
Hirschbeck, Michael 145
hockey 67, 71; *see also* National Hockey League
Hodges, Gil 43
Houston Astros 157, 176-181
Houston Colt 45s 176, 178
Hudson Valley Renegades 36-37
Hunt Auctions 90, 92, 220-222

Iassogna, Dan 122
International League 2, 141, 235
Ivy, Chris 223-224, 226, 228

Jackson, Joe 220
James, LeBron 73, 76
James Spence Authentication (JSA) 221
Jeter, Derek 176, 187-188, 201, 226, 228, 234, 237
Jiménez, Ubaldo 112
Johnson, Adrian 9
Johnson, Erynn 140, 157-158
Johnson, Lou 104
Johnson, Randy 171
Johnson, Walter 41, 89, 189, 210
Jones, Chipper 165
Judge, Aaron 9, 101-103, 138-139, 232, 234
Judge, Joe 40

Kansas City Royals 47, 85, 157
Karkovice, Ron 134-135
Karl, George 75
Karros, Eric 166
Kayser, Tom 126, 129-130
Kerr, Steve 75
Kershaw, Clayton 226
Kessinger, Don 106
Keuchel, Dallas 117, 122
Key, Nik 212
KeyMan Collectibles 1
Klem, Bill 89
Klett, Michael 101-103, 232
Koufax, Sandy 103-106, 181, 183-186
Kuenn, Harvey 106

Lachemann, Marcel 91, 141
Lajoie, Nap 39, 220

Index

Lake County Captains 135
Lakewood BlueClaws 129, 135
Larkin, Barry 204-205
La Russa, Tony 107, 113, 190, 205
Lasorda, Tommy 30, 113, 165, 167, 186, 190
Lazarus, Jeffrey 40, 92, 95-98, 140, 165, 179, 186-187, 189-191, 193-194, 198-201, 206-208, 210, 213, 217, 235
Lazzeri, Tony 191
Lederer, George 104
Leonard, Dutch 222
Lester, Jon 197-198
Levy, Rick 105-106, 181-186, 223, 238
Lewis, Duffy 220, 220
Lewis, Kyle 230
Leyland, Jim 57
Leyritz, Jim 163
Liga Mexicana de Beisbol (LMB) 153-155
Little League 10
Los Angeles Angels 12
Los Angeles Dodgers 30, 57, 95, 103-104, 106, 129, 162, 165-166, 178, 181, 183-186, 208, 234
Los Angeles Lakers 75
Lovitto, Joe 51
Lucas, Sky 98-100, 214
Lynn, Fred 176
Lynn Sailers 133

Mack, Connie 41, 89, 208, 210, 225-226
Macko, Steve 199
Maddon, Joe 115
Maddux, Mike 133
major league 113, 133-134, 141, 150, 171, 199, 202, 220
Major League Baseball (MLB) 3, 5, 7, 10, 12, 14-17, 19-21, 25, 28-30, 34, 37, 41-42, 51-53, 56, 59, 61-64, 67-68, 77, 83-84, 88, 94, 97, 99, 100-101, 104, 107-109, 112-113, 115-117, 121-125, 129, 132-133, 135, 139-140, 143-145, 147-150, 153, 155, 157-158, 160-161, 163, 166, 168-170, 174, 176-177, 180-181, 185, 188, 192-195, 198, 200, 203-205, 209, 212-214, 216-218, 220-221, 223, 226-227, 229, 232, 234, 237-240; MLB Auctions 98-99, 101, 212, 228-229, 232, 234; MLB Authentication 28-30, 112, 214, 216-217, 226-227; MLB.com 198, 221, 234
Major League Soccer 77
manager 1-2, 5-7, 10, 17, 23-25, 29-31, 34, 37-44, 47-51, 57-58, 63-66, 77-78, 83-84, 87-91, 100, 106-109, 113, 115-117, 123-126, 137, 139-143, 148-150, 153, 155, 157, 159-161, 164-165, 167-168, 171, 173, 176-178, 189-191,

198, 200, 203, 205-210, 214, 217-219, 221, 223, 225, 228-229, 232, 238, 240
Manchester United 78
Mantle, Mickey 186
Manush, Heinie 41
Maris, Roger 186
Martin, Billy 200-201
Martin, Mike 142
Martinez, Dave 217
Martinez, Marty 51
Martinez, Pedro 188, 212
Mason, Mark 51
Mattingly, Don 131
Mauch, Gene 123, 167
Mauer, Joe 29, 143, 228
Mays, Willie 178, 188
Mazeroski, Bill 49, 226
McCarthy, Joe 226
McCollum, C.J. 73
McEnaney, Will 51-53
McGowan, Bill 89
McGraw, John 41, 88-89, 226
McKechnie, Bill 41, 88-89
McMurtry, Craig 131
McNally, Dave 169
Memphis Chicks 235
Memphis Grizzlies 72, 75-76
Mercari 228
Mercker, Kent 165, 167
Meza, Scott 140, 175-180
Miami Marlins 13, 17, 141, 181, 235
Midwest League 159, 235
Miller, Kenneth 80
Milwaukee Braves 45
Milwaukee Brewers 48, 146, 148, 157, 210, 226-227, 234
Milwaukee Bulldozers 38
Minaya, Omar 129
Minneapolis Millers 123, 167-168
Minnesota Twins 18, 28-30, 58, 65, 141, 144, 149-150, 155-156, 181, 183
minor league (MiLB) 10-11, 25, 35, 37, 71, 123-127, 129-131, 133, 135, 137, 139, 148, 159-160, 166-167, 176, 179, 211, 228-229
Mississippi Braves 160
Molitor, Paul 157
Montoyo, Charlie 232
Montreal Expos 30-31, 108, 113, 129, 181, 235
Morris, Jack 48, 188
Murphy, Sean 230
Murray, Eddie 161
Musial, Stan 43

Narron, Jerry 84, 107, 109, 113, 117-122, 148, 150
Nashville Sounds 235
National Baseball Hall of Fame 1, 91, 97, 123, 140-143; *see also* hall of fame
National Basketball Association (NBA) 67, 71-76, 83, 238; NBA G League 71

National Collegiate Athletic Association (NCAA) 71, 76
National Football League (NFL) 71
National Hockey League (NHL) 67-69, 71, 83, 238
National League 38-39, 41, 53, 62, 88-89, 142, 166, 178, 237; Division Series 143
National Premier Soccer League 79-80; *see also* soccer
Negro League 198, 205
Net54baseball.com 1, 41, 214, 228
New Britain Red Sox 131-132
New Britain Bees 23
New York Clipper 38
New York Giants (baseball) 190, 191
New York Giants (football) 71, 164
New York Mets 33-34, 59, 161, 164-165, 201, 206, 217
New York-Penn League 10, 130
New York Yankees 37, 44, 49-51, 95, 101, 103, 121, 126, 138, 144, 161, 175-176, 181-182, 188, 190, 194, 196, 198, 200-201, 207, 225-226, 229, 232, 234, 235
Newcombe, Don 43
NHL Auctions 71
Niekro, Phil 200
Nieves, Juan 157
Nogosek, Stephen 34
Nomo, Hideo 178
non–Hodgkin's lymphoma 198
Northwest Arkansas Naturals 131
Northwestern League 38

Oakland Athletics 25-26, 29, 54, 141, 176, 186, 234
Oates, Johnny 119-120
Ohtani, Shohei 178, 234
Ontiveros, Steve 132
Ortiz, David 2-3, 212
Osborne, Todd 78, 80, 83, 140, 158-161
Ott, Mel 190

Pacific Association 141
Palmer, Jim 174
Pasquintino, Vinnie 157
Pawtucket Red Sox 123, 138, 141
Peoria Chiefs 235
Perez, Salvador 131
Perez, Tony 190
Perkins, Cy 206
Perry, Gaylord 188-189
Perry, Gerald 134
Philadelphia Athletics 40-41, 89, 187
Philadelphia Phillies 143, 166, 191, 219
Piazza, Mike 95, 161
pitchers' relief usage card 20, 150
Pittsburgh Pirates 35, 49, 51, 93-94

Index

Popovich, Gregg 75
Portland Trail Blazers 74
Premier League 76-77; *see also* soccer
Press and Daily Dakotian 38
Pressly, Ryan 30
Professional Sports Authenticator (PSA) 220-222
Puckett, Kirby 150, 152
Pujols, Albert 12, 93-94, 234

Raines, Tim 161, 236
Raines, Tim, Jr. 236
Ramirez, Manny 141
Reach Official American League Base Ball Guide, 1914 40
Reading Phillies 133
Reagan, Ronald 146
Redus, Gary 134
Regan, Phil 90-91, 141, 214
Renaudo, Anthony 136
Renteria, Rick 133
replica lineup card 20
Retrosheet 165, 221
Reynolds, Jim 42, 62-63, 65-66, 217-218, 238-240
Rhodes College 235
Riggs, Jeremy 34
Ripken, Billy 169-170
Ripken, Cal., Jr. 90-92, 97, 123, 141, 168-175, 227
Ripken, Cal, Sr. 169-170
Rivera, Mariano 144
Rizzuto, Phil 103
Roades-Brown, Peter 79
Robert Edwards Auctions 83, 226
Robinson, Brooks 168
Robinson, Frank 170, 173
Robinson, Jackie 43, 181, 215
Rochester Red Wings 123, 141
Rodriguez, Alex 148, 161, 176, 225, 234
Rodriguez, Ivan "Pudge" 192
Rodriguez, Julio 27
Rogers, Taylor 30
Rojas, Luis 206
Rondon, Hector 135
Rosen, Al 183
Ross, David 31
Roth, Richard 220-221
Roth Law Firm 220
Ruffing, Red 191
Runnells, Tom 107-113, 122
Ruth, Babe 41, 93-94, 140, 161, 213, 220-222; Birthplace and Museum 91
Rutschman, Adley 239
Ryan, Nolan 141

Sahlen Field 7, 141, 153-155
St. Louis Browns 41-42
St. Louis Cardinals 41-42, 45, 53, 93-94
Saint Paul Daily Globe 38
St. Paul Saints 38
Saltalamacchia, Jarrod 115
San Antonio Spurs 75

San Diego Padres 189
San Francisco Giants 22, 144, 178, 229, 234
Sandberg, Ryne 190-191
Santana, Ervin 30
Santo, Ron 104
Scherzer, Max 57
Schmidt, Mike 161
Scioscia, Mike 166
scorecard (score card) 23, 39-40
Scranton/Wilkes-Barre RailRiders 138
Scully, Vin 104, 106
Seattle Mariners 5-7, 17, 26-28, 84, 115, 170, 219, 225
September 11, 2001 attack (9/11) 96-98, 188
Serino, Bob "Bino" 127, 129, 131, 148
Servais, Scott 218-219
Severino, Anderson 122
Shaw, Travis 234
Shea Stadium 161, 165
Sheen, Charlie 161
Showalter, Buck 115, 131
Sioux Falls Skyforce 71
Sisler, George 40
Skowron, Moose 43
Smith, Lee 166
Smith, Ozzie 188-189
Snell, Blake 141
Snider, Duke 43
soccer 76-78, 80; *see also* Major League Soccer; Premier League; United Soccer League
softball 10, 80-81
Somerset Patriots 126, 235
Soto, Geovany 30
Soto, Juan 216
Sousa, Bennett 122
South Atlantic League 130, 134-136
Southern League 130-131, 235
Speier, Chris 203
Sports Collectors Digest 171, 173, 182-183, 223
Steinbrenner, George 122
Stengel, Casey 43, 49-50, 190, 207, 226
Stocking, Tyler 72-76, 83
Stompers, Sonoma 141
Story, Trevor 27
The Sunday Star 40
Sussex County Miners 34-35
Suzuki, Ichiro 112, 178
Swirsky, Seth 140, 161-164, 213-214, 220, 222-226

Tampa Bay Rays 141, 171
Tanner, Chuck 51, 53
Target Field 155-156
Tecolotes Dos Laredos (Owls of the Two Laredos) 154-55
Terry, Bill 190-191
Texas League 126, 129-131
Texas Rangers 14, 50-51, 101-102, 115, 192, 226, 229, 232, 234

Thomas, Frank 161, 194-195, 202
Thomas, Lane 34
Thomas's English Muffins 161
Timberlake, Justin 76
today's lineup card (clubhouse lineup card) 19-20, 54
Toronto Blue Jays 7, 96-97, 141, 155, 159-160, 232, 234
Torre, Joe 190
Tosi, Alex 31
Towson University 172
Trammell, Alan 176
Trout, Mike 12, 139, 148, 179, 193, 212
Tumpane, John 9

umpire 1, 2, 5, 7, 9-11, 25, 30-31, 34, 39-40, 42, 49, 58, 62-63, 65-66, 80, 88-89, 91, 108, 117, 122, 124-127, 129-130, 135, 137, 139-140, 142-144, 146-149, 153, 155-157, 165, 172, 176, 178, 180, 194, 198, 200, 205, 218, 220-223, 228-229, 235, 238, 240
United Soccer League (USL) 77, 80
U.S. Olympic Festival 129
University of Oklahoma 80-81
University of Texas 81, 132
Urias, Julio 235

Van Burkleo, Tyler 115
Vancil, Preston 161
Van Oeyen, Louis 221
Vargas, Jason 217
Vargas, Kennys 155
Venable, Will 86
Ventura, Robin 150
Verlander, Justin 57, 117
Viola, Frank 131
Voda, Tony 140, 150, 152-157
Volpe, Anthony 37

Wade, Dwyane 76
Wakamatsu, Don 107, 109, 113-117, 122, 215-216
Washington Nationals 17, 33-34, 144, 216-217, 231
Washington Senators 41, 189
Weaver, Earl 107, 194
Weiss, Phil 203, 213, 224, 226, 228
Weiss, Walt 108
Weiss Auctions 203, 213, 224
Wendelstedt, Hunter 122
West, Joe 122
Western Carolinas League 130, 134
Whitaker, Lou 176
White, Rick 130
Wiley, Mark 98
Williams, Billy 104
Williams, Ted 50-51
Wills, Maury 181, 185
Wilmington Blue Rocks 236
Wojtkun, Jim 76

World Series 4, 7, 20, 88, 95, 100, 117, 141, 143-145, 147, 169, 180-181, 183, 186, 191, 194, 213-214, 225; (1937) 191; (1944) 42-43; (1955) 44; (1960) 49-50, 226, 237; (1963) 49, 182, 184-185, 224; (1965) 183-185; (1969) 161; (1970) 169; (1974) 141; (1976) 194; (1977) 194; (1979) 194, 196; (1981) 194; (1985) 237; (1991) 194; (1995) 144; (1999) 95, 163, 188, 194, 196-197; (2000) 201; (2003) 194; (2004) 98-100, 198, 214, 224; (2006) 144; (2007) 194, 197-198; (2009) 194; (2010) 144; (2016) 20, 144; (2018) 186, 194

WorthPoint 41
Wrigley Field 41
Wynn, Randy 150

Yastrzemski, Carl 95, 144, 188
Young, Chris 18
Young, Don 104
YouTube 148, 229

www.ingramcontent.com/pod-product-compliance
Lightning Source LLC
Chambersburg PA
CBHW060339010526
44117CB00017B/2886